LIBRARY/NEW ENGLAND INST. OF TECHNOLOGY
3 0147 1
D0464309

PS 3555 .L58

Ell

NEW ENGLAND INSTITUTE
OF TECHNOLOGY
LIBRARY

The University and Corporate America

THE UNIVERSITY AND CORPORATE AMERICA

BRIDGING THE TWO WORLDS

BY

LLOYD H. ELLIOTT

NEW ENGLAND INSTITUTE OF TECHNOLOGY
LIBRARY

NATIONAL HERITAGE BOOKS

WASHINGTON, D.C.
2001

7-02 # 48805117

Copyright © 2001 by Lloyd H. Elliott
Published by
National Heritage Books
2700 Unicorn Lane, N.W.
Washington, D.C. 20015
Editorial Office:
8301 Alvord Street
McLean, Virginia 22102

All rights reserved. No part of this book may be reproduced or transmitted in any form or by any means, electronic or mechanical, including photocopying, without permission from the publisher.

Publisher's Cataloging-in-Publication
(Provided by Quality Books, Inc.)

Elliott, Lloyd H.
The university and corporate America : bridging the two worlds / by Lloyd H. Elliott. ~ 1st ed.
p. cm.
LCCN 2001091232
ISBN 0-9665234-7-4

1. Universities and colleges~United States~Fiction.
2. Corporations~United States~Fiction. 3. Education, Higher~United States~Administration~Fiction.
4. Universities and colleges~United States~Business management~Fiction. I. Title.

PS35554.L59185U55 2001 813'.6
QBI01-700811

Book design by Cynthia B. Scudder
Manufactured in the United States of America
October 2001

CONTENTS

This book is dedicated to my wife, Betty,
who earned her PHT–*putting husband through college*–
in the early years of our marriage.

Acknowledgments

Access to boardrooms, friendship with directors, trustees, CEOs and staff officers in colleges and universities, small and large corporations, numerous charities and, yes, a few public bodies—zoning boards, congressional committees, state and local authorities—made possible the machinations expressed in this volume. While each glimpse of managerial behavior recorded herein is fictional, the seed was planted by an actual incident which occurred somewhere in the four decades of the author's experience.

It was an exciting, challenging, sometimes frightening odyssey, replete with surprises, both pleasant and disappointing. But satisfaction far outweighed the disagreeable; plusses many times outnumbered the losses; and, looking back, it is easy to observe that private business and academe, with all their weaknesses, remain the backbone of American progress. In no other part of the world has the work of these two entities—or any other combination—served the people so well. For the opportunity to be part of this parade, the author will forever be grateful.

To help prepare the manuscript for this book, the writer called on a longtime friend and editor. Robert L. Breeden spent most of a distinguished career with the National Geographic Society, editing a long series of their most widely distributed books. He kindly put his considerable talents to work on this volume; the writer is most grateful.

Finally, it is with deep appreciation that I remind my wife, Betty, that the journey could not have been made without her constant support, extending all the way back to the days when she "put me through graduate school." We made the trip together, joined along the way by two children, each of whom added a special measure of love and satisfaction. More immediately, Betty's gentle prodding and her superb management of the household allowed me time for writing, along with my own inevitable procrastination.

For the shortcomings, and there are many, the author is alone to blame.

Introduction

This account is anecdotal, a composite of characters, real and imagined, put together by remembering and forgetting, imagining and experiencing, dreaming and, perhaps, hallucinating. Obviously, any reference to persons living or dead may be frightening, threatening, or promising—but most certainly, only coincidental!

For readers who want objective data, irrefutable facts, footnotes or scholarly references, this little exercise in fictional reporting will be a disappointment; for those who are looking for a bit of common sense, a suitable solution to a CEO's problem or an occasional glimpse of decency, it is the author's hope your reading time will not be wasted.

Since this book is about higher education and corporate America, the writer hopes to add some small measure of better understanding of these two immensely vital parts of our society to those brave enough to endure its rhetoric. Only tangentially is the interface of government with academe or government with business addressed. The writer offers no apology for evading such a frightening task!

It is further hoped that service on nine corporate boards and thirty years as a university president (seven at the University of Maine and twenty-three at George Washington University), will have equipped the writer to undertake this exercise. Broader understanding of business on the part of academicians and clearer insights by men and women in private enterprise of colleges and universities are the sole objectives of this volume. Whether the writer succeeded or not is for the reader to decide.

I

The University by Degrees

The president read the letter again. After years in the university's top office William Comstock couldn't decide whether it was the subject or the people it attracted that irritated him the more. At any rate few topics required a greater waste of time and energy than honorary degrees. Somebody, somewhere, seemed always to be wanting one—for himself, for a friend, or for someone known only through the media.

Which did this letter address? A political has-been, a budding artist badly in need of a boost, a public figure who needs to be made more public, an overlooked over-achiever, or one who is simply promoting himself? The president had seen too many such letters to take this one at face value—an innocent-looking, seemingly straightforward recommendation, written on personal stationery with name and home address jumping out from high quality paper, and a very select zip code. It came from a well-known estate in the hunt country of northern Virginia.

Irritation was the right word. Prexy, as he was addressed by his favorite dean, had long since learned that a dozen happenings could make him good and mad every day—if he allowed it to occur! How much better to control the anger, hold one's tongue—and pen—and see where all the culprits were coming from before showing one's hand. If he put the letter aside, it would just rest in that holding stack with a mounting mixture of messages until a phone call, another piece of paper, or a chance conversation stirred the subject again.

It came up the same day at an afternoon meeting of the board of directors of a local charity, raised by the CEO of a regional bank, also a trustee of the University.

"Say Bill, did Joe Hubbard write you about his former boss at the department of Agriculture? He told me he was going to."

So that's where it came from. Hubbard wasn't the most successful bureaucrat in Washington, but he had landed a series of presidential appointments. He always seemed to have friends in high places and could be seen at more receptions, luncheons, and dinners around town than most other government hangers-on.

"Yes, I got his letter," President Comstock replied, "and Mr. Hubbard said he would send along a copy of his boss's resume."

"Until then, I'm afraid I can't say much to our Committee on Ceremonies about the proposal," the president continued. "While I know the name, I never really got to know the man. He was retired when I first arrived in Washington."

Comstock had long since learned that honorary degrees were extremely important to many people outside academe and especially, it seemed, to business leaders.

As he drove home that evening, the president mused about some of the trials of leading a university. What a potpourri of matters come to the desk of a college or university CEO. The crises of the late sixties were vivid all across the campuses of America—and the whole world for that matter—but an honorary degree for a retired government worker was hardly a critical factor in the life of a university. Again, he decided to let the matter rest.

Just a few days, however.

Returning from a fundraising trip and feeling good about responses to an appeal for the library building fund, he found on the top of the second priority for reading, so classified by his very knowledgeable secretary, the resume of Floyd Gardiner Reynolds. Numbering ten pages, the "curriculum vitae" as it was labeled, gave the "highlights of the Professional Career" of Dr. Reynolds. Sure enough, there was an earned Ph.D., plus bachelor's and master's, too, all awarded by the University of Minnesota.

Dr. Comstock looked again. What is Reynolds' association with Midtown University? He must have missed it. He probably had read too much too fast. He would simply read the ten single-spaced pages again, this time carefully. Even after a second, tedious, reading there simply was no mention of the Midtown University.

Is this another case, thought the president, in which someone is trying to use the university? If it is, it wouldn't be the first time. Yes, it was true, as the president learned over the course of the next few days; a series of letters arrived, "supporting the nomination of Dr. Reynolds for the award of the honorary degree of Doctor of Public Service." The letter-writing campaign was well orchestrated. Some emphasized his contributions to basic research in plant genetics leading to new opportunities for American farmers. Others spelled out the personal dedication he gave in putting the country's welfare above personal gain. Still others observed that because he achieved these great things in Washington, any Washington area educational institution would really be honoring itself by honoring Floyd Gardiner Reynolds.

Such hogwash! And so well-ordered. Had it not been that a couple of the most flowery letters were marked b.c. (blind copy) to Dr. Reynolds, Comstock might not have seen through the nomination so clearly.

Reynolds wanted an honorary degree badly. In comparison with many who were awarded such honors, he undoubtedly deserved one. However, he had the misfortune to attend and to receive three earned degrees from a university that does not grant honorary degrees. Comstock simply did not believe that another institution, in this case Midtown University, should be used to meet another's obligations. He quietly buried the Reynolds file in the archives, never to be seen again.

Traditions die hard in academe, and institutional policy in honorary degrees is sacrosanct.

Certainly Comstock knew that Minnesota, Rice, and Cornell all followed the tradition of giving awards of various kinds but no honorary degrees. He knew, too, that Nicholas Murray Butler let it be known that an honorary degree from Columbia University could be gotten with a generous contribution. He claimed, in fact, in his later years that he "built Columbia by degrees!"

Who, indeed, had invented the honorary degree? It was more a curse than a blessing. How many entreaties had college presidents heard, "Give him an honorary degree, and big gifts will come to the institution."

Well, Comstock had learned that part the hard way. Give the degree after the gift was received, not the other way around. Too many, having received the honor, didn't even acknowledge requests for contributions thereafter. It was a game played by some with a con artist's skill and was still viewed in awe and wonder by the innocent and naïve.

He had also witnessed a little horse trading, too. In his first year as a university president, Comstock came face-to-face with the chicanery of academe when the president of a sister institution put it bluntly, "Bill, I'll invite you to give our summer commencement address this year and give you an honorary degree, and you can do the same for me next year." Before a reply could be voiced, he added, "After all, nobody pays any attention to the August commencement anyway."

Finding various excuses, Bill didn't succumb, but the proposition alerted him to the rules of the game. His suspicion that honorary degrees were as valuable to college and university presidents as to senior officers of business and industry was confirmed over and over. This proved to be true even though most of these presidents, both men and women, had earned doctoral degrees. The only people who seemed more eager than all others were the politicians. When a U.S. senator wrote him some years later, asking "to give a commencement address at Midtown University and to receive an honorary degree," Bill was no longer surprised. By that time the matter had become so routine that he didn't find it necessary to acknowledge a personal letter from a U.S. senator. And contrary to usual procedure, no follow-up call came from a member of the senator's staff. What business!

There was a rationale for awarding such honors. In fact, many universities had written criteria which were supposed to guide such consideration: Outstanding service to humanity, unusual dedication to the public good, special help to the institution concerned, or unique leadership in managing a difficult societal problem. These criteria were so high sounding that few could question the recognition of one who presented such credentials.

Comstock soon realized that committees in academe found it easy to read into unusual service such monetary terms as leading gift, timely pledge, patron of the arts, and philanthropist. He learned that a newly elected governor, mayor, or legislator would find colleges and universities within his jurisdiction vying for the honor of being the first to recognize the great accomplishments of the political winner. If the public official left office sometime later in dishonor or disgrace, the institution simply kept as quiet as possible all references about the previous association.

Captains of industry often seemed more awed by honorary degrees than public officials. Comstock was soon to learn that Midtown U, located a few blocks from the seat of government—perhaps the most influential capital city in the world—had become a special place where those from the private sector desired to strut upon the stage. With diplomats, trade experts, bankers, and potential buyers from around the globe, where better "to be recognized" for "my" achievements–and, incidentally, "my company" also. The degree-seeker would ask himself and others, "Do we have alumni from Midtown U employed in the top positions? Is there by chance a director with ties to the university?" Ambition turned to action: "Put the PR department to work, and, oh yes, don't forget to see how much Midtown receives in the way of federal funds. Some of our congressional delegation may be able to give us some leverage there."

That certainly was the scenario for one campaign, a campaign by the CEO of one of America's major corporations to get an honorary degree, not from any college or university, but from the institution located at the center of the world's stage.

A year later, Comstock reluctantly awarded the degree. Arriving the day of the ceremony by corporate jet, surrounded by public relations staff and personal aides, the CEO played to the galleries while the aides handed out folders stuffed with company fluff, glossy prints, and appropriate speech-writer quotes.

Arrogance flowed freely. The entire corporate delegation seemed hyped, swaggering through the day with condescension oozing from all contacts. None wore the emblem more blatantly than the CEO himself.

The Washington Press Corps, accustomed to such visits, and oriented to the politics of the nation and the world rather than to business, hardly yawned at the ceremony. All was chronicled, however, for the business world and the folks back home.

But this honorary degree had a particularly bitter residue. It was triggered as Comstock and his corporate visitor waited in line to enter the auditorium for the ceremony.

"Well, Mr. President," the attack began as the big business executive played his trump card, "I suppose you have to live with that plague called tenure. I've heard all about it from Joe Hickam, prexy of my alma mater.

"I used to think we had problems with unions, but when I learned about tenure–you see Joe asked me to come on his board a few years ago–I learned what having a job for life really means." Continuing, loudly enough for a dozen senior professors to hear, the self-appointed center-of-the-stage, drove home the hapless condition of academe. "How is it you put it? You can't fire a professor with tenure unless he is caught raping the dean of women on the library steps at high noon.

"Or that's about the way Joe described his dilemma to me. Believe me, Mr. President, I wouldn't put up with that crap."

"Tenure really has its defense," began Comstock, but he had no chance to finish; the marshal was waving the procession forward. He could see a wry smile on the faces of a few faculty members as he led the stage party to its place.

Academic freedom, which lives so vividly within the university, is only an abstract, philosophical will-of-the-wisp to many of the general public. It is not difficult, Comstock reasoned as he mulled over the matter in the days that followed, to see why academics are so easily branded as unrealistic, living outside the real world, and even arrogant in their demands for non-interference. So it is only to be expected that when specific threats arise, the public has little understanding of the precedent which may be set if the issue of the moment is handled poorly.

Why would professors refuse to take an oath of loyalty? Why require students to study foreign-isms? Americanism is good enough for the rest of us. And so, many citizens eye with suspicion the special treatment which the academic demands. At best it speaks of arrogance; at worst it displays disloyalty, a lack of patriotism, or even advocacy of another form of government.

To help a bit toward a better understanding of academe could be vital to the long-term well-being of the country. Comstock had learned from his own service on various corporate boards over a period of many years that underneath the veneer of professional uniforms—the proverbial tweed jacket and baggy slacks of the professor and the silk tie, monogrammed cuffs, and tailored suits of the business world—most players on both sides were intelligent, reasonable, and well-intentioned people. Each group, however, seemed to have an oversupply of uncertainty, jealousy, fear, and downright distrust for the other. Bridging the canyon, wide and deep, what a challenge! Somehow. Sometime. Somewhere. As for now....

Another commencement season had closed. Graduates scattered to the far-flung points of the globe. The faculty, too; but for Comstock and his immediate staff, the summer slowdown of campus life carried only a change of emphasis, not a lessening of tension-filled work. True, the period of temporary numbness brought on by ceremony after ceremony, speech after speech, handshake after handshake, and smile upon fixed smile did come to an end with graduation. With the change of pace, the president could tuck the cap and gown away, clear undelivered diplomas and copies of citations from his desk, and sign the many follow-up letters: "Your presence meant much to our graduates;" "Inspiration is the only appropriate word for your message;" and "Thank you for the example set with your unexpected gift." They all cleared the basket for a whole new range of summer activities.

But nagging like a sore-tailed pet, the honorary degree just wouldn't go away.

Was he so different? thought Comstock. Any number of his colleagues, some among the most respected of university presidents in the country, seemed comfortable with the degree. They used it, so it appeared, with grace and dignity—and with long-lasting positive results for their institutions. If such results were really being achieved by his colleagues, what was he doing wrong? Or was there the same trouble behind the scenes on other campuses, and were good public relations simply succeeding in the camouflage? Comstock had his doubts.

Having spent his life in the academy, Comstock had come to respect all awards for scholarship—degrees, citations, prizes, medals, and plaques—if they were earned. To Comstock, earning an award meant fulfilling the conditions: finishing the program, doing the complete job, competing with others for the prize, but, heaven forbid, having nothing given and having no shortcut allowed.

Yet, universities were giving away the highest awards within their reach for a passing moment of publicity, for a gift of questionable size or quality, for some imprecise future favor, or simply to please a friend or constituent.

Somewhere integrity kept looming out of the academic mist, but a bit of tarnish seemed always to mar the view. Feeling as he did about the university, Comstock wasn't comfortable with the tarnish, even though integrity appeared bright from so many other viewpoints.

As for Comstock himself, he could scarcely recall the institutions which had honored him, or the occasions. The events usually involved a speech sandwiched between stops on a cross-country trip which had other, more important purposes. And he remembered a colleague from one of the nation's most prestigious universities who called to ask if Comstock could attend a ceremony on a certain date. As he put it quite routinely over the phone: "I want to give you an honorary degree." Somewhat taken aback, Comstock could only reply, "But, my friend, I have one already from your institution." His fellow president didn't know that his own institution had given Comstock an honorary only a few years earlier! Embarrassing? Not necessarily. Honorary degrees just weren't very important to either of these presidents.

The misery for Comstock of giving away a degree remained: It wasn't like virginity because it kept occurring over and over.

To Comstock, the academic world had several manure-like things to hide, but none carried quite so strong an aroma; the honorary degree was distasteful, thoroughly nauseating, and undoubtedly dishonest. Feeling entrapped, he put the subject out of his mind.

It wouldn't go away.

There was always someone who wanted to bargain for a degree. Within the week, Comstock's assistant for international programs called, and, in his usual tone of excitement mixed with smugness, he wanted to come immediately to report great news.

And the news!

A Middle Eastern potentate with oil money dripping from his pockets wanted to establish a center at MU for the study of regional economics, politics, languages, literature, art, music, and, in fact, for any worthwhile scholarly interest which might evolve. "Centers" and "Institutes" were being formed to do everything under the sun—and under the academic umbrella of a university. One major state institution reported the presence of more than a hundred such creatures, all formed since World War II. Comstock, having heard it all before, simply waited in this case for the details to fall.

His assistant wasted no time.

"This world leader," quickly promoted by Comstock's international messenger from monarch to statesman, "wants a presence in Washington. He wants to send many of his young countrymen here for study." Almost breathlessly, Elwood Hillary Hutchenson, the fast-talking assistant continued, "His ambassador, with whom I've been on a first-name basis for many years, told me that. His Highness wants to start the center with an initial gift of several million dollars."

Skeptical but hopeful, Comstock listened as Hutchenson filled out the picture. The ruler, absolute ruler of a small country of some 30 million people, would purchase a presence in Washington. He proposed to come in by a respectable door–the academic. Perhaps young men and women from that country studying alongside American students and those from the other hundred or more countries represented at MU would sow seeds of world understanding and goodwill.

Wasn't this what Comstock himself had come to believe? Didn't he say essentially that while on a recruiting trip to the west coast only a few weeks before?

Hutchenson knew all of this, of course, and he played to the old man's weakness. (Why is it that the CEO no matter his age, is referred to as "the old man" in so many organizations? Another carryover from the military perhaps, so common as often to be forgotten.)

Seeing that Hutchenson was wound up and knowing that nothing pleased him quite so much as the sound of his own voice, Comstock interrupted with, "Well, where do we go from here?"

"It will be moved along quickly," said Hutchenson. "I only need to let the ambassador know that we are willing to proceed. He will take it from there."

The conversation had lasted less than 30 minutes, and the swirl of a new pipe dream filled the office. Would anything really come of it? There were so many hot air balloons let loose in Washington every day...and yet, sometimes.

As he left the office, Hutchenson missed by only a couple of minutes meeting the university's chief development officer who arrived for an appointment with Comstock. Prexy turned his full attention away from oil-rich potentates, not bothering to mention the possibility of five to ten million coming their way, even though raising money was the work of this veteran officer.

Comstock never liked to count the chickens before the eggs at least had been placed in the nest.

Always well organized, with ideas fully developed and committed to paper, the development vice president was especially welcome today. He would bring hard facts and realistic proposals to the president. One of the better selections Comstock had made in recent years, Ted McKiever had thoroughly demonstrated that he could organize and guide a successful fundraising program.

Every university president undoubtedly had a few such people on the staff. There never seemed to be enough, however.

The full hour with Ted quickly passed. From the session the president took for his briefcase only one small folder. It would stay there for the rest of the summer for handy reference—only a half-dozen typewritten pages, yet a complete blueprint for a full summer of development work. The role and responsibility of a dozen leaders and various groups was fully agreed upon, all parties had been advised and problems resolved, and only a half-dozen calls were necessary for the president to make, contacts no one else could handle.

How different from appointments with some deans, other senior staff, faculty members, student representatives, alumni emissaries, or even trustees. Academe seemed to be filled with procrastinators, windbags, fuzzy thinkers, puffed up toads.

Did private business have such baggage? It would be worth a look.

Comstock had forgotten Professor Hutchenson's early June visit—or he had just chosen to put it out of mind and move on to more promising activities. Summer was almost gone. Preparations were being readied for another opening of the fall semester when Bill, looking at his appointments for the day, viewed with mixed feelings a late morning appearance of Professor Hutchenson.

"'Trouble at home and threats from neighboring countries,'" Hutchenson quoted the ambassador, "had delayed considerations by His Highness of timely follow-up on the center. However, it is now back on track, and we can proceed with financing to the extent of some one to three million dollars, as his Excellency told me just yesterday."

For Edward Hillary Hutchenson using the correct and complete titles in the diplomatic world was not only proper, but it also conveyed his own sophistication to the ignorant—and Hutchenson considered Comstock and all other academics to be illiterate on such protocol. After all, several administrations, both Democratic and Republican, had sought this professor's services for various high-level diplomatic and other governmental responsibilities, as Hutchenson was quick to reveal.

Comstock doubted that Hutchenson had ever been offered even a dog catcher's job. He only wished that something or someone would take this self-anointed international expert, this supercilious snob out of his hair.

On the other hand, this lordly, contemptuous bastard could somehow attract money.

Building a university required money. And one of the ways to get money was to search it out with whatever kind of sleuth could do the job. Sometimes, Comstock had learned, this meant sending a skunk after another skunk.

Freshmen arrived, other undergrads stormed back with all the arrogance of perpetual sophomores, and the campus again took on the character of organized chaos.

And, as though he had been waiting for just such a period, Hutchenson called again.

"Ambassador Crispie says the King wants to proceed immediately. He would like to send $750,000 now, more money to come later—much more—and to show his philanthropic interest to the world, His Majesty wishes to come to Midtown University and receive an honorary degree."

Comstock, known for his calm, friendly demeanor, proud of holding his tongue and of his ability as a shrewd poker-faced player when the situation demanded, could hold himself no longer.

Here it was. A tinhorn dictator was buying his way to the center of the world's political stage at the lowest bargain-basement price. Several million had dwindled to less than one, and now he was adding the most irritating part of all—an honorary degree!

"Well, that does it," snapped Comstock.

"Tell the ambassador to forget the whole mess," the president continued. There was so much nausea in the president's voice that Hutchenson didn't dare interrupt.

"One million dollars is my absolute minimum, and so far as bringing him to campus for an honorary degree, the idea is asinine. We would be the laughingstock of the whole country. I can think of nothing that would cheapen this university more!"

Concluding, and perhaps inadvertently giving Hutchenson the parameters for the continued pursuit of a gift, Comstock elaborated, "Yes, one million is the minimum. Put it up front. We'll establish the center, get a minimum program going, wait to see what other support is forthcoming, and then think about honorary degrees—or possibly other ways of recognition."

Wasn't there another way to say thank you? Comstock never quite gave up the search.

Months later—following a series of exchanges with message after message going back and forth—the million-dollar grant arrived. A named professorship was quietly created in the potentate's name, and amicable relations were established.

And, the honorary degree was awarded, not in Washington but in the palace of the recipient, with the queen, the prime minister, and other dignitaries in attendance.

The luncheon following the ceremony was an elegant affair, but Comstock and members of his party were fully relaxed, put at ease by their warm welcome. The potentate spoke respectfully and enthusiastically about the importance of education for the citizens of his own country and for the world at large. Only when he reached the university in his observations—he did most of the talking—did he express any doubts. And his reference was one of hesitancy rather than downright disapproval. It was his observation that some professors were casting doubts on government policies, raising questions about prevailing religious beliefs, and, in some cases he had heard about, questioning individual property rights.

Turning to Comstock, the monarch put it tersely but kindly. "How do you control the faculty in your university?" Falling back on an old cliché, Prexy smiled as he replied, "In our country we say a professor is one who thinks otherwise."

At that point the queen wisely came to the rescue of all by observing, "That's what I have always said. A professor follows only himself." A round of hearty laughter revealed to all that new ideas, even those from professors, were welcome.

How incongruous, thought Comstock. Here is a dictator, in the eyes of the western world, who probably understands the meaning of academic freedom more clearly than many leaders of business and government back home.

As for the trip, Comstock and his small party traveled halfway around the world for the occasion, lived for some ten days in a lifestyle not usually experienced by an American university president, all at the monarch's expense. Hesitantly, perhaps even grudgingly, Comstock had to conclude that Hutchenson had delivered a major gift, the entire experience had given new insights into the way of life in at least one kingdom, a world removed from our own shores.

The honorary degree–maybe Butler at Columbia had something after all. At least the development officer found a more open mind when he broached the same old subject to the president not long after his return.

"He doesn't suspect it; he will be surprised, absolutely shocked if you even suggest that he might be given an honorary degree." Ed McKiever was speaking of Andy Pritt, a former MU student.

Have I been blind? Comstock wondered to himself. No, he reasoned, he had simply allowed himself to become prejudiced about honorary degrees to the extent that he refused to admit that such an award might be appropriate in some cases. Among all the friends and benefactors of a college or university could there be some to whom it would be a pleasure to make the award?

Andrew Jackson Pritt over the years had done so much for Midtown U. Leaving before even completing one semester of academic work, Pritt had gone to work building a small soft drink stand into a chain of fast-food outlets. His was another success story, and like so many other hardworking, grateful Americans, he had turned to philanthropy in later years.

Maybe it was the untimely death of his daughter, an only child, from a heart disease, or the effects of a dual loss–his wife died shortly thereafter–or perhaps it was his lifelong concern for all humanity. Whatever the reason, here was a businessman who used his wealth to help others.

Small in stature, energetic, bull-doggish in endurance, modest in his presumptions, yet realistic in his appraisal of human frailties, Andy lived his life ever-mindful of his early years in rural Missouri.

From his parents, first generation settlers from the old country and from two older sisters, Pritt knew firsthand of homesteader hardships, frontier survival necessities, and the richness of human mercy. Man's mortality was personal to Andy; he learned early of its reality. Where some became callused, Andy Pritt became compassionate.

Comstock felt like kicking himself. Here was an honest-to-goodness humanitarian without oratory, without fanfare, and without design. Here was a man who took for granted his own deeply felt concerns for other human beings to the point that he conscientiously denied his own endowment of this virtue while assuming it to be present in others.

There were those on the faculty who felt academicians had a corner on imagination, creativity, and innovation. How could this little man from the fast-food world rise to a point at which Midtown U. could rightfully give him an honorary degree? Comstock was off his rocker—again—was the way Professor John P. Boaker put it at the community table in the Faculty Club a few days before graduation. Among a dozen colleagues, only one could give a fairly complete accounting of Andy Pritt's success in business, philanthropy, innovations in marketing, or contributions to complex management and mass distribution.

Glancing round the table, Boaker could count on most of his colleagues to turn thumbs down on business, to rise above making money, and to reside in joyous smugness at the academy's monopoly on new ideas, truly creative thinking, and desirable cultural change.

The businessman lived in the real world where he had to meet the payroll, put the goods on the market, fire the incompetent, and keep government off his back. The professor had no deadline to meet. His was a world of meditation, daydreams, and air castles. Clichés covered ignorance both on campus and in business.

For one who had a lifetime in both worlds, Comstock could see the commonality, the likenesses as well as the differences, and maybe, just maybe, he thought he could someday add an ounce of understanding to both sides. Someone needs to build bridges. He resolved again to try.

For now Comstock knew Andy Pritt could stand tall in both worlds!

Years later, after both men had grown old, Andy would still say to his intimate friend, Bill Comstock, "Mr. President, I never in my wildest dreams imagined that an honorary degree would come to me."

And Comstock would still respond with honest enthusiasm, "Doctor Andy, in my three decades as a university president, I awarded more honorary degrees than I can remember, but none gave me more pleasure or was more rightly deserved than yours." And he would raise his glass to that good man and his lifelong friend as tears again appeared in Andy's eyes.

A.J. Pritt's list of good deeds seemed endless. Over a period of 40 years, he had financed a sizable research program on heart disease—his daughter's death from that disease before reaching her 21st birthday was a loss never to be forgotten—a museum, a public park, a children's playground, and an endowment for boys' and girls' clubs were but a few of the works he left to that rural county in Missouri where he began life's travels. One of the great hospitals of the country displayed his name prominently, in spite of his protest, for his generosity in financing a major addition.

These and many others were the public evidences of Andy's philanthropy. His greatest impact was felt, however, among the immigrants whom he helped to find jobs, homes, schools, and a new life in America. If a person wanted to study or to work, adult or youngster, Andy would give that person a chance.

How absentminded Comstock had been not to see Pritt in his full posture—an alum (colleges and universities had long since adopted the practice of claiming all who had ever registered as alumni), a former trustee, and a major donor. It was both embarrassing and unforgivable.

Owners and trainers of horses use blinders on their animals, or so Comstock was told, to prompt the animals to do desired things. What was his excuse for wearing them?

If anyone needed unimpeded peripheral vision, thought the president, it is the CEO of a university or of a profit-making enterprise. He was well aware that being blindsided was always a danger to the CEO.

But the junk that came to his desk, the piddling matters that seemed always to be yelling for attention—did other CEOs daily confront the same mountains of unimportant chaff? There were those with major administrative responsibilities who seemed to go about their tasks with more free time, with fewer distractions, or with the help of better organized staff than his. As a professor of management in his earlier years, Comstock had taught the values of delegation, decentralization, and placing decision making at the lowest possible levels of the organization.

Had the teaching been wrong, or was Comstock his own worst enemy? Somewhere along the way, Bill Comstock was determined to analyze the whole perplexing problem. In the meantime he could only look at two of those CEOs in the business world on whose boards he served and marvel at their administrative skills. Personally, the president knew he was endowed with adequate physical endurance and low blood pressure, and from his first days as an assistant professor in a very select Ivy League institution, Comstock had learned that he could hold his own in any academic debate. In fact, that first decade of his academic life had taught him many things that would serve him well in his career as a university president.

A knock at the door brought yet another surprise to the president.

"Bill," a loyal and outstanding vice president began, "John Turner has done more for this university than almost anyone I know. As we look ahead to the midyear convocation, where all schools and colleges will be together, why don't we give him an honorary degree?"

So help me, thought Comstock, it's happened a second time. I have allowed myself to think so much about the jackasses who get such honors but don't deserve them that I've missed the outstanding people who should be considered.

John Turner's complete career flashed across his imaginary screen as he responded. "Yes, Austin, I agree. It would be very much in order."

Here was truly an outstanding scholar and teacher. He had been "Mr. Greek and Latin" at Midtown for decades, serving for a dozen years, too, as university marshal. Public ceremonies, which John Lewis Turner handled, always had the right blend of dignity, good humor, and aplomb. Even in the days of student unrest, urban riots, and political upheaval, Turner had managed somehow to strike the right balance between chaos and good order. It was hard to envision another who exercised such a delicate touch in the midst of possible anarchy.

Yet, it was his scholarship that stood out above all else. During a period when students were turning to competitive high-tech and exotic science, when the whole of western tradition was being challenged, Professor Turner, as all who knew him addressed him, made students want more of the classics. And having tasted Greek or Latin with Turner, these young students, often in disreputable clothing, with disheveled hair and sandals flopping, came back for more of the origins of western civilization.

Now retired for some five years, John Turner built further goodwill for the university by shepherding faculty retirees, speaking to numerous alumni groups, greeting new students, and continuing to publish scholarly books in the field.

Comstock never forgot a single detail of the awards ceremony where Professor Turner was awarded the degree.

Escorted by the academic vice president to a spot at the president's right beside the podium, Turner listened as the citation was read. Comstock was barely through the first sentence when the faculty, sitting in the front rows just below the platform, men and women from all disciplines and rank, rose, a few at first and then all. Silently and unanimously, with facial expressions and stained handkerchiefs, they said, "Thank you, Professor Turner, for what you have done for our university."

Later, in the dressing room, as dignity gave way to relief, and caps and gowns gave way to red suspenders and comfortable dress, a spontaneous handshake said it all. Professor and president, two very articulate people, needed no words to explain the satisfaction and pleasure each felt.

Watching these two major players on Midtown U's academic stage, E.K. Lindstrom, the wise old chairman of the board, marveled at the bond of friendship and respect that their years together had molded. Here was the professor of classics whose entire life had been consumed with the ancients—the so-called dead languages, the philosophy of the Greeks, the laws of the Romans, and the Judeo-Christian ethic. Beside him walked the president of the university who, while a student of literature in his early years, had nonetheless become a pragmatic problem solver later in his career. Here were two men united as one in their combined zeal for MU. Each had lived long enough, had climbed the rungs of their respective career ladders to the point at which each understood the necessary ingredients of a great university. So, too, could each of these men relate to their colleagues—those dead and gone, those still active, and those yet to come. When a proposed action could damage a part of the university in any way, these two were always among the first to see and understand the implication. Comstock knew that a university's ever-present and overriding purpose was to bring the student into the influence of the John Turners of the campus. All else in the world of higher education is but means to that end.

From a gathering overflowing with goodwill and pride, Comstock was forced to turn to yet another matter involving honorary degrees. It was a simmering case so vulgar as it built to an ugly climax, that Midtown's president would wish again for an institutional policy of no such honors to anyone, like Minnesota, Cornell, and Rice.

Board Chairman Lindstrom and every other member of the assembly were free to enjoy the exhilaration of the occasion, but Comstock, while seeming to do the same, was all the while turning over in his mind the possible twists and turns that lay ahead.

An international plot was being hatched, and Jackson Lawrence Pickard was the mastermind. That Comstock was the key player was another of those unfortunate coincidences; he had an acquaintance in the wrong place at the wrong time.

Pickard's father chose Jackson (from Stonewall) for his newborn's first name, and then added Lawrence (from Arabia), undoubtedly preparing the way for a great military figure, diplomat, or politician. Jack Pickard must have been a bit of a disappointment, at least in his physical appearance. At twenty-five he stood only five feet, eight inches tall and weighed one hundred and forty pounds—far short of the commanding figure his father had envisioned.

But Jack Pickard, who let everyone know that Bill Comstock was his longtime friend, didn't allow his small stature to impede his plans. Comstock, on the other hand, was a bit uncomfortable with Pickard's public display of their friendship, especially as the relationship was reported to other university presidents in the Washington area.

It was true the two men had known each other for many years. The first meeting went back to the late thirties when both happened to be students on an Ivy League campus. Pickard was studying law and business, having come with all of his father's ambition from their well-to-do home in the Southwest. Comstock was spending only a few weeks, participating in an institute on problems of rural America. Although the next contact would not come for 15 years, neither man forgot the other.

With sparkling credentials in both law and business, Pickard was a natural to be hired early by the War Production Board as World War II burst open, consuming the country's complete attention. After four years in military service, Comstock returned to take up again his academic career; Pickard went home to prepare himself for his next opportunity in Washington.

Brilliant, ambitious, ruthless, but careful, Jack Pickard learned that ability alone was not enough for a complete career in the nation's capital. For the role he wished to play some future day he needed wealth—wealth beyond the comfortable well-to-do.

The myriad experiences gained in his five years with the War Production Board helped him in his climb to the top. In the years that followed, it was apparent this young entrepreneur had carefully mapped his strategy with uncanny foresight. Picking first the oil and gas industries of his native region, Pickard caught the wave of unparalleled expansion, moving with confidence into new markets where others hesitated. By the time President Dwight Eisenhower announced his plan to connect all 48 states with a system of superhighways, Pickard had bought an already successful trucking company. His fleet grew well ahead of the highway construction, and many contracts with shippers were signed before the railroads began to recognize their losses.

With generous contributions to both Eisenhower campaigns, Jack Pickard, personally and through each of his separate companies, all of which carried their owner's name, renewed contacts in Washington. Offered an ambassadorship, Pickard declined. He saw little to be gained from going off to some country halfway around the globe and living for four years out of touch with the political and economic forces of Washington. Furthermore, he considered such a post just a bit beneath his just reward; to wear the title of "Ambassador" for the rest of his life, an achievement which some spent a lifetime to secure, was not enough. But Jack Pickard knew, too, that as his wealth grew—and it was now moving toward the billion-dollar mark—the traffic to his door would increase. Besides, there was no need to hurry; he was still a young man.

Wealth meant power if a person chose to use it for that purpose, and Pickard had power foremost in his mind when he returned to the Southwest after the war. Otherwise, he would have remained in Washington, serving his years in some comfortable, reasonably high-level bureaucrat's chair until retirement brought additional years of pleasant living.

Economic power certainly came with great wealth, but Pickard had seen wealth used to gain political power, to get recognition in the arts, and to elevate an entire family to positions of leadership. This son of the Southwest wanted it all, and he now had acquired the wealth he believed necessary to gain the power he wanted.

Too shrewd to put all his political eggs in one basket, Pickard was already recognized as a major contributor to the Democratic party as well as to the Republicans by the time a young senator from Massachusetts was running for president. So when John Kennedy went to the White House, Jack Pickard and wife, Delores, were high on the list of regular guests. This was exactly as planned. In fact, the Pickard name was appearing with increasing frequency on government commissions, boards, advisory bodies, and special missions. No end was in sight.

Did Jack Pickard want to be president? If so, some columnists pointed out, he ought to run for congress or for governor, or at least accept a cabinet post, something it was said he had earlier rejected. Pickard was content to let the speculation go unchecked.

How much their lives had changed, thought Comstock, as he followed the news of Jack Pickard. He was hardly prepared for the warm, personal letter that reached his desk at New England University upon the announcement of his selection to the presidency of Midtown. Pickard wrote as if they had just had lunch together the previous week. Back in the fifties, the two men had exchanged brief greetings on two occasions when conferences in Washington brought business leaders and academics together to talk about ways of furthering mutual interests. But these were large groups numbering several hundred, with little opportunity for one-on-one exchanges.

"And when you take up your duties in Washington, I want to get together with you," Pickard's letter read, following a short, friendly reference to their initial meeting years earlier. "I have long been interested in Midtown U; it is a university ideally located to play a major role in national and international affairs," the message continued. The paragraph finished with the sentence, "Perhaps I can be helpful in a small way as you and your associates go to work."

What a message! How many university presidents receive such a letter from a billionaire? And one who proudly, so it appears, parades himself as a "longtime friend." Academics seem always to be chasing persons of wealth, not the other way around.

With a bit more than his usual cordiality, but stopping short of inviting a buddy-buddy relationship, Comstock replied, agreeing, of course, to a get-together when he reached Washington. It was a wait filled with curiosity. To an experienced academic, this billionaire seemed out of character.

"This is Dr. Comstock, the new president of Midtown," Pickard said as he introduced his guest to the manager of a very exclusive luncheon club in Washington. "He's going to do wonders for that university—and I'm going to help him," the genial host added before either of the others could comment.

Preparing for his meeting with Pickard, Comstock had learned that his wife, Delores, was serving as a trustee of their home state university where, incidentally, the two had met as undergraduates, and that Jack had served two terms as alumni trustee of his Ivy League alma mater. It was clear both Pickards were interested and active in university affairs. What then was Jack's relationship with Midtown? That was something Comstock would quickly learn.

"Since my first stay in Washington, beginning way back in World War II," Pickard began, "I have felt that Midtown University is the one institution in this part of the country best located to become a truly intellectual center for the nation's capital. World leaders—and they pass through here every day—need the help of scholarly evaluation, and such thoughtful assessment of proposed actions can best come from the academic community. Everybody else has an ax to grind. Our own leaders in government have platforms, policies, commitments; they come to Washington having made promises, most of which they can never hope to keep, of course. But the same is true of business and industry; we have our interests, too, and we aren't going to be objective in weighing all the alternatives. We need a great university with its community of scholars to keep us all honest; we need it right here at the seat of government."

Seldom had Comstock heard such forthrightness, but Pickard didn't stop there.

"University professors, protected by tenure, exercising their rights of academic freedom are the only people in our society who can speak their minds—truth as they see it—and not suffer irreparable harm. And, if one professor goes off the deep end, his colleagues take him to task."

Goodness, thought Comstock. Here is a man who understands a university; he knows what academic freedom means and the rationale for tenure. As for Midtown's mission, Pickard practically took the words out of Comstock's mouth. Those were the very reasons which persuaded this academic to leave the comforts of New England for the political crossfire and lousy weather of the Potomac.

"Now, Bill," Pickard turned personal, "I know that you have a hundred things before you at Midtown right now. When you have a chance to catch your breath and to think about some possible new thrusts that you want to make as you get hold of the university's problems, let me know what I can do to help. In the meantime I'll just sit on the sidelines and be quiet."

Thanking him for his interest, a nice lunch, and a warm welcome to Washington, and believing that both he and Midtown had an important friend in Jack Pickard, Comstock took his leave.

Five years later these two men would part company, their work and interest never to coincide again.

The drama involved honorary degrees—and many other things.

During President Lyndon Johnson's administration, Jack Pickard decided the time was ripe for his move to Washington. No one would know whether it was Lyndon's infamous arm-twisting skill that brought Pickard to his administration or whether this wealthy supporter of both parties came of his own accord. Whatever the reason, Pickard became a White House mastermind for Latin America. President Johnson found in Pickard a successful businessman, broadly experienced in working south of the border, one who spoke the language fluently—a by-product of youth spent with Mexican-American neighbors—and a self-educated cultural anthropologist. Even the professional foreign service would have been hard-pressed to find someone better prepared to undertake such a broad assignment on the Johnson staff.

He had one other notable attribute, a rare one indeed; Jack Pickard's gamesmanship was certainly on a par with that of Lyndon Johnson. It was in his first few months of service that Pickard once again took up serious discourse with Bill Comstock. The intervening period had been spent in watchful waiting.

"Delores and I," Jack began as the two sat down together again, "would like to encourage your Latin American program at Midtown, and we're thinking first of sponsoring a series, perhaps running a full year, of art exhibitions from Mexico and the other Latin countries. Your art gallery—and Delores and I have been there several times, thanks to your thoughtful invitations—would seem an ideal place for bringing such exhibits to the nation's capital.

"If you think well of the idea and, of course, if schedules would permit, Delores and I would be pleased to finance four or five of the shows. We did this a couple of times back home, and each show cost about a hundred thousand," Pickard concluded.

Unprepared, since he couldn't anticipate Pickard's agenda, Comstock expressed interest, thanked his host, and promised to get back immediately after conferring with the museum director and the head of the art department.

"Let me commit us to $500,000, Bill," were Pickard's parting words. "That might buy four or five shows. Whatever you can work into your schedule will be fine with us."

Midtown U's art faculty was ecstatic. They had been unable to find sponsors for a number of exhibitions, and especially difficult were those from Latin America. Yet, there was a world rich in the arts, one which was more difficult to reach than other places with similar treasures. Pickard's offer was quickly accepted.

With five carefully staged exhibitions, each from a different country or region of Latin America, every painting and piece of sculpture carefully researched and catalogued, Midtown's modest but adequate gallery gained immense new recognition. Newspapers in both New York and Washington carried reviews by leading critics, concentrating on various aspects of each show, all laudatory. As the news media picked up stories of the many artists and their works, Midtown University gained an entirely new dimension of academic visibility. Applications for both undergraduate and professional programs increased tenfold from students in Latin America. Within 12 months of the final exhibition, Midtown had replaced Texas and Florida as the preferred place for further study by Latin Americans, a development that did not go unnoticed among the country's academic leaders.

Having ingratiated himself to the other Washington area universities, although none to quite the level of Midtown, Pickard concluded it was time to play his trump card. He asked Bill Comstock if he would be so kind as to host a luncheon where he, Pickard, might discuss with all the other presidents still another Latin American initiative.

Comstock did so with pleasure, yet not completely free of concern. Was Jack Pickard just too smooth an operator, or was Bill Comstock simply unable to throw off an intuitive skepticism reinforced by his earlier years in Yankee territory? As the jovial group sat down to lunch at the Cosmos Club, Washington's home for intellectuals–a classification that the members willingly bestowed upon themselves–there seemed no reason for apprehension.

Pickard, confident that five university presidents had been adequately courted, wasted no time in laying out his plan for "further solidifying the relations with our neighbors to the south." "We can," he said, "if we only seize the opportunity, show these fellow citizens of the western hemisphere our genuine concern for their welfare, their way of life, and the common interests we all share. We can remove once and for all their strongly held belief that we in the United States look always to Europe for partners rather than to our south."

"I suggest, gentlemen, that we invite the five leading statesmen from that part of the world to Washington for a western hemisphere summit, a kind of assembly which has never, heretofore in history, taken place. President Johnson," the first inference of any kind Pickard made to possible interest or participation from the White House, "has been looking for some way to strengthen our relationships in that part of the world, and I think he will support such a summit when I take the idea to him."

"But where do we fit in?" the question on every president's tongue was voiced by Comstock only because the others deferred to him and because of the close relationship which Pickard had so carefully nurtured with others at the table.

"I would like to see each of our universities"—he slipped easily into the "our" posture when referring to the institutions represented by each of the five presidents—"honor one of these invited statesmen with a special convocation where he could give a major address and receive an honorary degree. Supporting activities such as seminars, art exhibitions, social events, and the like could be arranged as each campus might choose."

With a slight pause, Pickard concluded. "Let me stop there, and you gentlemen can tell me whether the idea is worth pursuing or whether we should forget it." While casually voiced, no one around the table was inclined to view the matter lightly. As a matter of fact, all five presidents were caught in a vise. They had to buy the package being offered or run the risk of alienating a man of great wealth, and lately of uncertain power, who had already demonstrated a willingness to use his own dollars to help their institutions.

Academics, when caught in such a predicament, must confer. Each voiced the need for advice, involvement, or commitment from faculty members—experts on Latin America—historians, political scientists, anthropologists, economists, linguists, and others among their associates.

But other words flowed freely. Imaginative, pioneering, bold, creative, dramatic, and a vast vocabulary of equally complimentary terms gushed from the presidents as each strove mightily to outshine the others in praise of Pickard's proposal. But, alas, in the end they all had to confer–find others with whom blame would be shared should the idea prove to be impractical, impossible, or just plain stupid.

What a box Pickard had built around five presidents! All left in a deep quandary. Maybe there was good reason that such a summit had never before taken place.

It was a proposal that would prove to be not just nauseating, but potentially embarrassing to half the world.

Addressing the presidents a week later, Pickard insisted the group move promptly. Each president had more questions, and Pickard had answers.

Who would pick the five statesmen? Which university would be host to which one? How would the White House placate the many other countries and their leaders who would not be included?

Key faculty members at Midtown U, whose advice Comstock had sought, had given their president an earful. Dictatorships were rampant in Latin America, something Bill Comstock already knew, of course. Did Pickard choose to call them statesmen, or did he have in mind the truly forward looking, humane leaders in that part of the world–writers, scholars, diplomats, and philosophers–who, if honored, would indeed show the world a fundamental understanding of freedom, integrity, and democracy?

"It would be a great summit, indeed," Comstock remembered one of Midtown's professors as saying, "if we could invite the very popular Belunde-Terry (then one of South America's great architects recently turned politician) as our statesman to be honored. But he is living abroad, in exile, because of his strong pro-democracy views."

But Jack Pickard was well ahead of the presidents.

It took the full two hours of exchange, interspersed with lunch, to reveal the details. With delicate questioning and appropriate reading between the lines, the White House blueprint, as it was being touted, was finally laid out in full view.

According to Pickard, President Johnson had bought the idea immediately and, in his words, "directed me to proceed with all deliberate speed. 'It is brilliant, timely, and exactly what we need to show our friendship and concern for our southern neighbors.'" Those were the words of the President of the United States, so said Jackson Lawrence Pickard. Pretty heady stuff for five academics, and from a man of great wealth, now special assistant to the leader of the free world!

Five statesmen, three of whom Comstock's advisers on the Midtown campus had described as ruthless dictators, were already picked. "No, it would not be possible," said Pickard, "to change the roster at this point. Preliminary conversations had already been held with the appropriate ambassadors," he added, obviously determined.

How much had taken place in one week! Too much. "There is no way," said another president who called Comstock following the luncheon, "that Pickard could have put all this together in one week." And, facing up to the unfolding dilemma, he added, "We are being set up."

Seldom had Bill Comstock felt so uncomfortable. Jack Pickard continued, more than ever, to present his relationship with Comstock as that of an old and trusted friend. Yes, the other presidents had responded to Pickard's overtures, and all had received significant financial contributions for their own campuses from this wealthy and seemingly generous man. Now, as Jack Pickard was putting the squeeze on all five presidents and their institutions, Comstock realized that, like the mice that concluded the cat should have a bell, he had to carry the message.

Early in his career, Bill Comstock had learned that unpleasant tasks should not be put off and allowed to fester because the dread was usually worse than the deed. Seldom had the stakes been higher—all the more reason for speedy resolution in this instance.

"It is my job to inform Pickard of our decision, and I shall do it just as soon as I can get an appointment to see him," was the way Comstock put the matter to each of the other four presidents. "I only need to know that you don't want to participate in the summit as Pickard proposed. Is that correct?"

It was a kind of signing off with each of his colleagues, something of a roll-call vote by telephone, that armed Comstock for his forthcoming encounter with Pickard.

"Jack, it won't fly," Comstock said firmly.

Seated in Pickard's comfortable office on the second floor of the Executive Office Building with full view of the White House, Midtown's president began with another of his own rules of conduct: If you have unwelcome news to deliver, do the dastardly deed and have it done. Let explanation, excuse, what-might-have-been, or rationalization come after. It was the way Midtown's president did business, and he certainly wasn't going to change when dealing with Jack Pickard. A long, drawn out discussion of the whys, and why nots, with the ultimate answer already a certainty, would only multiply the agony. Comstock often compared such a session to "cutting the dog's tail off, inch by inch."

But Jack Pickard seemed not to be surprised with Comstock's blunt announcement.

"Well, Comstock." It was the first time Pickard had ever greeted his longtime friend without putting Doctor or President alongside or calling him just plain Bill, and the obvious discourtesy registered clearly. "You have missed a great opportunity," Pickard continued, "one that will never come again. The forthcoming summit will mark an historic milestone for the entire western hemisphere. It is too bad the universities will not be there to participate."

Turning a bit red in the face, yet holding back his growing anger with a measured lowering of his voice, Jack Pickard went on.

"I learned long ago that you people on the campus are not practical. You live in a cocoon; you don't know the real world; and I doubt that you ever will." It was the beginning of a five-minute tirade, ending with neither handshake nor any other show of courtesy by the man behind the big desk. Midtown U's president was dismissed with a snarl, something he had never before seen from Pickard. They would never again speak to each other, being careful to stay beyond range, even while attending the same event, as happened frequently in Washington.

Glad that the bitter confrontation was over, Bill Comstock, nonetheless, felt the burden as he walked back to his office. He wanted to reply to Pickard's outburst; the answer was so clear. Only a year earlier, he and almost 500 other university presidents had attended a meeting in Moscow where the role of a university had been debated. Those presidents behind the then Iron Curtain argued that such an institution exists only to serve the state, while those from the west maintained that service to humanity, even if it means criticism of the state–one's own government–is the primary responsibility of the university. But he knew any rejoinder would only fall on deaf ears.

For Pickard universities could be used for political purposes; for Comstock such a use would be a surrender of integrity. Little wonder the two men never again had anything to say to each other.

No summit ever took place.

Had Lyndon Johnson really known about the grandiose strategy for putting Latin American affairs on a higher plane? When Comstock later leaned that Pickard had already held discussions with the ambassadors whose chiefs were to be honored, that host universities had been agreed upon even before the presidents assembled for their initial luncheon with Pickard, Midtown's president was happy that all relationships with him had been ended.

Months later, as the full story emerged, it became clear that Jack Pickard had actually come to Washington with his dream of giving a new birth to the Monroe Doctrine through his well-thought-out plan. President Johnson and five universities were only instruments for him to use. That he left government service soon afterward was not surprising; that he remained in Washington for the rest of his life only confirmed the strength of the virus known as Potomac fever.

But presidents, cabinet officers, and congressional committees can always make use of wealthy citizens, and Pickard was ever ready with continued generous contributions to both major parties. He remained busy, therefore, on special assignments, investigative commissions, and nonprofit enterprises. More than one charity saw fit to feature either Jack or Delores Pickard, or both, as sponsors, hosts, or special guests at their affairs. It was a life that kept this couple on the society pages of the daily press for the next two decades. From his carefully controlled distance, Bill Comstock could only conclude that Jack Pickard had achieved at least part of what he set out to do. If he fell short of reaching all the power he wanted, he at least got a full share of attention and recognition.

Whenever Comstock reflected on the whole Pickard affair, the fact that honorary degrees were to play an integral part irritated him deeply.

Honorary degrees! They were nothing but devilish appendages for higher education round the world, thought Comstock again and again. How many breaches of morality, compromises of principle, or acts of deception could be avoided if honorary degrees didn't exist? But the award of such an honor was a magnet too tempting for those in government, business, or academe itself to pass up. Boards and presidents of colleges and universities, those who carried the burden of selecting recipients, would be vulnerable to its abuses into eternity, Comstock concluded. But as one extreme followed another, so it was, even with honorary degrees.

Board Chairman E.K. Lindstrom continued to ponder the memorable ceremony in which an honorary degree had been bestowed upon Professor John Turner.

As one who had not taken his own college years very seriously—the gentleman's "C" was his readily admitted record, supplemented by a busy fraternity schedule and gung ho participation in athletics—Lindstrom kept replaying the Turner ceremony in his mind. Maybe, thought the old trustee, there is more to a college education than I realized; clearly, Comstock and Turner see the reach of a university much better than I do.

Neither Comstock nor anyone else could foresee the effects that a ceremony might have on a participant or observer. Like the observation often made of the teacher: "No one really knows where his or her influence ends." For EK the award to Turner possessed such a level of goodness—the right thing to do—that he could never forget the experience. To him it was the mountain peak, the just reward, the capping of a lifetime of superior service—it was all of these in his mind. He had never quite experienced such a moment in any other of life's activities.

Successful in business, EK had carved out a place at the top of Washington society for himself and his attractive and gracious wife. With enough money, yet not rich, they moved easily as equals among the economic, political, and social leadership of the great capital city. It had not been a particularly painful struggle. They arrived as a young couple, both graduates of recognized and socially accepted colleges, he from New England and she from Philadelphia. He was soon at work in a local business, and she was quickly accepted into appropriate ladies' charitable organizations and social groups.

It would be years before the simple act of awarding a degree would take EK's thoughts beyond the routine of a comfortable life in his chosen city. All that was changed when he saw a university at close range.

Within a few days of the ceremony which had so moved him, EK visited his attorney. There, he changed his will. He would leave his entire estate to Midtown University upon his death and that of his wife. Years later, Comstock, long since retired, learned of the sizable estate that came to the University after EK's widow passed away. Only then did the attorney share with him a full account of EK's actions.

Having moved routinely up the ladder of success to the honored and prestigious chairmanship of a university's board without any serious understanding or commitment to the cause of education, this man came to see the far-reaching effects of the institution whose creation was aimed squarely at the service of society itself. Perhaps it was a case in which a man, amply endowed with common sense, had never before thought seriously about this particular institution or the leadership which the greater society might get from the activities of a strong university.

"Seldom," said the attorney as he recounted EK's behavior from that visit years earlier, "have I seen a person so moved. EK said, 'I want everything that I own and all that I will ever own to go to Midtown University. I want it used for scholarships so that kids—kids from the whole country—can go to college. And please, Mr. Counselor, (a favorite approach to his good friend and designated executor) handle the estate carefully. We both want (including his wife in the collective pronoun for the first time) every possible cent to get to MU's scholarship fund after we're gone.'"

All nine members of the Development Committee of the Board were present for the report of the attorney, F. Elwood Smith. The estate had, indeed, been well handled; otherwise the final figures could not have been so large. Here was a lawyer who carefully guarded the assets, charged no fee—not even expenses—in order to deliver EK's estate to Midtown U in the best possible order.

How pleased Comstock felt that he had presided when EK, upon retirement from the board, was awarded an honorary degree. Some things appeared in order; the honor was a perfect fit.

There are many people, thought Comstock, and Elwood Smith is among them, who give their all to the cause of education. Universities provided the learning by which lawyers earned their living and, likewise, accountants, engineers, architects, and a host of other professionals. Comstock looked upon all as important links to private business.

But would the chasm ever be fully bridged between two fundamental parts of civilization where mutual misunderstanding prevailed? Private business on the one hand was seemingly always suspicious of the campus and the professor in the college and university forever perplexed by free enterprise. Neither seemed to understand or appreciate the other; and yet, the welfare of each was vital to the other. E.K. Lindstrom had come to see the university in all its glory—an institution of inestimable value to business. Could professors be made to see their dependency on business? More than a philosophical question, thought Comstock, one that must be addressed if the country is not to fall behind the rest of the world. Damn! It nagged and nagged.

II

Academic Freedom and Tenure: Saint or Satan?

"Tell me, Bill, just how in the world do you live with that thing called tenure?"

The question, again, but this time in a situation in which there were both time and need for an answer.

Gathered around the luncheon table, feeling a bit relaxed after a full morning of committee meetings, Comstock's seven colleagues on the board of National Charities, Inc., the coordinating body for more than a hundred of the country's public service organizations, were immediately attentive. Each director had some experience with, or knowledge of, tenure; only one in addition to Comstock understood its history and importance. Frank T. Wright had served as professor, dean, and president of one of the Boston area universities before retiring and coming to Washington as director of research for a leading think tank that dealt with economic and social problems on the world scene.

But the question had been directed to Comstock. And the common one-sentence answer, often flippant, would not suffice. Neither would a philosophical discourse, lengthy lecture, or even logical observation. Seven fully attentive people, all respectful of the Midtown president, waited for the reply. He knew before he began that five of the men were skeptical that tenure could be rightfully defended.

The response had to be thoughtful and complete, but brief.

"Perhaps the best way I can answer you," he said, as he looked his friend Harold Forsythe in the eye, "is to tell you about one incident that occurred during my years at New England University." All knew that Comstock had come to Midtown from the presidency of the institution in the Northeast and fully understood the reference.

"We had a professor there, a brilliant fellow in the school of forestry, who raised serious questions about acid rain and the damage it was causing wildlife, particularly fish in a number of lakes and ponds in the region. Now remember," admonished Comstock as he continued, "these were the early days of such research, years before the EPA and other such governmental agencies were born, so our professor quickly attracted a lot of critics. Furthermore, he had a reply for each criticism, sometimes quick and combative. He simply refused to be quiet about what he was learning.

"And as professors are prone to do, this fellow got many of his students all excited. Some of them began collecting data all over New England, and before we hardly knew it, civic clubs and even town meetings were clamoring for our professor to come and talk to them."

By this time the appetizer had been served and consumed, and the waiter was clearing the dishes for the next course. Comstock quickly finished his story.

"As you might expect, some industry leaders weren't happy. They went to a state legislator and persuaded an accommodating politician to introduce a bill that would cancel all appropriations for research in the school of forestry."

Comstock then returned to the original question, "Our professor was protected by tenure. Even the businessmen knew he couldn't be fired, so they set about to choke off his research by withholding funds."

"And Bill's example can be multiplied a thousand times," added Frank Wright, joining the discussion.

"You see," and Wright too addressed Forsythe, "tenure is necessary in campus life so scholars and researchers may have the freedom to investigate the unknown—or to challenge things already learned. We call it academic freedom; it is the right of the professor to pursue what he gloriously describes as the truth."

"I see," said Jim Collins, CEO of one of Pittsburgh's giant corporations, and also chairman of the board of one of the region's leading universities, "that tenure is a condition necessary for the professor to do his work. But we have had our share of problems with tenure on our campus with professors who do little or nothing, yet hide behind the protective wall of tenure. Then they scream to high heaven if anyone questions the practice."

"I don't understand it," added Pat Barnet, CEO of a major food chain, one which was started by his parents and was still controlled by the family. "I simply wouldn't put up with it in my business." Turning to Comstock, he added, "I'm sorry for you poor devils who must live with it. But keep the practice on the campus; don't let it spread to private business. It's the work of the devil." All knew that this man had given millions to his alma mater. Interested from a distance, yes, but he wasn't going to get bogged down with such things as academic freedom.

"When I went to Ivy Wall University, even though I was to hold a distinguished professorship, I certainly didn't ask for tenure," said Leon T. Border. As chief scientist for a leading-edge technology company, Border made his reputation as a pioneer in automation where he held a number of patents in the computer world. After four years in Washington as science advisor to the President, he chose to accept the prestigious position at Ivy Wall rather than return to industry. Everyone around the table knew that he didn't need the protection of tenure but he got it anyway. It came with the position.

As he listened to the discussion, William C. Clorety was clearly troubled with tenure and all that it implied. A quiet, thoughtful man, Bill Clorety had won the respect of the entire country. After a successful career on Wall Street, this investment banker gave up a colossal income to serve at the Federal Reserve. Clorety was also a trustee of a small denominational college in his home state. He did not fully understand how tenure affected the smaller campus, and he was seeking new insights.

"Bill, as you know," Clorety addressed Midtown's president with an aside to the others—"Bill and I have compared notes on several campus matters—I am a trustee of a small Christian college in mid-America, and, frankly, our president becomes quite worried from time to time about this practice of tenure. He and the board want to be fair to the professors; on the other hand, we have certain beliefs and rules of behavior which we have agreed are important for our students. We make these things clear at the outset to incoming students. If they fail to conform to those standards, we feel justified in sending them home. Now, can we do the same with faculty members, or is there something in academic freedom that works against the principle?" Obviously troubled, Bill Clorety wanted guidance for his college

As he addressed Clorety's questions, Comstock was aware, as were the others around the table, that Clorety was more than a trustee to his college. He was its chief benefactor, having supplied the money several years earlier to move the institution from a two-year college to the full four years of undergraduate study. Clorety had personally picked the current president, recruiting him from a prestigious campus, further strengthening his bonds to the growing college. Fully committed to their religious denomination, each man trusted the other implicitly.

"Bill," Comstock began, "yours is the classic dilemma of every church-related campus in the country. How do you respect the freedom of the scholar, in this case the professor, and still protect the mission of the institution? Add to that the purpose of the educational experience at the college for the student, and we have the makings of a continuing problem. A faculty member may join the staff, fully informed about the special purposes of the college and those purposes may correspond to his own beliefs; the same may be said of an incoming student. But later, either or both may become dissatisfied. Beliefs are subject to challenge, learning goes on and on, opening new options, revealing new directions. Intellectual curiosity has an insatiable appetite. We are always looking to the unknown."

Faces around the table were a bit grim. Two of the group were Roman Catholic, one was Jewish, the others ranged from the conservative Clorety to at least one who questioned the validity of all religions.

"When I entered college," injected Jerry Holmes, the insurance executive who had listened attentively but had said nothing, "I assumed I was there to learn from my professors, some of whom were laymen, but many were men of the collar. It was a Catholic college, and I, being a Catholic, never questioned such things as the freedom of the professor or the behavior of students. Taught by nuns in the early years and members of various Catholic teaching orders in high school, I simply continued in college the same basic education I had started. There were non-Catholics in my college classes, but they accepted the campus as I did."

Not feeling comfortable discussing a subject about which he felt least informed, Holmes hurried to his conclusion. "I guess I was spared the stresses and strains which you gentlemen must handle."

Sensing his friend's uneasiness, Harold Forsythe quickly picked up with his own experience.

"Jerry," he began, "I, too, went through Catholic schools and college, but I was so hell-bent on becoming an engineer that I can't tell you whether it was a priest or a layman who was lecturing. I only knew that I had my nose in the books and the labs 24 hours a day." A good laugh provided momentary, welcome relief.

"Neither tenure nor academic freedom meant a thing to me at that time, but now," Forsythe continued to outline his predicament, "I'm on the board of my alma mater, and we're having a terrible time with a professor who seems to be defying the Bishop, the Church, and even Rome. And we can't fire him."

Both Wright and Comstock were familiar with the case; it had received considerable publicity in reports from campuses and the academic grapevine. In fact, most of the country's major newspapers had carried at least one sizable story on the professor. Everyone around the table registered knowing glances, with most saying in one way or another, "That's exactly the problem with tenure."

"Remember Joseph McCarthy, the senator from Wisconsin?" asked Frank Wright. The mere mention of that name was enough to bring sobering reality to the eight directors of National Charities. Each could personally remember one or more lamentable cases involving individual professors—often the most noted and from the greatest universities—who were cited as security risks, disloyal eggheads, or downright communists by the infamous senator. "Altogether, more than one hundred faculty members across the country were branded as 'poisoners of young minds, unfit to wear the academic robes, traitors, pinkos, and betrayers of America.'"

Bill Comstock instantly recalled the case of a friend and colleague at Ivy Wall in those days.

Riley Gibbons was a highly respected professor of zoology, an excellent teacher, and a zealous researcher. For more than ten years he had studied dolphins, those uncanny saltwater creatures that seemed to have a language almost as definitive as that of humans. Each summer Gibbons would hunt these intriguing animals, recording their grunts, barks, and coughs in an effort to unravel their unique ways of communicating with each other. Since Gibbons' travels took him to various oceans in search of these animals, McCarthy accused him of carrying on clandestine work with the communists. Furthermore, the senator had learned that Gibbons had held membership in what he labeled a "communist cell" when a graduate student at Harvard. That was the clincher.

Academic Freedom and Tenure: Saint or Satan?

A blast like an erupting volcano hit the Ivy Wall campus. Comstock remembered so vividly. Ivy Wall was a complex, multi-purpose institution—one of the world's great universities. Those who knew Riley Gibbons were shocked by McCarthy's charges; a more knowledgeable, intelligent, or patriotic American would be hard to find. They were incensed at the foul play by a senator who was hiding behind the cloak of congressional immunity, literally destroying a dedicated citizen and teacher.

But what could they do?

While Gibbons survived the crisis, as did Ivy Wall, and McCarthy got his comeuppance, the umbrella of tenure, with its ensuing protection of academic freedom, was again reaffirmed but not without its price.

Meeting with senior officers of the university on the day following McCarthy's accusations, the president of Ivy Wall decided the best course of action would be to place Gibbons on administrative leave with pay until the matter was resolved.

The action did not have unanimous support.

Voices were loud in chastising the president for caving in to the demagogue McCarthy; an immediate cry went up that Gibbons' academic freedom was being unjustly denied; and yet another just as vocal opinion came from other groups, mainly parents with encouragement from the conservative press, declaring that college students must be protected from the influence of communist professors. Comstock, serving in a minor administrative post at the time, saw the dilemma of Ivy Wall's beleaguered president. He had the support of those he did not wish and the enmity of those whose understanding he needed. For a university president, or the CEO of any enterprise for that matter, it was the most uncomfortable of all possible positions.

How may a CEO avoid such a trap? Comstock concluded that forces beyond the control of top corporate officers can, at times, even with the most astute planning, simply roll over almost any leader. Such was the incident at Ivy Wall.

Fortunately, damage was limited.

But as Comstock revisited the Ivy Wall campus in his nostalgic reverie of an event which took place some 30 years earlier, the luncheon group continued to pursue the controversial priest on the faculty of Forsythe's alma mater.

The Rev. Charles E. Curran was the center of the mini-crisis in Catholic higher education. A theological scholar, with a reputation for original thinking and brilliant writing, Curran expounded views that began to diverge from those of the Church. In due time the Vatican declared him ineligible to teach Catholic theology. As he resisted the prohibition against his teaching, a number of supporters accused the Catholic University of America, his academic home for many years, of denying his academic freedom, his right to pursue the truth. And, of course, he was protected by tenure—that uncertain and confounding condition of academic employment.

As would be expected, the president of the university, the Rev. William J. Byron, had to intercede, along with the cardinal. It was Byron who drew the limits on the principles of academic freedom at the unversity by declaring, "Freedom is a value, but it's not unlimited. We are a Catholic institution, and you [any professor] have a duty to maintain consistency with the Church."

The legal challenge to the university took almost five years to reach a conclusion: The rights of the institution prevailed. Still, the debate in academe over the meaning of tenure, with its ethical and moral limits, continues unabated.

"On what we call a private, independent campus, that is, one without church affiliation, and in the public college or university," Frank Wright added by way of further elucidation, "a professor with tenure can do almost anything he chooses so long as he breaks no law. You may remember," he continued, "the case at Harvard, involving a man named O'Leary. Harvard was able to fire him without repercussions because he was experimenting, along with some of his students, with illegal drugs. In other words he was breaking the law."

"Like I said," it was Pat Barnett again, "I'll let you academics deal with tenure. I want no part of it!"

"I wish we had never heard of tenure," Leon Border chimed in. "As for academic freedom, I've never felt any inhibitions on my work, either in private industry or at Ivy Wall."

It was the voice again of a brilliant and aggressive researcher, one whose scientific field had the full support of the general public and one who, unfortunately, believed that the humanities and social sciences had little to offer in the way of new knowledge. Genetic engineering had not yet reached a controversial stage, and neither was he familiar with the language of dolphins. As for Senator McCarthy, the whole escapade had been only a media event, embellished by politics, and had come to a predictable end. "Nothing to get upset about," was the way Border put it.

While there was little agreement around the table for Border's position, neither did his comments help to clarify the issues.

It had been another discussion of tenure and academic freedom without much headway in gaining understanding by those outside the campus. But Comstock realized he must continue to live with its ambiguities, as indeed he would when he returned to his office. While the others could forget the luncheon conversation, Midtown's president faced what was called an active case of challenge to tenure.

A powerful, effective trustee was demanding that a controversial professor of law be fired. Of course, the faculty member had been given tenure some ten years earlier. A classic case? Maybe. For Comstock, each challenge to academic freedom seemed to be different. He thought he had seen them all, but Professor Horace Ambling had added his own twist. He was counseling young men to avoid military service by leaving the country.

Protests against the Vietnam conflict were at a peak. College students were being given deferments until completion of their courses of study, so Ambling decided the most effective protest of all would be for each male student to leave the country just as soon as he finished. To that end, the professor of law—he claimed to be expert in the Selective Service Act and its provisions—held meetings in Midtown's student center each Thursday evening to discuss ways to avoid the military service for those who would be called by their draft boards.

Was his action illegal? Or was it within the law? Robert Dinwiddie Yost, the trustee, and a famous trial lawyer himself, argued that to "counsel, advise, or otherwise encourage others to break the law was in itself a breach of the statute."

"I want the SOB fired!" Trustee Yost demanded, sitting across his desk from Comstock. Midtown's leader had gone to Yost's office in an attempt to bring some restraint into this key trustee.

But Yost was more than a powerful trustee. He was one of Midtown's most illustrious alumni. Now in his early seventies, he was nationally recognized as a great trial lawyer, perhaps the best in Washington, a place that attracts the most skillful attorneys. Comstock had learned, too, that he was unstinting in service to his alma mater, where he served as chairman of the board's finance committee. Midtown had long benefited from his generosity of time, talent, and money. He was not a trustee to be alienated.

"Bob," Comstock began, "I want a little time to work out the Ambling problem. He is protected by tenure, and to fire him now would set off a violent storm with the AAUP (the American Association of University Professors, with which Yost was very familiar), and it is a spotlight which Midtown University does not need."

In view of Yost's obvious dissatisfaction, Comstock continued.

"I have a couple of ideas that might bear fruit and avoid what I fear would be a real black eye for our campus. Give me a couple of weeks. If I can't make any progress, we'll go your route."

"Bill I'm skeptical, but out of respect for Midtown and for you, I'll wait. I've been accused of being hot-headed," and his chuckle indicated a bit of pride in being quick on the trigger, "so I'll be quiet."

Yost would be quiet, Comstock knew, but not for long. Midtown's president would have to move fast, or the trustee's road would do far-reaching damage to the institution. Washington's most brilliant trial lawyer couldn't envisage its full extent; the academic knew clearly.

Comstock had a plan in mind. Was it a bit sinister? Perhaps. Would it work? Maybe.

The plan innocently unfolded only two days after Comstock's visit with Yost. A law student named Richard Cartwright sought Ambling's advice, following another of the professor's Thursday evening sessions.

"Professor Ambling," Cartwright began, "you obviously feel very strongly that we should leave the country as soon as we get that diploma."

"That is my advice, young man. Graduate and get out of the country." Ambling's firmness left no doubt as to the soundness of his counsel. He began to close his fat briefcase as the audience headed for the exits.

"Let me tell you, then, a bit more about myself," Cartwright continued.

"My name is Richard Cartwright, and I'll be graduating in two weeks from the law school. I've prepared this memorandum of understanding. If you will sign it, I will have considerable peace of mind while I'm away." He placed a one-page, typewritten statement on the table before the professor.

"What does it say? What kind of understanding are you talking about? Who gave you license to put my name on such a memorandum? I've never heard of such a thing." As his voice rose, a half-dozen other students began to listen.

"This simply says that you will defend me when I return as soon as the Vietnam War is over." By now more students had joined the circle. "It further states that you will defend me without charge. You can be sure," Cartwright was also talking a bit louder at that point, "that I won't have any money after running around the world hiding from the authorities."

Ambling grabbed the sheet of paper and crumpled it with both hands. He was furious.

"Get out of here," he yelled, catching the attention of even those students who had already made it to the outside corridor. Tugging at the bulging briefcase, Ambling made a dash for the nearest exit, but the only way out led through the more than a hundred students who had attended his session. They all stood aside, leaving a clear path for the professor as he headed to the parking lot.

"This is what I asked Ambling to sign," explained Cartwright to the dumbfounded students quickly surrounding him. He laid a second copy on the table. The crumpled copy had gone into the professor's pocket.

"I figured that Ambling wouldn't want to be saddled with any continuing responsibility for those of us who took his advice and left the country." Cartwright said. "But I wanted to find out for myself, and I did."

He continued as the sheet of paper was being passed around, "Ambling may be giving us the best advice in the world, but before I take it, I want to know what comes later."

It was a worry shared by the whole group.

Neither Cartwright nor any of the other students realized that Ambling had never been in a courtroom as a judge, prosecutor, or defense attorney. He had gone directly from student of law to teacher of law, and he was simply terrified at the prospects of a court in which he would have to match his skill and knowledge with practicing attorneys.

Having failed his limited legal encounter with Cartwright, a law student not yet a graduate, Horace Ambling went back to the classroom where he took up again his well developed lectures on constitutional law, at least its theoretical phases.

Of more immediate concern to Midtown's president, Ambling ended his Thursday evening counseling sessions, choosing not to risk requests or questions from the Cartwrights among his listeners.

On a call to trustee Yost, Comstock reported the end of Ambling's counseling sessions. Bob Yost chuckled and said, "I don't know how you did it, Bill, but you have my congratulations."

"Let's just say, I had very little to do with it. The matter sort of worked itself out," Comstock concluded the call.

Professor Horace Ambling couldn't recover from the experience. Not able to face his colleagues, continuing questions from the news media, and the prospects of another year at Midtown where his personal debacle had taken place, Ambling quietly accepted appointment to the faculty of another law school in a less prestigious university, still protected with tenure. Maintaining a low profile, he spent the next 20 years quietly teaching constitutional law, awaiting the time when age and annuity would permit his retirement.

Upon receiving a copy of Ambling's letter of resignation, the dean had alerted Comstock that the message was on its way. Midtown's president decided to let the matter go unnoticed. When students returned for the fall semester, the whole episode had become history.

Only in the privacy of a closed meeting of the board's finance committee, chaired by trustee Yost, was the departing Ambling even mentioned.

Coming together only two days after Ambling's letter arrived, the trustees were unaware of the news. Before Chairman Yost called the meeting to order, Comstock reported that he had received Ambling's resignation—to the delight and relief of everyone on the committee.

Flashing a satisfied glance toward Comstock, Bob Yost turned to the agenda.

After a lengthy but routine meeting, the trustees, with Comstock and a half-dozen staff members, moved next door for lunch.

"Tell me, Mr. President," asked Trustee Vince Burdette, a highly respected banker and also a member of the finance committee, who was always bothered by the topic of tenure. "Must we protect a fellow like Ambling with tenure when he is obviously misleading students? Giving them advice that could ruin their lives? It just doesn't seem right to me."

"I guess," he added, getting to the heart of the matter, "it's almost impossible to fire a faculty member after he has been given tenure. Isn't that right?" now addressing the entire group.

Prescott Vogel, the shrewd old treasurer, smiled broadly. He had seen so many professors outlive their effectiveness during his 43 years at Midtown U that he was accused of having created his own vocabulary to describe them. Without further invitation, he held forth.

"Burned out, caked over, run down, left behind, hiding out. That's what happens to people with lifetime guarantees of their jobs. I have seen it time and time again. It's a disgrace to our colleges and universities. But then Prexy," as he nodded toward Comstock, "has heard me rant about this matter a hundred times."

"Sounds like you don't like tenure," said Bob Yost, pulling Vogel's leg a bit since he had heard him at other times, too.

"We have set up all sorts of evaluating devices in an effort to award tenure only to those who have proven themselves, but it's still a chancy business," Comstock commented as he tried to bring the discussion back to some rational base.

"Our problem is that we can't foresee the future," he continued. "We simply can't guess what will happen to a person in the final 30 or more years of his career. Most institutions must make these decisions when a faculty member is in his thirties, hoping that a good start on an academic career will continue for another three to four decades." Midtown's president voiced the dilemma experienced throughout academe: "Tenure is necessary to protect academic freedom, but it also protects too much deadwood in the halls of America's colleges and universities."

But Comstock knew that trustees like Bob Yost and Vince Burdette, as well as the entire board, were deeply worried about the type of job protection that seemed to put faculty members in such a unique position, beyond the reach of all university authority. To many citizens, professors seemed to have a stranglehold on the campus, but the same audience held the university in both awe and respect.

Still working to bring further understanding of tenure and its corollary, academic freedom, Comstock reached out for support in this, another unscheduled, informal, but important discussion of the subject. He turned to Harold Bridges, the blunt-spoken, much respected academic vice president of Midtown U.

"Harold," addressing the vice president, "you fight these battles every day. How do you live with tenure?"

"It's a crazy system. We are forced to protect the incompetent and to ignore some of the laziest people in the world. Then we give them regular raises and sweeten their fringe benefits. I don't like it, and the whole campus knows how I feel," Bridges replied.

True to form, thought Comstock. He had heard the academic vice president explode on the subject many times. He could be counted on to overstate the case, a technique he used to make his point. His bark was clearly worse than his bite, and everyone on Midtown's campus, especially the faculty, knew Harold's blustery, exaggerated way of voicing most problems.

But professors had a friend in Bridges. He was one of them!

Mathematician, researcher, superb teacher—few university administrators understood the unusual role of an institution of higher learning so clearly as Harold Bridges. Comstock had quickly identified these characteristics when the two men first became acquainted. It didn't take the president of Midtown long to recruit Bridges for the position which he had filled so successfully for some fifteen years.

"But, as Churchill said of democracy," Bridges proceeded to explain, "it is a lousy way to govern, except when compared with all the rest." And the group joined in a collective smile of understanding.

"We all know," Harold continued in a calm, serious voice, "of case after case in which a faculty member was fired, ostracized, blackballed, or literally turned out on the street because he expressed a different opinion from that of the politicians or community leaders on his campus. Whether it's evolution—and that one has cost many a professor his job—or abortion, or some other subject, a faculty member must be very careful about what he says or what research he undertakes in many colleges and universities.

"Unless one is tuned in to the campus grapevine, or reads the publications in higher education regularly, it's almost impossible to discern the extent to which faculty members are harassed and criticized. Most of the time the things that plague a professor have nothing to do with the quality of his teaching or the value of his research."

Having launched his comments, Bridges moved easily into his own soliloquy on the subject. Expressions, unanimous from the group, left no doubt as to the interest in the subject and the respect for the speaker.

"Now we have with us the most insane threat of all to academic freedom–political correctness! It's the most asinine idea to come along in a hundred years." Blustery, colorful, booming–Harold Bridges was all of these. But he was more. This academic was a through-and-through hardliner, a staunch defender with gritted teeth of the right of a professor to search out new ideas, to look behind every rock for possible clues to an unanswered question.

But he was equally demanding of faculty members. Nothing seemed to please him more than to challenge the assumption of a professor's proposal for a piece of research, insisting upon a defense of the plan. The exchange between them was much like a courtroom confrontation between the accused and a prosecutor.

The president smiled as he recalled the first such incident upon his arrival at Midtown U.

As a new leader, he was an easy target for faculty members who were seeking funds for pet projects, often proposals which had been turned down by previous administrators. It was just such a request, carefully packaged by a senior professor from engineering, that first brought Bridges to the attention of Bill Comstock.

Asking for university funds to get his research started, only a few hundred thousand dollars, he explained, the professor predicted the proposal would attract millions from the defense department once its importance was revealed. Comstock never forgot the unique circumstances.

The new president had serious doubts about the proposal, but for the moment he kept them to himself. He didn't want to insult a leading member of Midtown's faculty and the chairman of an important faculty senate committee. He would have been on thin ice with any answer he gave, but he knew that the institution was in no position to use its scarce funds to jump start even the most promising proposal.

Dr. Robert V. Perkins was not one to yell and scream about his research. With two decades of experience at Midtown, a wide acquaintance among the faculties of arts and sciences, law, business, and medicine, as well as among his own colleagues in engineering, he seemed, at least to Comstock, to hold all the aces in this, the first serious meeting of the two men.

What was a new president to do?

Bill Comstock would repeat the story for years to come, not to illustrate his own ingenuity or the ineptitude of a professor of engineering, but to show how Harold Bridges came to be chosen as the chief academic officer of Midtown.

Feigning rapt attention, the president spent the last half of his hour with Dr. Perkins hearing little of the explanations offered, but searching for a way out of a potentially embarrassing problem.

"By the way," Comstock finally flagged down the unending salesmanship, "do you know Dr. Bridges, the associate dean of faculties?"

"Oh, yes," came the quick reply, "I know Harold very well," and nailing down the relationship, added, "He is a friend of mine."

"Would you mind discussing this proposal with him?" asked Comstock. "The matter seems very timely and important, but since I'm illiterate on the subject, I would feel much more comfortable if he had a chance to study it."

The new president had bought some time without insulting an obviously important faculty member, and the rush of new problems moved the matter to the back burner.

Heading out of his office to lunch a week later, Comstock happened to meet Bridges walking across the yard. It was a chance reminder of the research proposal.

"By the way, Harold, (Bridges was not one to be addressed more formally) did Professor Perkins see you about his research proposal?"

"Oh, you mean the fellow from engineering?"

"Yes," replied the president.

"He came in just yesterday afternoon," was Harold's reply.

"And what did you tell him about the proposal?" Comstock was anxious to see what difficulties lay ahead.

"Hell," Bridges saw no reason to moderate his language just because he was talking to the president, "I told him it was the stupidest damn thing I had seen in a long time. It's a crazy idea, and the research design won't hold water."

That was it. The two went separate ways for lunch, each meeting others at the entrance to the faculty dining room.

Back in his office, Comstock waited for the next call from engineering, undoubtedly a complaint of insult to a senior professor, probably joined in by the dean, the man's department head, and who knows how many others?

No complaint ever came. Only after weeks of waiting did Midtown's president conclude that he would hear nothing more of the 20-page research proposal, so carefully constructed by Dr. Perkins.

If a man as knowledgeable as Bridges could be as blunt and critical of other professors and still retain the respect of the academic community, he deserved watching. He could be useful to a president; he could be especially useful to an institution in which the strengthening of academic programs all across the campus was the chief objective.

Eighteen months into his presidency, Comstock asked Harold Bridges to become vice president of Midtown for academic affairs. Now fifteen years later, discussing tenure with a group of trustees, Bridges was unchanged.

"You see, PC once stood for personal computer; now it stands for putridly correct," and Bridges continued to educate his listeners about the latest campus insult.

"We had one just last week which nauseated me. A faculty member in anthropology explained to his class that some Asian cultures historically place a higher premium on the family than some others, particularly most ethnic groups in western societies. He inferred, so some students concluded, that some of our western cultures might come up short when compared. The very next day I had a delegation in my office to tell me the professor was prejudiced, pushing one group above others."

"And what did you tell them, Harold?" Comstock, who already knew of the incident, inquired.

"I asked them if the professor was correct. When they said they didn't know, I told them to find out. Go wherever you want, talk with any authorities you can find, and when you determine that the professor is wrong, come back and see me. Until then, don't bother me." It was typical of Harold Bridges. Pull no punches; talk around no question; bite the bullet; take the consequences.

But do all such things in a non-combative manner, adding even a smile or genuine belly laugh as the conversation permits. Too, self derision was always present. He could call himself stupid as easily as he could any luncheon companion. It was a manner which few other people could use; with Bridges it was his unique nature.

CEOs who couldn't stand criticism, who wanted only associates who agreed with them, wouldn't want Bridges around. Comstock couldn't remember how many times during their 15 years together that Harold had used stupid, a favorite word to describe a presidential action or proposal. But it was always spoken without malice.

"Some institutions have tied themselves in knots over political correctness," explained Bridges as he warmed to the topic. "They can't find common ground between freedom of speech and slander."

Some trustees had seen press accounts of flare-ups at the University of Pennsylvania, Brown, and other campuses, but none understood what the fuss was all about. Harold's comments fell on welcome ears.

"I've always felt that the best way to refute chicanery, propaganda, or misinformation is to parade it in full daylight and let the chips fall where they may. I just love to see some pompous, self-righteous bigot put in his place with a few facts or basic truths right there on the stage in front of the world." And those who had seen Bridges cut down impostors over the years could attest to the pleasure with which he acted.

Comstock sometimes compared an argument with Bridges to a tennis game, and the two men, quite evenly matched, thoroughly enjoyed the give and take. Harold never pulled a punch in his effort to win, but he never claimed a questionable call, always deferring to fairness for any opponent on the other side of the net.

"Theoretically," the academic VP was quite at home discussing philosophy as well as mathematics, "academic freedom is there to protect the professor who wishes to speculate on some new answer to a problem, whether it be a new black hole in the universe or another way to handle rural poverty. In so doing, that same faculty member can illustrate to his students that other ways may be found, perhaps better ways, to resolve the problems around us.

"But professors, too, can get carried away. Once in a while an idea or prospective solution may be so persuasive to the professor that he accepts it as better and becomes an aggressive advocate before he has any proof beyond his own conviction. Good land," nailing down his point, "I've seen them become stark raving fanatics at times before they had a single new piece of evidence to support their position."

A pause, a change of pace, but with full attention still focused on him, Bridges concluded his discourse.

"I look upon my job as a kind of referee. When I see a professor protected by tenure going beyond reasonable boundaries of academic freedom, kind of thumbing his nose at common sense, I call him to task. I want a rational and defensible explanation of his actions. If he can't defend himself in that situation, I'm going to challenge his tenure. And sometimes, as you can guess," Harold added with a big laugh, "I find I'm holding a skunk!"

Academic freedom to some could indeed be as dull as dishwater, but for Harold Bridges it was a vital protection for those who taught and searched for knowledge. The few trustees who had the chance to talk with him about tenure left convinced that the institution is at no risk so long as people like Bridges were monitoring the campus. As for Bill Comstock, he could pursue the many other facets of a president's work without fighting weekly battles with the faculty over academic freedom and without fear that tenure would be abused.

But Comstock saw more important results coming from the atmosphere of confidence which Midtown's faculty held for Harold Bridges. It was the removal of fear that caused professors on many campuses to build their own defenses, their own fortifications, so to speak, against the possible infringement on their rights of free inquiry. Through organizing and supporting local chapters of the AAUP, faculty members on campuses throughout the country were able to enlist the help of their own powerful organization in meeting institutional violations wherever they occurred. Where the AAUP was strong, threats to academic freedom were frequent; where professors felt no cause for alarm, the AAUP attracted little interest. At Midtown the local chapter had been inactive for more than a decade.

In spite of an occasional long, drawn out battle over the denial of tenure to a member of the faculty, the entire academic community remained relaxed, unworried that any real danger to their professional interests was present. In President Comstock and Vice President Bridges, the faculty felt they had leaders who fully understood the role of tenure in a university, and that such challenges as might come—there was always an alumnus or trustee willing to criticize the system—would easily be shunted aside.

President Comstock knew clearly the conditions necessary for maximum faculty success, both in teaching and in research, and while he would not mount the stump to yell about such matters, his complete support of the principles was taken for granted. On these issues the president and the faculty had learned to live together in mutual respect and complete trust.

In view of essentially ideal relationships between administrators and faculty leaders, it was ironic that Midtown's most notorious case of faculty challenge to the university's personnel policies had nothing to do with tenure or academic freedom. It was the failure of an associate professor who had already been granted tenure to be promoted.

Arnold C. Schmidt came to Midtown after two years as an instructor in a highly respected midwestern university where he did his Ph.D. After only three years as an assistant professor, half the usual period in that rank in first-line institutions, he was promoted to associate professor, which carried tenure at Midtown. A more promising young appointee had not joined the faculty of engineering in a long time.

But things changed! The same dean, chairman, and faculty that together had hired him and promoted him said that it was Schmidt who had changed. Not so, replied the young associate professor; it was the others who had strayed, and in so doing, he alleged, they had brought great harm to a vulnerable academic so early in his career that he could never hope to recover.

When he first failed promotion, Schmidt brought a grievance against the chairman and members of his department. It was a formal action, a procedure available to any faculty member who feels aggrieved, and the next step following the failure of all informal efforts to reach a mutually satisfactory settlement.

It would be ten years before the case was finally concluded.

Midtown required that the promotion of a faculty member be initiated by the departmental faculty. All members senior to the candidate were eligible to join in the appraisal. In the case of Schmidt, the same group that had voted unanimously to promote him and give him tenure unanimously went on record five years later to deny him further promotion.

The appellate process eventually carried the grievance to the personnel committee of Midtown U's board of trustees. It was the first time that some members of the group had ever experienced the nitty-gritty of faculty organization.

"You mean," asked the newest trustee, a businessman attending his first meeting, "that Dr. Comstock and Dr. Bridges don't make promotions on the faculty?"

With knowing but sympathetic glances, others around the table simply looked at Harold Bridges, knowing the chairman would turn to him for a kindly, knowledgeable answer.

"When I was at General Electric," Harold began his reply, "all assessments of one's performance came from the top down. It really didn't seem to matter what the people on my own level thought of my work." Bridges had left academe for five years at GE where he put his mathematics to work in setting up a statistical framework for testing a number of the company's research efforts. Harold always referred to GE with great respect, but he soon found that the corporate world was too confining for him; hence he returned to the campus.

"But a university is different," Bridges stated, as a way of reminding the committee that authority over the faculty is authority which the faculty itself holds in great measure. In the case of Arnold Schmidt, it was his immediate colleagues, those senior to him, and people working next door to him year in and year out who must, in accordance with long established procedures, pass judgment on his performance. Without a vote of confidence from those closest to him Schmidt would always fight an uphill battle.

And so, after all arguments had been heard, and the trustees on the personnel committee had gotten another firsthand lesson in academic management, the formal grievance was remanded to the faculty of civil engineering for review. Nothing special was asked, only that the faculty "review the performance of Associate Professor Schmidt during its next regular assessment period." No special review was called for, no shortened time frames. It would be another year before such a review took place.

When the time came, the results were the same. By unanimous vote the senior colleagues of Arthur Schmidt "failed to find sufficient improvement in teaching, adequate substance in completed research, or broadened professional activities" to justify promotion to full professor.

In spite of widespread publicity and interest throughout the campus, Midtown U's faculty saw no reason for concern. They had witnessed another example of the governing board, through its personnel committee, returning decision-making authority to the faculty, this time to the faculty of civil engineering. And while all members of the community knew that the case would require further time and effort, it was a price worth paying.

Even with the Arthur Schmidt case continuing, and it seemed endless, not a single voice could be heard warning of possible loss of faculty authority, and neither could interest be found in activating the long-disbanded chapter of the AAUP. Turning to the courts for relief, Arthur Schmidt lost there as well. He had invested a full decade in his battle for promotion while neglecting his teaching and research. With his final disappointment at Midtown, he left academic life for a belated entry-level job in private industry. It was ironic that tenure, job promotion for a professor, should lead to such an unexpected conclusion.

Years later, Comstock would see signs that greater care should be exercised in awarding tenure on many campuses. When enrollment was growing, either on a single campus or in a state-wide system, tenure slots could be allowed to increase. But populations were shifting. While California and Florida and others were growing, some states were losing residents or remaining stable. Then, too, many students were being attracted to off-campus sites for instruction, taking courses for credit without living in the vicinity or even visiting professors' classrooms or laboratories. Experiments in distance learning were being tried out, not only in America, but all around the world.

What did all these developments mean for professors? And for tenure?

Perhaps private institutions could control such changes in enrollment. Since they could set limits on class size without evoking citizen revolt, public colleges and universities would have to respond to a growing student population by increasing capacity. Likewise, they could more easily be caught with too many tenured faculty members if registrations on the public campuses shifted unexpectedly.

Numerous reasons, which were given as challenges to tenure, had erupted over the years. Shifting enrollment was only one; lack of confidence on the part of governing boards in the necessity for such job security seemed ever present. The new factors of rapidly moving technology, the use of more part-time instructors, distance learning, and all the other innovations were beginning to converge, threatening the long-standing tenure system again.

If the job guarantee is weakened, will academic freedom suffer?

Comstock wondered. Will a professor without the security of his position feel free to offer new ideas, contrary theories, or challenging findings?

Unfortunately, even with protection of tenure, many researchers down through the years had lost their jobs by challenging accepted truths. Without adequate safeguards, professors would likely face an uncertain future. Yet the general public still seemed unable to grasp the value that academics attach to tenure. Unneeded mischief to some, simply misunderstood by others!

III

The CEO: Getting and Losing Power

"Borrowed power" were the words used by Barbara Bush to describe the commanding position of the President of the United States shortly after her husband's departure from office. A better description of a chief executive officer's role in government, business, or academe would be hard to find.

It is easy to read into "borrowed power" certain important restraints. It refers to the position, not the person. There is a time restriction vital to every CEO; it is time in office. For elected officials—mayors, governors, and presidents—it is a specific number of years, most likely two or four; for CEOs in business or academe the term may be indefinite. However, the person occupying the office holds the power of the office from the day he takes the oath or other appropriate ceremonial commitment until another person arrives.

It isn't easy to circumscribe the exact power of any CEO; the occupant frequently does much of his own defining of its limits. As Bill Comstock learned over the years, the limits of a university president's power differed, sometimes widely, depending upon the constituency.

He recalled an appeal from an applicant to Midtown's medical school that suggested power this academic leader never quite imagined.

"Dr. Comstock, I have always wanted to go to medical school," began Richard E. Miller, as he opened the conversation in the president's office. "When I finished college 20 years ago, there was simply no way I could finance any further education. My father had just died, we were in debt, and I had to begin immediately to try to keep the small family business from going into bankruptcy."

Upon checking Miller's record at Midtown U, a routine procedure when an alumnus made an appointment, Comstock's secretary found only an undergraduate record. Sure enough, it was a pre-med course with a major in chemistry, and with very high marks. No entry of any kind in the intervening years, not even a note among alumni records. Gene Miller, as he introduced himself, had disappeared for two decades. But with his usual patience the president heard the rest of the story.

Rushing on, Miller laid out his case, not wasting a single sentence. "I immersed myself completely in the family business, doing little else in these 20 years. Now I'm back hoping to go to medical school."

"But we have no record of an application from you. Has it been lost?" Comstock interrupted.

"No, no," hastened Miller. "I'm now 41 years old, and I know medical schools will not admit people my age. That's the reason I'm here to see you. If you will let me in your medical school, I will give Midtown University one-half of my estate. My business is now worth 20 million dollars; it doesn't need my day-to-day management; and I want to devote the rest of my life to medicine—something I've always wanted to do."

Comstock was hardly prepared for Miller's proposition. He knew that some university presidents, or so he had been led to believe, actually used the power of their office to place special applicants in medical school or law school or some other desired spot. It was a power which Midtown U's president neither sought nor ever accepted. His answer to Miller, therefore, had to be a disappointment.

"I never interfere in the admissions process," Comstock explained. "Why don't you apply just as the other candidates do? You had an excellent undergraduate record; I checked it before you came in today."

"I would," Miller quickly responded, "but I know I could never pass the entrance exam after 20 years away from my studies. No, I have no chance of studying medicine if I must go that route."

"Let me make another suggestion," said Comstock, trying to be helpful. "Why don't you take a year, enter a graduate program in pathology, biochemistry, or another basic science, hire yourself a tutor, and get ready for the entrance exams a year hence?"

"I've thought of that," Miller replied. "But I would be a year older, which would make my case even weaker than it is now, and I'm afraid the prejudice against age would keep me out no matter how well I might do."

Bill Comstock was well aware, and obviously Miller was also, of the feeling of admissions officers in medical schools: Since the course is so long—seven or more years beyond the undergraduate period—it was desirable to get applicants into the study of medicine as early as possible. Such a policy would give the physician more years in which to practice.

Gene Miller, if success in business and his undergraduate studies were any indication, would undoubtedly be an outstanding physician; that his career would be shorter than most other physicians was also a reasonable certainty. What was the best answer? Unfortunately, Comstock didn't know. Did he have the power to add ten million to Midtown's assets? Did he have the power to place a student in medical school whose profile represented a departure from present policy? And what about the entrance exam? Such questions represented limits of the president's power, which Midtown's president had no desire to test.

Since no word ever came back, Miller's future activities remained unknown to all at MU—never a note or a call nor a request for a transcript of his undergraduate record.

Comstock had been a member of the university president's circle long enough to know that some presidents, in fact, presidents of some of America's most illustrious institutions, always kept a few vacancies in first-year classes to be filled at their own discretion. Since appointment to the office, Comstock had been asked by two newly selected presidents the very question: How many slots do you have for your law school? For your business school? For undergraduate colleges?

One case involved a good friend, Lew Thompson, who had just taken office but who had not yet been formally inaugurated as president of a highly respected private institution. He had agreed to buy lunch in exchange for advice on one of the many decisions he would soon be making.

Seated in a quiet corner of a restaurant conveniently located near the Midtown campus, Thompson asked quite matter of factly: "Tell me, Bill, what my role should be in the admissions process. My predecessor, as you undoubtedly know, kept 20 places that he could use anywhere in the university, and I'm wondering if I should ask the board for more. If I want any change, the chairman tells me now is the time to ask for it."

Then, zeroing in on his colleague, whom he had known for several years and from whom he felt he could get wise counsel, he added, "Bill, how many do you have at Midtown?"

"Lew, my answer may disappoint you," Comstock replied, "You see, I don't have any, and, furthermore, I don't want any."

"Just what do you do when Midtown's athletic director has filled his quota and the then son of the president of your boosters' club can't get in through the normal admissions procedure? You're in Washington, Bill, so what do you do when the son or daughter of a cabinet officer or perhaps even the President of the United States doesn't get an application filed on time or scores too low on an entrance exam? Don't tell me you turn such applicants down?"

"As I said," Comstock began, explaining his position very calmly. "I don't have any such slots anywhere in the university, not even in our athletic department. I have made it a policy over the years never to interfere in the admissions process. I ask admissions officers in our various schools to alert me to potential problem cases so I won't be caught off guard, but I make it clear that each applicant must be admitted or denied on his or her merits—not because some important politician, alumnus, or donor is pushing the case. And I want to be informed after the decision has been made, not before."

It was a topic which this president was comfortable discussing with a newcomer to the presidential ranks. Midtown's leader had seen all sides of the issue.

"I have withstood the pressures of the White House on admissions cases," confided Comstock. "Early in my tenure at Midtown, we found it necessary to deny admission to a nephew of the President. Yes, I was personally beseeched to admit the applicant, but I didn't. No volcanoes erupted; no orders went out to quarantine Midtown; and donors didn't quit giving to the university.

"You see," he continued, "the White House wasn't eager to let the world know that a member of the family had failed to gain admission to Midtown; the nephew simply enrolled elsewhere.

"But the message was clear to every admissions officer on our campus, and it got around quickly: Comstock can be counted on to support our decisions. It was, of course, a vote of confidence in the many people who are involved in admitting students to our professional and graduate schools as well as undergraduate programs."

It was a new line of thinking for a president not yet formally installed.

Lew's predecessor not only had such power, but he also exercised it fully. And it was well known within the institution that the number 20 meant nothing. If the president wanted someone to be admitted, that was it. Neither faculty committees nor admissions officers challenged the president's action. Otherwise, some sons and daughters of the noted, famous, and sometimes notorious probably wouldn't be there. It was an established part of that university's culture.

Should the president's role be changed? Did he want to be the one to reverse a hundred years of practice?

"It has been my experience," and Midtown's president couldn't refrain from looking back over the years, "that once admitted, an unqualified or poorly prepared student is likely to be skating on thin ice for his entire course of study. When academic trouble comes, and it does all too frequently, I like to ask, 'Is the family, including the student, ready to face academic dismissal?' Flunking out has greater stigma than falling short of admission."

It was apparent the new president had not focused on many aspects of the matter, one of many problems he would face for the first time.

"I shall never forget a case at New England U," Comstock continued as Thompson listened intently. "The applicant was the son of a powerful state legislator, and when he was turned down for admission to our engineering school, the legislator threatened to block the annual appropriation to the university. Unfortunately, I had to tell the politician that the son had no chance whatsoever of doing satisfactory work in engineering. The family could expect the young man to flunk out by Thanksgiving or, at the very latest, by Christmas. I then offered to evaluate his son's academic strengths and to advise him of what we thought his best choice might be for further education.

"The father relented, finally, and the boy ended up in a vocational school in Boston, but only after a lengthy struggle."

Thompson was still all ears.

"Look," Comstock finally had to say to his friend who appeared to be settling in for a full afternoon, "I must get back to the campus to keep an appointment. I don't know what you should do about your role in admissions in your new job. I can only tell you how I have handled the matter, and it's entirely different from what's been done on your campus." Then, leaving the door open for a return to the topic and wanting to be helpful to the newcomer if possible, he added, "Let's talk again. I'll make myself available at your convenience."

"Bill, I deeply appreciate your advice, and as soon as the inaugural ceremonies are over, I'll call you."

The call never came.

Long before Thompson had his inaugural activities lined up, the grandson of a powerful U.S. senator, one who had steered millions of dollars to the institution, didn't have the academic credentials for admission to law school. Lew used a presidential slot to admit the young man. Having turned the corner toward the practices of his predecessors, in this instance at the request of his law school dean, there was no turning back.

From the academic grapevine, a circuit to which Comstock was well connected, Midtown's president heard the news within days. Another two years passed before the two presidents again discussed the subject. It was Thompson this time who reviewed his action. He confided to Comstock what he had done, and with some apology he acknowledged the practice of his institution, which he didn't feel he should attempt to change.

Was Comstock simply a coward, unwilling to exercise a power of the presidency that other university leaders—Thompson was by no means alone—used to enhance their institutions? Each time he wrestled with the dilemma, he ended up with the same conclusion. He would stay out of the admissions process, and Midtown, in so far as was humanly possible, would admit applicants on merit, not on influence.

And then came the case of the judge's son.

Thomas Rogers had been on the federal bench for only five years, but already he had become widely known as a brilliant judge, uncanny in his ability to cut through the confusing legalese of the country's craftiest lawyers and promptly write decisions, something which took some of his colleagues months or even years to do. His penetrating questions to those attorneys who appeared before him often turned the toughest, most devious litigators into wimps. Then, too, Tom Rogers was one of the four or five names mentioned for possible appointment to the next vacancy on the Supreme Court.

This time, however, it was Judge Rogers, sitting on the couch in Comstock's office, who was pleading the case. He asked that his son be admitted to Midtown's law school. The rejection letter had already reached the Rogers' home.

"I have always been proud of my association with Midtown University," explained Rogers. "Wherever I have gone, I have never failed to mention the fact that whatever success I have enjoyed in the legal profession was all due to the outstanding preparation I received while a student at Midtown law school. And, as you know, Bill, (the two men had long known each other on a first-name basis) I have been active in alumni work, helping the university as often as I could."

"I know all those things," agreed Comstock, "and as Midtown's president, I can tell you that everyone in the institution is grateful for your help. You have helped me, personally, I want to add, in furthering many of my own ideas for strengthening this university."

It was a pleasant exchange so far. But Comstock questioned whether such an atmosphere would last. He soon got his answer.

"I would like you to admit my son to your law school," the judge stated his case. "I know his record is not strong; on the other hand, I have done so much for the school that I feel you owe it to me to do this."

Tom Rogers had put the matter entirely on a personal plane. Simply put, Comstock thought, Rogers is asking me to repay my debt to him—his help to Midtown and to me over the years—by admitting his son.

Facts had been avoided up to that point in the conversation, but the president was prepared.

"Judge," a salutation which he had long used in addressing Rogers, instead of the first name that Rogers always used in speaking to Comstock, "do you know where your son stands in the list of applicants for law school?"

"No," came the quick, emphatic reply. "And I don't care. It doesn't matter where he stands. I only know that he can do the work and he will make a good lawyer." Rogers' impatience was evident, but Comstock refused to be intimidated.

"As you know, Judge, we get about ten applications for each place in the law school. Unfortunately, your son didn't make the admitted group, and neither could he be put on the waiting list. He simply had to be turned down. I'm sorry." Comstock got no further. Rogers exploded. Fortunately, the office door was closed.

"Don't ever expect me to do anything for Midtown again! I should have known that all my work for this university would be a one-way street. You academicians are all alike. You sit here in your ivory tower, protected from the world. And those lazy, stodgy professors in the law school! What a bunch! I sat in their classes bored to death."

"Comstock," the judge put all of the condescension, frustration, and anger he could muster into the conclusion of his outburst, "my son will go to law school—a good one. And he'll do well. You see, I won't depend on the faculty to teach him. I'll do it myself."

Bill Comstock tried never to plunge the knife into someone unless he was driven to it. In this case he felt compelled.

"Just remember, Judge," he said calmly, "a thousand applicants ranked ahead of your son when all the grades and scores were compiled. Do you think justice would be served by pushing your son ahead of a thousand others," and the president added, "or even one for that matter?"

Judge Rogers turned and left without a word. He was never seen again on the Midtown campus, nor did he attend any of the university's activities around the city.

For 25 years the name of Judge Thomas Hillard Rogers continued to play prominently in legal circles and the daily press. He never made it to the Supreme Court, but all along the way, Comstock wondered what justice really meant in his court.

Midtown's president continued to stay clear of any interference with admissions to the institution. He believed it was a power in the presidency with moral, ethical, and practical limitations; it was a power that, when exercised, created dilemmas.

Should a CEO, whether in academe, government, or business, back away from the power of the office, or should he grasp every opportunity to exercise such powers as exist when he assumes the office, and then drive to expand such outreach ever further? And what about sharing power? What happens to others when the CEO pushes his own power to the limit? Each CEO must find his own answer, Comstock concluded. As for himself, he had come to believe that to share power, responsibility, decision making—all the actions of management and operations—was the only position with which he was comfortable. How else can the energy and ingenuity of associates be put to work in the interest of the enterprise? It was a way of working that served Midtown University well for all the years of Comstock's tenure.

But the CEO must face some responsibilities alone. Comstock's first challenge at Midtown had confronted him even before he took office. It came from the dean of the university's school of science.

"We have some serious problems in our school," Dean Cummings spoke ominously as he sat down with Comstock at New England University shortly after the announcement that he had been selected to fill the Midtown vacancy. Cummings had made the trip, as it turned out, hopeful of striking a preemptive blow in his own behalf before the new president had a chance to make commitments to others or to find out what the real problems were at Midtown's school of science.

"But I can't really do anything about them until I know whether or not you will support me in my decisions," Cummings continued.

Not wishing to insult Cummings and knowing nothing about any problems in the school of science, the president simply said he would have to wait until he got to Washington, became familiar with Midtown U, and had a chance to assess the situation. To him it was the only reasonable answer he could give, so after exchanging the usual amenities, Dean Cummings departed.

To the faculty of Midtown's school of science, Cummings had another story to tell: The incoming president was very concerned about the school, he would assess its place in the university as soon as he came to Washington, and would then decide its future. A very unsettled faculty of the school greeted the new executive upon his arrival some weeks later. Matt Cummings, as he was known to the faculty, had sought the new president's support for himself, knowing full well that his own faculty had lost confidence in him. He had done it at the expense of Comstock, painting him as a certain enemy of the school of science and its faculty.

But Bill Comstock had seen too much of academic politics already to be fooled easily. Within three months after his arrival, he went before the faculty of the school of science to inform them that he had asked for and received Dean Cummings' resignation. The faculty was now free to find the best person in the country for the deanship, and he would help them in the search. The choice would be theirs, however, not that of the new president.

When the first choice of the faculty search committee was appointed, the new president had made his point. The selection of a new leader for one of Midtown's schools is responsibility—power—to be shared, in this case delegated to the faculty.

But the executive power of the CEO, as exercised by Midtown's president, paled when compared with that of Phil Polson whose career at Meridian Financial Services left the company on the brink of bankruptcy. As a long-time director, Comstock was in no position to challenge the selection of Polson to head Meridian when Jason Burwell retired. After all, the search had been nationwide, and Polson, a personable and knowledgeable 45-year-old candidate, brought all the right training and experience to the job. Furthermore, at Jake Burwell's request, Polson had served a full year of apprenticeship at Meridian in preparation for the upcoming change in leadership.

Bill Comstock especially enjoyed this directorship. It was a company with a hundred years of stable growth, quietly serving a clientele that reached into the fifty states with never a blotch of any kind. His fellow directors, who came from a broad cross section of business and the professions, had worked together without serious disagreement or discord for all of the 20 years since he first came aboard. In spite of the fact that retirement and other reasons had brought an almost complete turnover in the board's membership in those two decades, the directors had worked smoothly through two CEO changes and a number of market upheavals in the financial services industry.

Retiring after more than 40 years with Meridian, the last 6 spent as CEO, Jake Burwell felt good about both the company and about having Phil Polson as his successor. So did every other director. For Comstock it was the third such change he had seen, and, looking ahead, it was, just maybe, the best choice of all.

Such were the promises with which Polson began his long-term contractual relationship with Meridian.

Whether he felt it necessary to use the power of the CEO's office to establish himself immediately, whether he saw threats from other senior officers at Meridian, or whether he brought his own blueprint for remaking the company, no one would ever know. For whatever reason, Polson wasted no time in exercising the full powers of his new office.

The first weekend of his tenure found all senior officers working until midnight on Saturday, something unheard of in previous years. They were hammering out, as the new CEO put it, a revised business and marketing plan that would put Meridian in the forefront of all financial services companies in the country.

"This company has been coasting too long. We are now going to get to work," was the way he confronted his senior staff members when he summoned them to the unusual and unscheduled Saturday session.

It all happened in the first week of July during the slowest time of the year for the industry. Everyone in senior management had to scurry to change weekend plans, inconvenience family, or disrupt Independence Day activities.

More than one senior officer came face-to-face with the CEO's power. Each silently raised the same questions: Should he go ahead with already-made plans for himself and the family? If so, what might be the consequences? Could he be fired? Would Polson do such a thing? It was a dilemma faced by every subordinate. Not one of them knew what the new CEO had in mind, what the results would be if anyone failed to respond to the order. With one executive action the new CEO had sent a shocking message to the entire organization. Was this his purpose? Did he simply want to scare everyone?

Phil Polson was using the power of the office to rock the complacency of Meridian's senior leadership. But why? Was his action limited to an awakening shock? Might it not also erode the pride they all had in the company, the confidence and trust that all had come to have in each other and their work?

With his tie loosened and his sleeves rolled up Polson welcomed each of his staff to the boardroom, the appointed place of work. He left no misunderstanding; he was set for a long session.

The lengthy agenda set the tone for the meeting.

Each man found, as he sat down at his designated place, a well-marked copy of the company's plan, the blueprint of the work to be accomplished in the fiscal year only just begun—July first. It was a boldly marked copy with big question marks, with pages and paragraphs crossed out, and with requests for more details, all in Polson's handwriting.

Saturday was a full day, interrupted only with a Spartan lunch. But it ended with a sumptuous dinner; the group learned that evening their new CEO liked rich food and adequate drink. The session finally ended just before midnight.

Through it all, Polson had directed each rewrite, whether a single sentence or a full paragraph. After the first hour, during which each suggestion was met with disapproval, the remarks became almost a monologue. "I want marketing to follow the program I've outlined. My managers (it didn't take long for Meridian to become Polson's company) must carry the right message to clients. You," directing his orders to each person around the table, "can't allow any of your people to do the following," and he spelled out a half-dozen examples of personal behavior that had nothing to do with job performance. "Never let them forget that they represent Meridian wherever they are seen or heard."

That first Saturday in July was never forgotten, but it was only the beginning. Polson's executive manner became a way of life at Meridian: unexpected summons to the corporate secretary, the chief financial officer, a first level supervisor, or a regional vice president on either coast. Everyone soon became braced for the CEO's call. It came at the end of the working day, in the middle of the night, or during vacation. It was truly a summons: Meet me in such and such a place, or come to company headquarters (located midway between Washington and Baltimore, and fortunately, convenient to Baltimore-Washington International Airport), and bring all the information (usually an armload) with you.

Did the directors know what Phil Polson was doing to the company? While senior officers asked such questions among themselves, employees in lower level jobs and many who staffed the offices of Meridian around the country simply assumed that the CEO was carrying out the board's orders. And the senior officers did, too. Dared one complain to a director? An atmosphere of uncertainty, downright fear in many cases, had pervaded the entire company.

Directors of Meridian knew their new CEO was working hard, that he was delving into every department, visiting each field office, forwarding new reports with more details. Judging from his own comments to board committees and meetings of the full board, the company was exhibiting new life, new vitality, and a higher level of intensity. Who among the directors could criticize such developments? Wasn't that what all board members wanted to see? Maybe Meridian had grown a little too complacent under good old Jake Burwell. After all, most successful business enterprises share a tendency to grow a bit fat and lazy.

It was a full two years before two members of the board were visited by the executive vice president of Meridian. He had been fired by Polson for his "inability to handle the competition in the new, more demanding world of financial services. He just refused to go along with our more aggressive philosophy," explained Polson to a meeting of the executive committee of the board. It was a bit sad, two or three members of the committee agreed, that one who had done so much for the company, one who had come up through the ranks with 27 years at Meridian, could not adjust to the changing times.

"We are giving him a good severance package, and he will have the benefit of our out-placement service," Polson further explained.

Most directors were satisfied that George Mahoney had been treated fairly; although the old-timers, including Comstock, weren't able to forget the matter.

George Mahoney didn't leave quietly.

Within a few days of the firing, the Baltimore-Washington business community was fully abuzz with the news. Such was Mahoney's reputation that he had offers of three jobs within two weeks. He accepted one, settled into a new responsibility, and received a 50 percent increase in compensation. Shortly afterward, Mahoney arranged to meet Comstock and one other senior director for lunch.

"If I were not so deeply concerned for Meridian, I would not have asked to see you," he said as the three sipped hot soup on a brisk fall day. Some two years and a few months had passed since that July change of the guard.

"Meridian is a good company supplying a much needed service to thousands of clients. In a small way, I helped to make it what it is. But if Polson's left unchecked, I'm afraid it's headed for the rocks."

George Mahoney had no reason to beat around the bush. He continued. "Two senior vice presidents got their walking papers last week, but you may not hear about it until the next meeting of the executive committee. Phil Polson is in no hurry to inform directors. Just how he may choose to present the actions to you, I'm only able to guess; but it will be some kind of unusual story. Their jobs are being folded into the responsibilities of others, making them expendable, or they have failed to see the importance of the company's new directions. I would urge you to question Polson," and as if he had to apologize for airing such matters to directors, he added, "I probably have no business banging your ears with these comments, but I just hate to see Meridian Finance sucked down the bilge."

"How satisfied or, on the other side, how unhappy is the staff these days? What about morale? Isn't business slipping a bit?" These and other questions set Mahoney off again.

"Things are in a mess. Actually, Polson's problems began with his first week in the chair. Have you heard about his Saturday meeting just before the Fourth of July holiday two years ago?" Well, there had been some reference to it but no details, both directors recalled.

George Mahoney filled in the long story. It was not pleasant for the directors to hear. Clearly they had not been tuned in to the workings of a company which they were responsible for controlling.

Genuinely grateful to Mahoney, yet embarrassed because they had been so inattentive to their duties as directors, the two men departed, worried and puzzled.

"If only half of what George told us is true, and I have no reason to doubt any of it," Comstock remarked to his fellow director, "then we have a job on our hands."

"Call me at home tonight," he said as they planned to confer further on the disturbing news.

It was late that night when they agreed that other directors, at least two or three, must be alerted to Meridian's problems. And it must be done before the upcoming meeting of the full board just five days hence.

Five senior directors briefed with Mahoney's full story arrived at the board meeting ready to question the CEO. Without rehearsal each waited for the propitious moment.

As usual, Phil Polson began the meeting with his report.

"With the reorganization which I have been doing, I find it is now possible to eliminate two vice presidencies, saving their salaries and all the expenses of their offices and staffs. The work in each case can easily be absorbed by other officers without overloading anyone. Truth is," the CEO emphasized with considerable enthusiasm, "we are becoming lean and mean—no longer slow and sluggish!"

The five directors became even more uneasy; others of the board, while unable to challenge Polson, felt increasingly uncertain of their new CEO's actions and motives.

Continuing with his report—no director yet felt the right moment had arrived for a challenge—Phil Polson moved into his regular update of the company's quarterly performance. There were enough signs of slowing business to evoke more than the usual round of general comments. Gross income had dropped 8 percent from the corresponding quarter a year earlier; in net income the decline was 12 percent. But in manpower the loss was even more dramatic; 50 financial planners, company agents who actually counseled individual clients, were gone. How can a company grow and offer financial services to an ever increasing clientele, with fewer people? Hadn't the deadwood among these planners already been cleaned out? Directors remembered that Polson had done that in his first year, or at least that's what he reported to the board.

"You see, it's more than deadwood," the CEO carefully explained, perhaps anticipating the board's reaction, "These agents were representing more than one company. They were selling other financial products as well as those from Meridian. I refuse to put up with that kind of business. You see," he seemed to be trying very hard to get the obviously ignorant directors tuned in to his special world, "that's disloyalty to Meridian. Either our reps work only for us, or they work someplace else.

"And we'll have more separations to make in the months ahead. I've warned them all. Take your choice; work exclusively for us or get lost." Phil Polson had spoken, and his law had been laid down.

How many directors, if any, would challenge him? Had the five board members already forgotten the vice presidents and their departure?

Quiet settled around the table, but not a person was relaxed.

"Tell me, Phil," Melvin Packard, a soft-spoken lawyer, asked casually, "am I correct that our representatives try their best, at least the most sincere of them, to advise a client on the full range of things he or she might do to put together the best possible financial plan for that individual?"

"Exactly," replied Polson, "and if we do our job well, that person will have a sound plan for his financial future, and, incidentally, Meridian will have a lifelong client."

"Yet, if I understand that matter clearly, and I'm never sure that I do,"

Packard spoke deferentially only to camouflage the point of his questions, "neither Meridian nor any other single financial services company handles all of the possible instruments that might go to make up an individual portfolio of holdings. Is that correct?" Packard's intonation was still innocent, an inquiry by one seeking information.

"We have all the products any client will ever need," was Polson's quick retort.

"But what do we do with a client who wants and may insist upon some financial instrument that we don't offer? Does he go to another planner from some other company who has the product he wants? Must he find the other agent himself?" Packard's questions were beginning to sound like those of the astute lawyer he was.

Unaccustomed to penetrating questions from directors, Polson began to show his irritation. Instead of striking back, however, he clammed up, obviously a bit shocked by the unusual behavior of an otherwise gracious and friendly director.

"Phil, you say we have all the financial products any client will ever need," the comment came from Bob Walpole, a relative newcomer to the board but one considered a real catch when he agreed to join Meridian some five years earlier.

Robert T. Walpole had made a sizable fortune on Wall Street, and at 45 years of age he was lured to Washington by a new administration, moving into a senior position at the treasury department. Four years later, with his party voted out of office, he chose to stay in the capital where he had found new interest in the performing arts. Almost from the day of their arrival, both Walpole and his wife immersed themselves in the activities of the Kennedy Center and the Corporation for Public Broadcasting. That Bob brought his knowledge of the financial world to Meridian was due to the foresight of Jake Burwell.

Bill Comstock remembered the pursuit very well because Burwell enlisted his help in courting Walpole.

"He knows a part of the financial world which I will never know," Jake explained to Comstock. "I want his help in managing Meridian, but he certainly doesn't need the pittance which a director's fee would be to him. Bill, you know him better than I do. Will you get us together?"

And so Bob Walpole had joined the board, and here he was, entering a discussion with Polson on a subject which had been his own professional interest through a most successful career.

"In my own experience," Walpole continued as he addressed the entire board as well as Polson, "I found clients who had their own ideas as to the best instruments in which to invest. Many times, too, I was not able to sell a client another product even though to me it was a much more suitable one for his portfolio. What happens when a Meridian agent runs up against a person who wants something Meridian has but he also wants a product which we don't have? That is to me the question we are all asking."

"Listen," Polson's patience was wearing thin, "if we let our agents sell other products, they will lose their loyalty to our own company. I won't have it! I won't stand for it!"

"How many of our agents now sell products of other companies?" The question came from Laban Meyer, a young engineer-builder with just six months on the board.

"Oh, I guess every agent occasionally sells some other product. But it's not a regular thing," the CEO continued.

"Is there a company rule one way or another?" It was Packard who had let others carry the questioning after he set the stage.

"No," replied Polson, "And that's our problem. Going forward, I'm determined that agents will do all their business with Meridian products, or they can leave. I wanted the word to get around about the new policy, so I made an example of the 50 who were separated."

Going through the minds of many directors was the litany of the problems with agents—recruitment, training, rewarding—a most difficult and treacherous course. It seemed each CEO and every marketing vice president had the same complaint: Costs were too high and casualties along the way were too unpredictable. Polson himself had said more than once to the directors, "If we can get one good agent from every five recruited, we feel we are doing well."

And so, to drive home something of an arbitrary point, or so it seemed to some directors, Polson had fired some 7 to 8 percent of the entire group.

"Were these representatives of Meridian our poorest performers, are they mediocre, or would they rank among the best producers? Were they beginners or old-timers?" Melvin Packard pressed the matter, much to Polson's discomfort.

An hour later, after a shaken CEO had faltered with fuzzy, imprecise, and sometimes downright misleading responses to the many questions that came from the board, the meeting was adjourned. Every outside director had reached the conclusion that Polson's leadership, or lack of it, was seriously damaging the company; every inside director was loyal to Polson, having no choice but to remain or leave Meridian.

Immediate action was necessary. The outside directors, due in part to the mind-set of the five who came to the meeting already unhappy with other actions of the CEO, moved promptly to change matters.

By quick exchanges in the elevator, in the lobby, and on the sidewalk outside, several directors set the stage for an emergency meeting. It would be a rump session of as many outside directors as possible—as soon as possible. It took place the next morning with an early breakfast at the Oxbranch Club.

"I called Jake Burwell last evening," Mel Packard began. "I wanted to see if he had heard of developments at Meridian, and, yes, I got an earful. It turned out that Bob Walpole has been in touch with him, and more recently some ten or twelve of the agents who were fired have called him."

Laban Meyers spoke up to report that two of the group had called him as well. As he listened, Comstock, who had become alarmed at Mahoney's separation and that of the two vice presidents, knew that he had made a mistake when he refused to see two of the fired agents who had sought an appointment with him.

"Jake is a very disappointed man," Packard continued. "You remember that Polson was his choice," a fact they all knew.

It didn't take long for the group to decide their next step. It was to convince Burwell that he must return to Meridian, and that he must do so immediately. His retirement had to be interrupted. Burwell must again take over the management of the company, and this time do a better job of finding his own replacement!

Within 48 hours Polson's departure had been arranged, Burwell's return was on schedule, and Walpole had been persuaded by Jake Burwell, of course, to come back to the EVP's office.

Unfortunately, the directors who took the decisive actions, but not in time to prevent serious damage, were still learning of Polson's misguided decisions many months after his departure. In addition to firing 50 agents, he had placed another 200 on notice that they would be separated by the end of the month if they did not stop selling other products. No, Burwell explained, Meridian agents had always had the freedom to find another company's product for a client if he wanted it or if the agent himself thought another product was better for the client's portfolio. Giving agents such responsibility was only common sense, Jake said in describing the long-standing practice.

Whatever prompted Phil Polson to take such actions? Comstock and other directors would discuss that question for years. When Burwell turned the CEO's chair over to another, a year later, clear guidelines as to selection of appropriate products were in place. Some 41 of the 50 departed agents came back on board, but 9, all top producers of the company, had gone elsewhere.

Jake Burwell had decided to share some of the CEO's power, too. He asked five outside directors to serve with him as a selection committee to find his successor. The collective judgment of six, he said, would be much better than that of only one. He could have added that blame could be shared also if the new leader should fail. Midtown's president considered himself fortunate to have been one of the five.

Comstock saw that the use of power by the CEO can be quite arbitrary. At Meridian Polson had simply grabbed it. In every walk of life, so it seemed, some people had to establish their power over others, to show who is boss, to grind a heel on a subordinate, to keep personnel of the organization in fear, or by every means available to hammer away at others' inferiority.

But after acquiring power, Comstock noted that ways must be found to consolidate, to hold, and to keep this ever elusive entity. With amusement he recalled his appointment and assumption of office at New England U. High on the agenda of the friendly and helpful board chairman who selected Comstock was the matter of consolidating the power of the office.

"I assume," routinely commented the chief trustee, "that you will be bringing some people with you. You may want an EVP, financial officer, or personal assistant. The matter is entirely in your hands."

When Comstock replied, "No, I'll come alone," the chairman, also the CEO of a sizable merchandising chain, seemed disappointed. He thought such an arrangement would leave Comstock unprotected, a bit too vulnerable to the vagaries of faculty, students, or alumni. After all, each constituency had its own interest, and a new president would be an easy target. He might need help, the kind that could be supplied by already tested loyal colleagues.

"No," said Comstock, "I'll fight my own battles," and went on to elaborate further when he saw the chairman's worried look.

"If I bring a team with me," the new president explained, "I am immediately creating a 'we' and 'they' situation. I am inviting opposition to me and my team by those who are already part of New England University. There is at least a suggestion that I'm bringing my own bodyguards, not trusting to fair play by new associates. Then, too, it may appear to some that I'm putting the institution, NEU, below loyalty to me in the total frame of things.

"You see, Mr. Chairman," Comstock continued, "I have no personal agenda that I am bringing to NEU. The agenda is already here. It is further development and strengthening of the institution, not anything personal with Bill Comstock. I will be joining the family and friends of New England U in pushing the interests of the institution. In that way I would hope to become a partner with them, not an adversary."

It took only a few months for Comstock to allay the chairman's concerns. Ironically, it was the chairman himself who was among the first to disagree with the new president. The chairman wanted more money for football; the president wanted more books for the library. What was best for NEU? In this case the faculty and the president won out; the alumni, students, and board chairman lost. The difference of opinion was settled—amicably. Years later, long after retirement from business and from the board of trustees, the former chairman made a multi-million dollar gift to New England U earmarked for its library. Comstock had long felt that the chairman was only playing to the alumni in his support of football, that deep inside he knew learning to be the real work of a university.

During his first year in office, NEU's new president faced a challenge from outside the university; it came from one of the state's leading politicians. Seth Lowery, chairman of the legislative committee on education and labor, made a speech before the Capital Rotary Club in which he attacked the admissions standards of New England U. A graduate of Harvard law school, by way of Choate and Williams, Senator Lowery had little use for public institutions. They admitted applicants who couldn't get into real colleges and universities, he believed, constituted an unjustifiable drain on the public purse, and ought to be restricted to vocational programs where they could be useful. Drawing a bead on NEU, Lowery's attack seemed aimed squarely at Bill Comstock, who had taken up his new duties just a month earlier.

As might be predicted, NEU's trustees and alumni rushed to Comstock's side, offering various pieces of advice, most of which suggested that he ignore the senator's criticism. One of the first to reach the new president was the sage old dean of agriculture, long since retired, but one who wore many scars from previous legislative battles. He was also, as Comstock later told the story, his best friend in all of New England.

"Don't touch him," was the dean's advice. "He is simply baiting you. If you ignore him, he probably won't say another word."

Thanking the dean for his advice, Bill Comstock had already mapped out his course of action. He would ask the Capital Rotary Club for a chance to speak on the same subject before the same luncheon audience as soon as a date could be arranged. He directed the university's public information officer to make the arrangements. Before details were announced to the public, Comstock called Lowery, whom he had not yet met, and invited him to share the dais with him on the upcoming date. The senator could hardly refuse.

Armed with data on costs, admissions, and graduation rates of both public and private higher education in all of New England, Comstock simply buried Lowery with facts. But he did it all in a kindly and understanding way.

"Facing the unknown world which is before our youth and our country," Comstock told the group," we simply must find more ways to educate more of our citizens to higher levels than ever before in our history. And I want Senator Lowery to help in that monumental task. We all know something else: Such a goal can never be achieved unless the distinguished senator and his colleagues join wholeheartedly in the pursuit of that goal," Bill Comstock concluded his first important public appearance.

Publicity about the luncheon had attracted an unusual number of reporters from around the state. They lingered for another hour, asking questions, making notes, and following up on details. Already, they were asking the senator about possible legislative action in the forthcoming session. Although he was noncommittal, it was apparent he was shaken by the face-to-face yet courteous challenge the new academic leader had issued.

Private schools simply can't handle the total responsibility facing education, particularly higher education, Comstock had argued. All jurisdictions, he believed, should be served by both public and private institutions. In the case of NEU he had all the hard facts; in any such discussion he was able to add arguments from the heart. Before the Capital Rotary Club, in that unusual August heat, Comstock put them together and won the day.

After five more years in the senate, where he continued to hold his chairmanship, Lowery retired from politics. Those five years were marked by a 500 percent increase in public funds to New England University. It could not have happened without the senator's support. Years later, Comstock would concede that at the time of the Rotary meeting he didn't know whether he would be president of NEU for 60 days or 6 months. He only knew that he had a message that must be told. As it turned out it fell on the right ears.

It was another case of the use of power by the CEO of a university, this time the power of fact and persuasion, to win over a politician. Comstock continued to study in theory and in practice the power of the CEO, always comparing his own methods with those of others.

His concept for consolidating a CEO's power was far from being universally accepted. Some presidents and chairmen behaved otherwise. They brought their own spies to the university or to the company, sometimes entire armies of them.

Such was the case of Joseph T. Riley, newly chosen head of Seminole Paperboard, Inc., with headquarters in Boston. It was through his good friend Arthur Howery that Comstock joined the board.

"We have just selected a dynamic new CEO, and during the same meeting, the other directors voted unanimously to invite you to join the board," Howery told Comstock. "I have taken the liberty to run it past Joe Riley, our new chairman, and he's all in favor."

"I'm flattered, Art," was Comstock's initial response. "I've long regarded Seminole as a solid company, but as you know, I'm already over committed, keeping a very hectic schedule."

"This is not going to take much of your time, and it will be good for New England U. There are several directors whom you already know, and they are people who can be useful to your institution. I hope you will agree to serve."

All of what Arthur Howery said was true, and Bill Comstock knew it. Seminole was much more than a paper company. In the last decade it had become a vast conglomerate, having branched by way of acquisitions into textiles, food processing, auto parts distribution, and cosmetics. Its board counted some of New England and New York's leading industrialists. For the president to be sitting on the board would give New England U additional recognition and respect in the world of private business. For the good of the university Comstock accepted.

It was a mistake, one which neither Howery nor any other director of Seminole could foresee. Joe Riley brought to his new assignment an entirely personal and unexpected agenda. It included a lifelong career for himself and, surprisingly, for other members of his family.

Bringing three key players with him, so different from Comstock's arrival at NEU, his team as he called it, Riley lost no time in getting hold of finance, marketing, and manufacturing with the strategic placement of his three associates. Each was placed high enough to learn all the details of his assigned department, yet not high enough to replace a key officer.

New job descriptions with redefined responsibilities would come later, but not much later. Within months the three "Friends of Joe," FOJ as they and others not yet employed would come to be known, were scattered throughout the company. Several went virtually unnoticed. Until they were well established in their departments, their relationship with Riley was kept under wraps. Since it was such a large enterprise with several unrelated business activities and a considerable turnover of senior officers, Riley had infiltrated the whole company with some 25 key appointments before the directors were aware of his mischief. Even then, most were unconcerned since Seminole's bottom line was ever stronger.

With increasing frequency the grapevine carried the news that yet another FOJ had turned up in some key spot within the far-reaching activities of the very large and still growing conglomerate. Just maybe Riley had the ability to pick able lieutenants, place them in the right spots, and, thereby, keep Seminole moving toward both continued growth and efficiency.

Until something changed for the worse, board members weren't about to challenge success; they had best let Joe Riley play his cards. Handling a large conglomerate was no easy task, and the world was full of failures to prove it. Directors had no reason to second-guess their still new CEO. Instead, it was Riley who challenged the board.

"It has now been two years since I came to Seminole," Joe announced as he opened the monthly meeting of the executive committee. "I believe I have done all that was asked of me in these two years. I would argue that I have done considerably more. Therefore, I want my contract examined. It is not exactly a renegotiation because you indicated that my situation would merit a new look if things were going well after a couple of years."

Joe Riley was indeed right. Yet his unexpected request, voiced in such a hard-nosed, demanding way, caught the directors by surprise. They had collectively settled into the complacency common to such boards when the enterprise is growing, profits are increasing, and, as in the case of Seminole, all signs point to the company's continuing vitality.

But something far more vital had occurred. Under the directors' very noses, their new CEO had taken control of the company. His army of lieutenants and key appointees throughout the business all shared a common trait: unquestioned loyalty to Riley. Seminole was new to them, but Riley was not. Each knew their boss from previous associations, and each knew that loyalty was foremost. If they did as Riley wanted, they would be well rewarded. Furthermore, if one had a question, he always had access to the boss—a casual meeting, a late-night phone call, or a personal note.

Would the executive committee consider a new contract? Yes, of course. They had no choice. But the directors who were present—six outsiders and Riley constituted the group—thought they had been quite generous with the initial compensation package. Was something missing?

Negotiations proved difficult. But why couldn't Riley be difficult? He controlled the company. Armed with data from three consulting firms, Riley's representative (he had hired a longtime friend and knowledgeable attorney to act in his behalf) was able to show that his client was greatly underpaid. Companies of comparable size and complexity were giving their CEO's as much as double Seminole's compensation to Riley.

Arthur Howery, selected to head a special committee to examine their CEO's contract, was by no means a match for the skillful lawyer. After weeks of haggling and stacks of reports, Joe Riley had a new five-year contract that placed him at the top of the group of CEO's with whom his representative had compared him. The fact that most of the other CEOs had been in office for many years, some close to retirement, was overlooked in the comparisons.

"My client," so the argument went, "is a hot property. Unless you want to lose him to one of your competitors, you must act now." Of course, the thought of going into the business world to find another leader sent shivers up the backs of most directors. They didn't have the time, nor were they confident of their own skill and knowledge in finding a good one. Several directors felt that Riley was taking them for a ride, but accepting his new contract was easier than risking the results of another nationwide search. Within a few weeks the grumbling ceased, and directors focused again on profitability. It was good that they did.

Very peculiar, surprising, unbelievable were the comments heard around the table as first one area of Seminole's business and then another turned sour only six months after Riley's new contract was signed and directors had become somewhat relaxed from the apprehension surrounding its provisions; cracks began to appear in the financial results.

First it was paper products, the historical business of Seminole for more than a hundred years. Riley explained the quarter's loss as a temporary blip brought about by the erratic behavior of the Japanese market. "It is nothing to be concerned about," he assured the board. Archie Halpin, a director who followed the pulp and paper industry for his investment firm, wasn't so sure. Other companies in the industry were not suffering. In fact, they were making money. What was so peculiar about Seminole?

Another quarter brought another loss to Seminole in the paper products division. It also brought another challenge from Halpin.

"What are we doing about the paper division? I see our losses are growing," Halpin addressed the chairman.

"Archie, it's a long story." How many times had Comstock heard CEOs use that answer. It could mean many things: "I don't have the time to explain it to you people who are uninformed; you wouldn't understand;

it isn't important enough to discuss;" or, just maybe, "I don't know the real answer to your question."

"Can you give us the short version," Halpin asked in a way to lighten the exchange.

"How about it, George? You're closer to this problem than I am," and he turned to George Dinsmore, the president of the paper products division who was sitting at the back of the room, an area regularly occupied by subordinates. They were rarely invited–or allowed–to speak.

Dinsmore was clearly surprised. His rambling comments only spread Halpin's concerns among more directors. Even with kindly prodding from Riley, he failed to lay out distinctly whatever problems might exist. He succeeded only in raising serious doubts about his own knowledge of the business he headed. Directors did not learn until much later that George Dinsmore was one of the early "Friends of Joe."

Dinsmore's division never recovered from its downward stumble. When it reached marginal profitability a year later, Riley chose to ignore both that part of Seminole and Dinsmore as well. It appeared only coincidental that Dinsmore was absent for each of the next three quarterly meetings of the board. What the directors did not know was that Joe Riley was protecting him from any further embarrassment, something he never did for the non-FOJs.

But Archie Halpin knew too much about paper products–the background and performance of all the companies, their senior officers, and their major stockholders–to be satisfied. It took only a few telephone calls to friends in the industry to learn that Dinsmore, as a newcomer, more or less appeared out of the blue to fill a senior vacancy in the accounting division; from there he had gone to the presidency with Riley's reorganization of the division. A strike among the employees of a major supplier to Seminole's biggest mill and the loss of a longtime customer, a well known national magazine, together had brought the loss of earnings. He also learned that Seminole did not yet have its problems under control. It came as no surprise to Halpin when Riley proposed some three months later that Seminole sell its paper products division.

"Conglomerates are beginning to slim down," the CEO began. "Since paper products are the least profitable part of our company, it makes sense to drop them and concentrate where we can make the most money."

It was pretty straightforward talk coming from Seminole's CEO. But directors weren't buying; nostalgia ran deep.

"I have numbers here from the five largest paper companies in the country, and all continue to be very profitable. Sure there is a cyclical nature to their earnings, but that's the nature of this business. Why, Joe," Archie Halpin aimed his question straight at Riley, "can't we do as well?"

"I just thought–" Riley began his reply, but he didn't get to finish. For the first time since he sat in the chairman's seat, he had to listen while the directors talked. More pointedly, he had to hear their flat rejection of his proposal. No vote ever came; that formality was unnecessary.

As the forces against him began to build, Joe Riley speeded up his own personal agenda. Unbeknown to anyone in the company, Riley had placed his son-in-law in a key position in Seminole's San Francisco office, the key marketing center for the West Coast as well as all of Asia. Total business from that single office accounted for 45 percent of Seminole' gross income and 50 percent of company profits. Keith Nichols, who had married the oldest Riley daughter some ten years earlier, was in the right place at the right time–put there by Seminole's CEO. Of course, it didn't hurt that the chief marketing officer was an FOJ, brought on only months after Riley became CEO.

Knowing that his own well-being was directly dependent on Nichols' advancement, he saw to it that the son-in-law moved rapidly, so fast, in fact, that he was in charge of all Pacific Rim sales in three years after joining the company.

Back at Seminole's Boston headquarters, it was easy for Joe Riley to praise the San Francisco office and all its personnel, and to turn up the wattage when he pointed the spotlight on Keith Nichols. Every director soon learned his name and knew more than the usual about his successes; they did not learn until later he was a member of the Riley family.

No one ever accused Joe Riley of being a slow learner. He read the messages from the company's directors with 100 percent clarity. Shoring up the weak spots while reigning in his horns became his modus operandi for the next 18 months. With continuing growth out of the San Francisco office, Seminole gave all appearances of a complete turnaround.

While directors relaxed, their CEO proceeded with his agenda. He proposed a reorganization of the company. Another year, Riley said, and he would like to turn daily operations over to a president. He would give up that part of his title, he explained, and would continue as CEO, but with only "Chairman" to distinguish his office. It was not an unusual move in the corporate world, so the directors were not deeply concerned. After all, Seminole had three EVPs, each responsible for a major division of the company and all reporting to Riley. Most directors assumed that one of the three would be Riley's choice when the time came for the change. Some directors were especially pleased because, as they said, "Should Joe be hit by a truck, which of the three is best equipped to move into the CEO's seat?" Riley, chairman and president, had carefully avoided showing any preference.

Nine months passed, and the directors still didn't know. With only a quarter remaining before the president and second-in-command was to be named, two directors with reorganization very much on their minds asked Riley if there had been a change of plans.

"No, no, no," the CEO replied. "I have simply been unable to come to a decision. But in the process of weighing all the possibilities and looking throughout the company for the best possible president, I have found at least two people beyond the EVPs who are worth considering." Then, as if to show how hard he was working on the problem and how difficult it was, he offered his next steps.

"Give me another 30 days, and I'll have a report for you. In fact, I promise you I'll come with a firm recommendation at that time." Fair enough, all agreed.

Keith Nichols was elected president of Seminole a month later. Joe Riley's personal agenda had been completed, almost.

It was another two years before chairman Riley turned over control to his son-in-law, the goal he had been working toward for a decade. Directors learned of the family relationship, but too late for it to affect their decisions.

Had the board of Seminole been misled? Absolutely. Had the deceit hurt the company? Yes, substantially. After only two years of his five-year contract, the directors bought Nichols out because of his continuous blunders. They named a former EVP as chairman and president and then set about the almost impossible task of restoring integrity to the company.

Arthur Howery never stopped apologizing to Comstock for recruiting him for the Seminole board. For New England U's president it was another learning experience, "and a personal view of corporate America I would never have witnessed had you not invited me," he told Howery. For years to come both men would smile about their trials with the conglomerate. As Seminole again became calm and as it gradually regained respect, they were able to relax.

Could it happen in the academic world? Comstock had his doubts. With faculty members enjoying the protection of tenure, with academic freedom shielding them when voicing opinions on almost any subject, he took a certain pride in his belief that such protections of the faculty, plus the indigenous integrity of the university, would never allow a president or chancellor to get away with such chicanery.

Comstock carried that belief with him for much of his career, well into his years at Midtown. It was shaken when he heard about Midwestern Institute of Technology.

The call came from Silas Broyhill in New York, perhaps the most highly respected consultant in higher education in the country. He had served as president of two universities, one on the West Coast and the other in New England, and every university leader in the country knew and respected Broyhill. Over the decades, Comstock tried to join his friend in at least one consulting assignment each year because he felt indebted to him for the many things he had learned about colleges and universities from this most astute former president.

"Bill, have you heard about what's going on at Midwestern Tech?" Si Broyhill asked the president. Midwestern Institute of Technology in Omaha was well known throughout the world of higher education. Ranking close behind MIT and Cal Tech, Midwestern had come up fast in the fields of science, engineering, and technology during the past quarter century. Its progress was due primarily to the generosity of five wealthy families who lived in the great expanse of prairie between the Ohio River and the Rocky Mountains.

"Why," one of the group said, as he had pledged 100 million dollars to Midwestern some years earlier, "should only the East and West Coasts be home to America's scientific brainpower? We are determined," and he spoke for all five families, "to put a great scientific research and teaching institution in the country's heartland."

Now Midwestern was attracting its share of the most promising students and hiring faculty away from both Cal Tech and MIT, as well as from Carnegie-Melon and Johns Hopkins.

"Have I heard what's happening at Midwestern?" Comstock had to repeat the question from Broyhill; he had heard nothing in recent months about the Omaha institution.

"What's happening?" He knew from Broyhill's tone of voice that it wasn't good.

"Bill," and Si became very serious, "they are in trouble, and I have agreed to try to help them. And," continuing before Comstock could reply, "I want you to go with me."

"Si, if I can possibly get away, I'll do it." Running through Comstock's mind was the knowledge that he had turned down his friend on the last two invitations, and he genuinely missed such opportunities because each one brought forth some new wrinkle to the problems of a university. Interviewing new people, discussing recommendations, writing reports, traveling at all hours—each assignment was a backbreaker but rewarding. There seemed no end to the problems of a campus, Comstock thought. Yes, Midtown's president would go; he had to find a way.

He arrived in Omaha the same day as the rest of the five-member team—two sitting presidents, one retired chancellor, Broyhill, and Tony Bacchus, chief of staff to Higher Education Associates, Inc., the consulting firm. Comstock was soon immersed in Midwestern's problems. They all centered on Timothy J. Mason, the president.

Mason, now in his sixth year as president, was boasting a new seven-year contract with compensation and fringe benefits that placed him among the highest paid of all university leaders in the country. Then why such an upheaval? That was the question posed by the trustees of Mid Tech—the short name used to distinguish Midwestern from MIT and Cal Tech—to the five consultants. Finding the answer was the mission for Si Broyhill, Bill Comstock, and their three associates.

Rumblings had been heard during Mason's first five years. Some were quite loud during his beginning months, but things had settled down after that, or so the academic grapevine had conveyed. And the higher education community had grown accustomed to flare-ups here and there as presidents moved from one campus to another, retired, were fired, or simply fought continuing battles for an entire career on the same campus.

But Joe Mason had come to Mid Tech with more than the usual fanfare. Following a nationwide search, Mason had been selected to lead this new upstart but already distinguished institution to the very pinnacle of world leadership. Unlike MIT and Cal Tech, which were still beholden to programs and contracts reaching back to World War II, Mid Tech was unrestrained by tradition and free of burdens imposed by an overage faculty. It was now positioned, thanks to the support of the five wealthy and farsighted families, to take over the summit. Timothy Mason arrived to take command of the assault. He came with impeccable credentials.

Mason's selection was announced with blaring trumpets, none louder than his own.

In a forced attempt of familiarity, he insisted upon being called "Joe." After all, if a president of the United States can be "Jimmy," then the president of a university can be "Joe," as Mason explained to many audiences. Mason had touched all the right bases on his way to the presidency of Mid Tech. An undergraduate degree from Rice with a major in chemistry was followed by an MBA from Harvard, that capped with a law degree from Chicago. He had the science, the management, and the legal preparation to lead in a world that required understanding of fast-moving research discoveries, changing managerial skills, and ever dangerous litigation. Rounding out his preparation were seven years as president of a smaller but well-respected multi-purpose university.

Again, the question, what went wrong? Or was anything really wrong? Some great moments in American university life had occurred amid intense controversy—Hutchins at Chicago, Rainey at Texas, and Meikeljohn at Antioch. These and many others were well known to the consultants facing the challenge of unraveling Mid Tech's apparent upheaval.

First came a meeting with the special committee of the governing board, a five-member group of honest, well-meaning trustees, all of whom believed, with the exception of one quiet old lawyer, that academics wore halos, campuses were sacred grounds, and everyone who worked in a university was there for only idealistic purposes.

The cautious Francis Pillsbury had been invited to join Mid Tech's board as something of a courtesy. Having done pro bono work for the institution over the years, this Harvard-trained lawyer, one of Omaha's most respected, was rewarded with a seat on the board. That he was placed on the executive committee came as further recognition of his high standing in the legal community. Personally, however, Pillsbury chose to stay in the background, letting others do most of the talking, responding with well-reasoned comments only when requested. He had doubts about Mason, but he kept his silence.

The goodwill and altruistic sentiments surrounding the institution were the very conditions that brought Joe Mason to Mid Tech. He had read the situation perfectly. That he took advantage of all the constituencies was revealed only later. It took Si Broyhill's team to get to the facts.

Exhilaration ran so high when Mason accepted the board's invitation to become president of Mid Tech that the announcement was made at a special press conference. It was presided over by the chairman and held before any mention was made by either party of salary, compensation, or financial condition. Joe Mason clearly had the upper hand—and he never relinquished the grip.

First, he called a lawyer who had represented a number of highly paid professional athletes in contract bargaining to represent him. Melvyn Douglas, the trustees soon learned, looked upon a university president as he did any other client. He was involved for only one purpose—to get everything he could from the employer. It didn't hurt that Mason was a longtime personal friend, another fact which was then unknown to Mid Tech's board members.

When it was all over several months later, Joe Mason had a compensation package that put him among the ten most highly paid academics in the country. Furthermore, it was for five years. Nothing like "serving at the pleasure of the board," or "being mutually satisfied" with institutional progress. Such phrases had no place in this contract, Douglas carefully but firmly explained.

The pill was a bit bitter for some trustees to swallow, but swallow it they did. After all, they had already made the public commitments. Mid Tech's constituencies were all aglow with the ballyhoo that had surrounded the selection, so it was impossible for trustees to turn back. Joe Mason had played the board like the proverbial violin, and early in the relationship, they had unwittingly surrendered much of their power.

Now in his sixth year, he had repeated his earlier contractual performance. This time, however, after another lengthy negotiation period, the everyday "Joe," as he still introduced himself, had a seven-year contract with an option to extend it for three more, should he choose. Mumbling and grumbling echoed here and there among students and faculty, alumni, and trustees—the campus was abuzz. Joe Mason was on everyone's lips: his latest memorandum, a comment on academic freedom, a call on alumni to increase contributions, the quality of the freshmen class—it was always going up under his leadership. The air seemed filled with "Timothy Joseph Mason," the full name with which he signed every letter or university document. A simple "Joe" was not enough for anything on paper.

Tony Bacchus had much to tell his four colleagues as he brought the group up to date on their first meeting at their hotel just off Mid Tech's campus in Omaha. Bacchus had been asked by Broyhill to assemble reports, gather a file of faculty complaints, review minutes of board meetings, and set up initial appointments for others on the team.

"The faculty is very unhappy with Mason," was Tony's first comment. "But their concerns range all over the board. Some don't like what they see as a very dictatorial president who has made a mockery of faculty participation in decision making. Some say he is strangling the library and computer center while spending too much on athletics and public relations, and a few still like the guy. Like most faculties, however, this one can't seem to come together. Resolutions of all kinds have been introduced in their faculty senate, resolutions that call for this or demand that, but all have ended up with amendments or attachments which obfuscate or placate the very problem they set out to address."

"Sounds just like a faculty," chimed in Si Broyhill. "They can talk around every bush in the universe without ever agreeing on what to do."

"What about the trustees," Broyhill inquired, shifting the focus of the conversation.

"I have gone through the minutes of recent meetings rather carefully, and it is apparent that too many board members are kept in the dark about a lot of important matters. They have a pattern of appointing a special committee, usually just three members, to look into a problem. They let that little group work out an answer and then accept the proposed solution without ever discussing, much less understanding, what the sub group has done," Tony explained.

"That was the way the faculty's gripes were handled a year ago,"

Bacchus continued. "And, believe it or not, it was only three people out of a total board of thirty-seven who did all the negotiations with Joe Mason on his contracts."

"Surely the chairman must know what all these special committees are doing. After all, he is the same chairman who selected Mason in the first place," Broyhill spoke up, again focusing on the place where ultimate authority and responsibility lay. "I really don't know," Tony replied. "All I have is what I found in minutes and other official records the secretary shared with me. Your first appointment tomorrow is an hour with the chairman. It should be interesting."

Comstock drew the chairman of the faculty senate to begin his day of interviews. It was to be like many other consulting visits, a very busy three days—and nights!

So central was the faculty's role to the educational mission of Mid Tech that Comstock was only able in his first meeting with its senate chairman to scratch the surface of the many fundamental breaches he saw in the way Joe Mason treated Mid Tech's most vital resource, the teaching and research personnel. It was this body of men and women who furnished the learning experience for every student who entered, the lowliest freshman or the most advanced scholar. Mason ignored them or, worse yet, vetoed every initiative they advanced. Sensing the gravity of the developing confrontation with faculty, Comstock asked that members of the senate, five senior professors from various parts of the campus, join him for dinner at the end of his first day in Omaha.

"At least six times since President Mason arrived, I gather the senate has considered, and on three of those occasions debated at length, a resolution of no confidence in your president. Is that correct?" Bill Comstock asked as they began dinner. It was a question centering on the ultimate weapon of a faculty—not just on their happiness, their satisfaction, or their general feeling toward their leader, but a question that clearly confronted them with their own responsibility to their institution. Without voicing his own assessment of the faculty's behavior, Comstock's questions challenged these five senior members who had been chosen to represent the interest of all their colleagues to defend their inaction toward their leader. Griping, complaining, wringing their hands, or blowing off steam in no way substituted for action appropriate to the severity of the situation.

A kind of group guilt spread over the five as each waited for another to reply. When comments did begin to flow, and each of the five felt compelled to say something, the answers fell far short.

"Tell me, were you afraid to go on record as having no confidence in Joe Mason?" Comstock pressed the point. He knew that few academic leaders could survive such a vote. There had been cases in which governing boards had simply thumbed their noses at faculties for going on record against their leaders, but they were rare. A vote of no confidence by faculty is customarily followed by the leader's departure from office. It happens with deans, vice presidents, presidents, and chancellors.

"To tell you the truth, Dr. Comstock, we didn't know and we don't yet know where the board of trustees stands," began the chairman of the senate, an outstanding professor of electrical engineering and computer science with a professional reputation that reached around the world

Alonzo H. Lockard was one of those academic stars, recruited to Mid Tech a decade earlier because he had a new idea to try out. The dean who persuaded him to come offered him the freedom and financial support necessary for his pursuit. Little did he dream that he would be spending endless hours agonizing over the performance of a president, wasting precious time in faculty politics, and worrying about governing boards. Yet his colleagues had put him in the most forward position to protect their rights. It was a new experience, one for which Lockard was completely unprepared; but a strong sense of duty, coupled with a lifelong respect for universities, would not let him shirk his perceived academic responsibility.

Here was a great scientist who could only flounder when faced with the give-and-take, the tugging and hauling of petty campus politics. Where did the trustees stand? Neither Lockard nor any of his faculty colleagues knew for sure. Comstock had found one of the broken-down power lines of Mid Tech—the faculty and governing board weren't communicating.

"So not knowing what the relationship between the board and the president might be, you were afraid to go on record with a vote of no confidence. Is that a fair way to state your predicament?" Comstock asked. All five professors reluctantly agreed, but only after considerable prodding.

Attempts to communicate with trustees had proved futile. Two faculty members had approached the chairman of the board before the end of Mason's first year. "Take up your complaints with the president," he said.

The chairman clearly had no time to interfere in the relations of the faculty and president. “Besides,” he added, “President Mason is just learning the culture of Mid Tech. I’m sure you will find him to be one who always puts the welfare of the institution first in whatever he does.” Comstock could see that not one of the five agreed with the chairman’s assessment. Lack of confidence had long since given way to animosity.

Other attempts over five years ended with the same results. Not only did the trustees seem satisfied with Mason’s performance, but they also appeared enthusiastic.

Reporting what he had learned to Si Broyhill later in the evening—the two not having seen each other since breakfast—Bill Comstock got an earful in return.

“Callahan is a personable guy, and probably a good CEO of his company, but he doesn’t know what’s going on at Mid Tech,” Broyhill began.

Chairman-elect of Mid Tech’s board at the time the search for a president was just getting underway, and waiting in the wings to succeed to the chairmanship, James O. Callahan seemed the logical candidate to head the search committee. And so it was that Mason and Callahan began their service together, one as chairman of the board, the other as president of the institute.

Callahan was no small-town businessman. He was CEO of Standard Oil of the Midwest, the largest corporation between Detroit and Houston. His was a big company, his was a big staff, and, naturally, his was a big salary. Where others might think in thousands or even millions, Callahan was accustomed to measuring in the billions. Mid Tech’s budget or the salary which its president might draw would be small change in Callahan’s world. Serving as chairman of its board was of some importance to Callahan, but it wasn’t anything so big or complex as to take more than a few hours of his time each month.

It took more than five years for him to learn that an academic institution may be one of man’s most complex creations. When chaos threatened in Mason’s sixth year, Callahan became alarmed—thus, the call to Broyhill. But he still didn’t know exactly what was wrong.

“Tell me,” he asked Broyhill in their first meeting, “are campuses always in turmoil? Is it the natural order of academic work to have every single constituency up in arms?

"In business we have stockholders," Callahan plowed ahead before Broyhill could reply. "But who owns a university? Students claim it's theirs; alumni are always yelling about something. And the faculty! I'll never understand where professors are coming from."

It was a voice of futility. Comstock and Broyhill had seen it before. A well-meaning corporate leader, successful in his business, willing to be of service to education, recruited by presidents and trustees because of his access to big money and wealthy friends, ending up in a position of vital importance to an institution of higher learning, but totally unprepared to perform even at a minimum level of satisfaction. So it was for Mr. Callahan, whom no one in Omaha addressed by his first name. That privilege was reserved for CEOs of other large corporations—and Joe Mason.

After two days of interviews, stacks of reports, and constant interplay, the five consultants met with the executive committee of the board of trustees. It was a session given over to checking impressions, confirming factual information, reviewing recent history, and securing to the extent possible the committee's confidential assessments of problems and people.

Broyhill and Comstock could have written their report before sitting down with the five trustees, so clear was the picture to them. With variations here and there both men had seen similar messes before at other universities. That an institution which had come so far so fast should be derailed, even momentarily, was a bad commentary on the academic field. It would take some drastic surgery to save the patient, but the cause of Mid Tech's illness was diagnosed; the medical team of five visitors prepared to apply the cure.

In retrospect it had been so easy for Joe Mason to perform his magic. A new board chairman, eager to put his stamp on Mid Tech, had felt good about awarding Mason what he had asked for—a longtime contract with very generous compensation. And then, after weathering the smaller eruptions of Mason's early years, he rewarded him with an even longer and more generous contract for the future. Callahan succumbed to the folklore: Academics were always grousing about something, campuses were forever in some kind of disorder, and every group concerned—alumni, students, faculty, even the townspeople—had their own claims to campus priorities. Here was another governing board chairman who turned a deaf ear to the sounds from an unhappy campus.

Having placed Mason in office, Mid Tech's chairman had only one remaining role to fill, that of supporting the new president. That's the way it was done in business, and that's the way it should be done on campus. Let the faculty shut up, and let the students and alumni enjoy their athletics. With that Callahan turned back to the oil business.

Joe Mason read the chairman perfectly and proceeded to take full advantage of his new position.

Within days of his arrival he began to bring new people to key positions on the Mid Tech campus. First, it was an assistant comptroller, then an assistant vice president for research, quickly followed by the arrival of an experienced lawyer who got the title of special assistant to the president. A new vice president for planning was brought aboard, an increasingly vital function for Mid Tech's growth, so Mason explained as he introduced the new man at a meeting of the board. That all were longtime friends of Joe Mason was a detail not mentioned. More than 30 such people, strategically placed throughout the campus, all previously associated with Mason, joined Mid Tech's staff in the new president's first 12 months in office.

For Bill Comstock the ghosts of Joe Riley and Seminole Paper were coming out all over. Midtown's president could hardly believe what a parallel the campus and the big corporation made.

Joe Mason's grip on Mid Tech had become a stranglehold. It's release would be a test of will, that of an arrogant, bull-doggish president arrayed against a recently awakened corporate tycoon wearing the hat of board chairman. While all constituencies continued to debate, Mr. Callahan prepared for the showdown. Si Broyhill in his confidential report following the consultants' visit had given him no choice.

Like many such reviews, the report written by Tony Bacchus simply stated the conditions that the visiting team found at Mid Tech: faculty morale dangerously low, other employees cowed with fear over uncertainty about their jobs, alumni openly apologetic for the sad state of campus affairs, and students unusually critical of both Mason and other senior officers. Bacchus had put it all in written form, couched, however, in the artistic language of the diplomat. It took no genius to find the culprit; he was Joe Mason.

Having forwarded a preliminary copy of the report to Callahan, a usual courtesy before putting on the final touches, Broyhill found the chairman ready to accept his advice.

"I gather the best way to dig ourselves out of the hole we're in is to separate Mason from the institution. Is that not the bottom line of this report?" Callahan asked Broyhill. The two were meeting ten days after the team's departure from the campus to wind up the assignment; it was the usual procedure followed by Higher Education Associates, Inc.

"Frankly, Mr. Callahan, we don't see any other way for Mid Tech to return to the life of a normal campus without Mason's departure. Not only is the place in an uproar, but there is also enough substance to some of the rumors regarding his actions to raise serious questions about his ethical conduct. Whether anything illegal has taken place, our team can't tell you with certainty. We do know strong suspicions exist in several quarters."

"Yes, I've heard the rumors, too," Callahan injected. Then, hurrying to the conclusion he had already reached, the chairman told Broyhill what his next action would be.

"I hired Joe Mason," said Callahan, "and, by God, I'll fire him. He has let me down, and I'm through with him."

Mr. Callahan, the calm, well-organized business leader was mad, a condition few outside the oil business had ever witnessed. His own judgment had been wrong. Having picked Mason as the right man for the job, having brushed aside the many hints over the years that raised doubts about his choice, this very important man in a very high place was having to admit his mistake. It was hard to swallow, but when he was forced to face up to the results of his terribly wrong action, he was ready to strike back with vengeance.

Getting hold of himself however, he quickly returned to his usually reasonable outward composure.

"I haven't had any practice in firing university presidents," he explained. "I'll need your help in getting rid of Mason."

"I'll be glad to advise," Broyhill offered.

Separating a president who had just signed a new and lucrative seven-year contract, whose compensation put him at the top among his colleagues across the country, and whose record was quite laudable, at least so far as his own well-oiled public relations machine had projected it, would not be an easy task.

Broyhill prepared to advise Callahan a few days after the consultant's report was delivered to Mid Tech's governing board. Its contents were widely reported on campus and throughout Omaha, "I would recommend," Broyhill began, "that you hire the toughest negotiator in the country to represent the board. I assume Mason will again call on Melvyn Douglas. After all, they are longtime buddies," something which had finally become known around Mid Tech.

"You can bet that Timothy Joseph Mason," Si Broyhill was reading the signature and mimicking the glaring handlebar, "will fight like a cornered skunk for everything he can get from any settlement."

Broyhill had names to suggest, but here was a field in which Callahan also was experienced. They settled on a Chicago attorney who had represented the big three auto makers in various libel cases, and as it turned out, he was a personal friend of Francis Pillsbury of Mid Tech's board. Callahan, upon learning of that relationship, asked Pillsbury to serve as well. It quickly proved to be the right choice.

As expected, when Callahan called Mason to his office and asked for his resignation, a step in the procedure that Broyhill had recommended and that was usual in such circumstances, the academic objected angrily. He made it clear he had a binding contract; the board of Mid Tech couldn't force him out; he would fight the action all the way; and, yes, he would get Melvyn Douglas to represent him.

"Take it to my lawyer; I'll see you in court!" Mason exclaimed as he hurried to the door. "Callahan, you'll be sorry," was his parting shot.

Relieved of his duties, with an acting president already in place, Joe Mason began rounding up support for his cause. The news surrounding events on the Mid Tech campus pushed everything else into insignificance on radio and television and in newspapers in and around Omaha for the next several days.

While Mason had trouble garnering support for retaining his position, he had no trouble attracting headlines. With pronouncements at each change of the news, he became louder and louder with charges that grew wilder with each recounting. Ironically, his letter of resignation came out of the first meeting of the negotiators.

Francis Pillsbury had been quiet, but he had not been remiss. Having checked signals with his friend from Chicago, he simply informed Melvyn

Douglas that if matters were carried to court, his client would be asked a few questions:

"I shall introduce these matters. You can take them to your client to ascertain his responses," Pillsbury began to state his case.

"We shall demand to know, and, of course, his answers will all be in the public domain, what he knows about the 20-million-dollar contract that was awarded one year ago for the operation of the computer center. What is your client's relationship with the consultants who drew up the new campus development plan some two years ago? We want to know, too, where the supplies and labor came from for the renovation of Mason's summer home. We have some other questions, as well, but these should give your client a flavor of the full-fledged investigation which we are prepared to launch."

Pillsbury's work, which really meant taking his time to listen to a few complaints over the previous two years, was Mason's undoing. He stood ready to disclose that the computer center contract had been given to a company in Boston headed by Mason's brother-in-law, whose bid was far from the lowest, that he personally owned 20 percent of the company which did the new campus plan, and that Mid Tech employees had done some $25,000 in work on his summer home, bringing materials from the campus as they traveled back and forth. Faced with having his client answer such irrefutable charges, Melvyn Douglas wisely advised Mason to leave quietly, quite uncharacteristic of anything he had ever done.

So with no place to hide and fresh out of alibis, Joe Mason affixed his full name to a letter surrendering claim to any further obligations from the institution. Mid Tech's constituencies began the solemn and lengthy task of repairing the damage.

Few among the campus family, and even fewer in the greater Omaha community, ever learned that the quiet Francis Pillsbury, with his usual pro bono badge, had rendered such monumental service to Midwestern Institute of Technology. Before leaving the chairmanship of the board some years later, Callahan tried, with the help of his fellow trustees, to award an honorary degree to Pillsbury. The lawyer quietly but firmly declined. "It is something I don't need," he said firmly within the confines of the closed meeting where the action was proposed.

Yes, some people did turn down such honors. Surprisingly it was usually those who most deserved the recognition. As for Bill Comstock, who continued to follow the affairs of Mid Tech for the rest of his career, the three-day visit provided another case study in the winding path of an academic institution. Each seemed so different, and yet had so much in common with other colleges and universities—and with private corporations.

But Midtowns' president couldn't forget POWER. It was so important to so many CEOs, but a few simply walked around it. Influencing others, controlling others—was it a question of fear, inferiority, arrogance, mistrust? Were CEOs driven to intimidate or even to destroy the careers of others in order to satisfy their own appetites for power? For those who behaved in such a way, did they really believe that authority was gained and retained only by using the club?

Bill Comstock could never bring himself to accept such conclusions. He had too much respect for others. He made a conscious effort to treat individuals as he wanted them to treat him. So easy, he observed many times, for the one in authority to take advantage of those below. How to get the job done, how to involve others, how to benefit from their insights, and how to keep the Rileys and Masons of the world out of positions of power—this was the chess game, Comstock concluded, that every responsible citizen was required to play. It was present wherever he turned—public service, business and industry, or academe.

IV

The Chairman, the President, the CEO: A Close-up

For 50 years William H. Comstock had observed, studied, assessed, and puzzled over the performance of managers—men and women who headed the big enterprises and the little ones, the simple endeavors, and the complex entities, the profit-making efforts and the non-profits. Although he still remained baffled as to what constituted success in leading an enterprise, he had at least learned what he liked to see in a CEO.

Several years had passed between his service in World War II and his first experience with a corporate board. The Navy had exposed him to a succession of commanding officers and had given him a view he later described as periscope-like, looking up at the leader. His perspective changed when he ventured into the business world.

Recalling his first corporate board, he remembered how he had struggled to understand the enterprise and his role in it. He felt like a college freshman on the first day of classes. For Comstock, however, that first board was a quick study in business, not because this academic was so knowledgeable but because the CEO was such an able leader and an outstanding manager.

It took only a few meetings of the board, a short visit with senior officers of the company, and one all-day field trip for Comstock to feel comfortable with this new environment. What a teacher H. Grover Robertson turned out to be and how much professors could learn from him if they could only come together, thought the campus leader. A New England based company, doing less than a hundred million annually in sales, it was nonetheless engaged in a half-dozen different manufacturing lines. Robertson was an unlikely corporate builder. He had arrived in this country from his native Scotland at 18 years of age with 25 cents in his pocket, all that was left from working for his passage on an old freighter. He sought no campus, no further formal education. Instead he followed his childhood sweetheart, who had come to Canada a year earlier with her family, determined to marry her first and leave all other decisions regarding his future until later.

Grover stopped in northern Maine and earned his first wages. It was potato-planting time, and the grower hired for the season every able-bodied passerby. The young immigrant learned basic economics, finance, and management, not from a textbook or classroom, but from the marketplace—and with a sore back. Geography was kind to romance. He took up anew the courtship of his young lady who was comfortably settled with her family just across the border in Canada. Her father, another Scot, who felt that a growing savings account was the best recommendation for a suitor of his daughter, was not ecstatic at the prospects of having a potato picker for a son-in-law. Grover set about to qualify.

Winter came early to the potato fields of Maine. It was always a race to get the tubers out of the ground and into storage houses before they were covered with heavy snow or frozen in the earth. When the harvest was finished, the young adventurer had time on his hands, full days with nothing to do. Fortunately, he had a place to live. The grower for whom he worked liked the way the young man conducted himself and offered him the use of a spare room in exchange for doing minor chores on the farm through the long winter months. The grower and his wife spent January and February of each year in the Florida sun, and they shrewdly concluded that young Robertson—reliable, honest, intelligent, and hard-working—was their best possible prospect for minding the farm in the winter. Aside from his weekly trip across the border to attend church and spend Sunday with his girlfriend and her family, he turned the other six days of the week into preparing for the absence of his hosts. By Christmas Grover was a paid caretaker, fully prepared to market the crop, now safely in storage, to do all the chores, and to solve the problems of his first Maine winter with confidence.

With his first paycheck Grover had opened an account at the local bank, and with each passing week the balance continued to grow. His frugality was soon noticed by the cashier; the larger share of the deposits was going into a savings account. Robertson had already learned that money, even a little of it, can earn more money if properly handled.

As the long winter dragged on, Grover reflected on his first season. Some things had become obvious to him: Only the growers really made money; laborers could earn only what one strong back could bear; some growers seemed ever to be gambling, borrowing heavily to raise a maximum acreage and suffering near disaster in a poor season, and bankers and truckers were those in a no-lose situation. Truckers were paid for hauling the crop, and bankers could always take the farm if the borrower couldn't pay back the loan. Then there were growers who seemed to be the most sensible. They ventured just enough with each crop to make a reasonable return in a mediocre year or a handsome profit if a shortage shot prices up, yet not enough to wipe them out should the season prove to be a complete disaster.

Grover laid his plans on five acres of rented land, a small bank loan, leveraged by his small savings account and made possible by his already recognized reputation for integrity. Thus, in only his second season, young Robertson became a potato grower instead of a hired hand. Prices held steady through the fall, and the crop was sold early—no point in chancing a late-season loss just to play the long shot of a shortage that would put prices through the roof. So he paid off his loan, cleared all debts—mainly rentals on the land and equipment, plus storage and loading fees—and signed another lease for the following year on 25 acres. He stuck his bank statements in his pocket and headed across the border to ask his sweetheart's father for his daughter's hand in marriage.

And here he was, some 25 years later, heading an enterprise of nearly 100 million dollars, a business which he had put together part by part a little at a time with no business administration degree and no MBA. In fact, his only formal association with higher education was as trustee of New England University where he had proved to be among its most constructive members.

It took another decade for Robertson, who would be 60 in a couple of years, to grow his company to a billion-dollar enterprise. By that time he was tutoring two young vice presidents to succeed him as CEO. One VP, the more promising one, was 10 years out of Harvard business school and had done his formal study in industrial engineering at Massachusetts Institute of Technology. Comstock enjoyed reminding Robertson that his native Scotland might have been a better recruiting ground for the next generation of managers than America's premier educational institutions, but his friend disagreed.

"I was just lucky," Grover would always say. "I came to this country following Christine," and he would nod to the partner he had married and brought back across the Canadian border to share his potato-growing years with him. "Yes, I do go back to Scotland regularly. We both have many family members there, and my directors like for me to go back so the Scot thriftiness won't fade too much. They want me re-treaded in the ways of saving money."

Grover and Christine both loved their native Scotland. As soon as their finances and business would permit, a trip back became an annual event. All three of their children were introduced early to the familiar haunts of the old country—the ballads, the poetry, and the crisp air.

As Robertson and Comstock and their wives came to know each other, a lifelong friendship emerged. Mutual respect, common interests—tennis turned out to be the shared recreation—and wide-ranging conversation served to bring four quite different people together. But the backbone of the relationship was the integrity the four individuals shared. Relaxed social get-togethers with good humor and inquisitive conversation were all pleasant, but it was the knowledge that the four people could trust each other, believe each other—no role playing, no hypocrisy—that bound them together in friendship.

How fortunate thought Comstock that his first experience as corporate director should be so rewarding—not in a financial way since board fees came in the form of a crisp twenty-dollar bill in a bank envelope clipped to the agenda sheet just inside each director's monthly meeting folder—but rewarding in so many other ways.

The only academic among the nine men—women had not yet entered the boardrooms of corporate America—Comstock saw a well-managed company and an honest and able CEO working effectively with directors from various walks of life. From every meeting and from many casual conversations with other directors and senior officers, Comstock seemed to be forever learning something that would be beneficial back on campus. Labor relations, employee benefits, building contracts, legal opinions, financial planning—everything discussed seemed relevant to the university. Was academe so far removed from business that neither knew about the other? It did indeed appear to be, and yet the two enterprises followed very similar routes.

Not all directorships would prove to be so pleasant down through the years. In his contacts with directors of other companies, Comstock had already begun to glimpse the ugly parts and to realize some shortcomings. But his initiation with Robertson wore so well that he left the board with great reluctance and only because the geography made it impossible for him to continue to serve after moving to Midtown U.

Another directorship did give New England U's popular president a different view of corporate America. Comstock was becoming known as an academic with knowledge of matters beyond the campus, possessing something of a fresh view of the private corporation. He was invited and agreed to accept a seat on the board of a local bank.

Still feeling somewhat inadequate but nonetheless curious, Comstock listened, read, and questioned with a casualness that betrayed his insights. He soon learned much about the world of banking. Every town had one or more banks, big cities many. Financial centers like London, Geneva, and Wall Street might just as well have been among the hidden mysteries of ancient Egypt so far as this academic was concerned. He simply had never expected to understand more about the world of finance than he did by watching carefully his own bank account, living within his means, saving for retirement or a more immediate crisis, and handling the budget of New England U.

Comstock believed that those were the simple truths of financial management. He came by them naturally; his father and mother saw to it that he learned them well. It wasn't until much later, after he became acquainted with the operation of a small New England bank through service as a director, that he realized what had come from his parents was all that one needed to know about money. How many people he would see through the years—CEOs, directors, professors—who had failed to learn those basic guidelines.

But the new director found in the CEO of the bank a manager much different from Robertson. John Granville was short of stature, short on words—never venturing a single sentence beyond the minimum required for any explanation—and low in camaraderie. Granville was the personification of the adage, often attributed to people in Maine: "If you can't improve upon silence, don't break it." It followed naturally that meetings of boards and committees and conversations with the CEO were all brief. In fact, a blueprint for the business of banking was drawn for him by another director, not Granville.

"The banker has the simplest business in the world," the director explained, speaking at the sandwich lunch which followed each board meeting. Granville just grinned, a kind of cat-and-the-canary grin, as Paul Chaplick continued.

"You persuade depositors to put money in your bank," he said. "Then you pay them as little as possible for the use of that money. You find other people who will pay you more, hopefully much more, than you must pay depositors for that same money. And so a banker just sits back and collects that interest." It was a good-natured ribbing for his quiet banker friend. Chaplick, who was himself the CEO of a sizable paper company, and a very likable and amiable fellow, played the role of the entrapped borrower, living always at the mercy of the banker. Doing business through the years, these two men needed only each other's word, no stacks of signed contracts, to conclude an agreement.

Some years later, as banks and bankers got into deep trouble and Comstock became director of yet another and much larger bank, he recalled with nostalgia the quiet honesty and pleasant dignity of John Granville. Symbolic of the changes in banking from Granville's era was the report Granville made at each meeting on loan losses. The number was always so low as to be inconsequential. This banker just didn't lose money on loans; he didn't chase high risks in order to get a higher return. Maybe, as Comstock recalled those calm, worry-free days in banking, Granville just wasn't so greedy.

Another not-so-greedy CEO whom Comstock would come to know and to admire was John A. Baker, the man who built Regional Banking and Trust Company into a solid mid-size institution, starting with the proverbial single door, hole-in-the-wall, storefront bank. Maneuvering his small company through the financial minefields of the nation's capital offered Baker, a small-town lad from Ohio, the chance of a lifetime. Rough-hewn, he made no serious attempt to polish his image or drawing-room manners; instead, he spoke a well-understood language with the likes of Harry Truman, Dwight Eisenhower, and Lyndon Johnson—three presidents who became regular customers of RBTC, as Baker's company came to be known.

Among the political hangers-on, as well as those in high office who didn't always pay their bills, Baker could smell a crook or deadbeat a block away. He was uncanny in picking those who always paid their loans on time, usually home mortgages, and those who left town with a string of never-to-be-paid debts. Short on words, but loud with the few he used, Baker made his point sharply and, if necessary, belligerently. Looking back at John Granville in New England and putting Baker and Granville side by side, Comstock saw two effective and very successful bankers with uncanny insights into human behavior but as different in both business and social behavior as day and night.

Short, blunt, and intimidating, Baker quickly separated the crooks from those who might enjoy a high-stakes game of poker, steal an election, or fudge the national budget, but would pay their personal bills. Granville was equally shrewd in sizing up the candidate for a loan, but if the loan was rejected, the applicant left without realizing just how or when he had taken the anesthesia.

Devoid of any sense of humor, John Baker didn't appreciate small talk. He was quick to make decisions and had little patience for reviewing a matter. Given a task, any subordinate would do well to leave and complete the job before coming back to see the boss. Whereas Granville was patient and careful to explain any innuendoes or possible hidden factors when discussing a problem with an associate, Baker was just the opposite. "Go now and do the job, and don't bother me until it's finished," was the unmistakable message from John Baker to an associate. However, if one of his subordinates performed well, Baker could be a bulldog in coming to his aid when a competitor or a customer appeared to be taking advantage of one of John's boys. "Ruthless in business," was a common description of Baker, and invariably the speaker would add, "but honest as the day is long."

Leaving the bank at the end of each long day, John Baker became a recluse. Rarely was he seen on the social circuit of Washington. If a key customer were hosting a cocktail reception—the capital's typical form of political stagecraft—and Baker simply could not ignore the affair, he would come early and leave quickly. Finding sanctuary with a special ladyfriend,

John closed the door on the bargaining and bustle of business with strong drink, good food, and quiet companionship.

Medics labeled Baker a prime candidate for a heart attack. They were right. Just at the time he was to retire from the pressures, many brought on by his own way of life, he died of a massive stroke while vacationing in a warmer climate. To his directors he left only trouble—no successor in view, no subordinate with broad knowledge of the business, and a host of deals that he carried to his grave in his vest pocket.

What a difference from the other banker, the other John. Granville retired on schedule and "kicked himself upstairs," as he said when he outlined the reorganization of NEB&T to his directors. He would continue to serve as chairman, putting his own carefully groomed and personally picked CEO in place. Granville quietly left the board after two more years, yielding that office, too, with grace and pleasure. The fact that he also enjoyed a long period of good health and satisfying living after his career in banking seemed to convey a strong message about his life-style, physical makeup, mental outlook, and calm demeanor.

Comstock saw a number of other CEOs before his own retirement many years later. He had witnessed wide variations in top managers and their personal behavior: the cool, shrewd, poker-player type; the quiet, dignified, always gracious, always forthright and honest leader; the boisterous, flamboyant, loud, and showy individual; the intellectually analytical person who made decisions only after the exhaustive research that textbooks on planning seemed invariably to teach.

Having spent ten years as a professor teaching administration in educational organizations, he had become both a student of management and a practitioner with some thirty-five years experience at all levels of executive responsibility. He continued to be a serious observer of the subject and a constant questioner of his own actions. Familiar with the efforts of his friend, John Gardiner, to examine all dimensions of leadership, Comstock remained a sympathetic critic of management in the many areas of life where it came into use as a function of human activity.

Gardiner, a highly respected public servant and the founder of Common Cause, joined Comstock at lunch one day to discuss leadership. John was then writing a book on the subject. Midtown's president took the opportunity to use one of his own favorite examples to illustrate a theory then in vogue regarding the preparation of managers. He said no one should be asked to manage a corner grocery store—even the mom and pop variety—unless he knows something, preferable a lot, about groceries. Within some of the country's most highly regarded business schools, a theory of management was being taught which held that business administration had a scientific basis sufficiently common to all public and private enterprises and that the professional manager could move successfully from one field to another. The CEO of an insurance company should be equally at home as the head of a chemical company. So went the theory if the manager faithfully followed sound practices of management.

Both Comstock and Gardiner had been on hand when the famous general, Dwight Eisenhower, was appointed president of Columbia University. Having directed the allied forces in Europe in World War II in one of the most complex and comprehensive undertakings in history, the general, it was pointed out, could certainly direct and manage the affairs of a much smaller entity, a university. To these two observers, however, the assumptions regarding the new CEO of Columbia University didn't go nearly far enough. They, and many others at the time, wanted to know what "Ike" was really hired to do. And the answer quickly became clear. The general was hired to raise money in a multi-million-dollar fund drive—not to "run the university." A chief academic officer, the financial officer, deans, and others—all below the rank of president—actually ran the institution, and Eisenhower, exhibiting judgment that would serve him well when he became CEO of the country, let others manage both the academic and the financial affairs of Columbia without looking over their shoulders and second-guessing them.

Although Eisenhower didn't complete the fund-raising mission before leaving Columbia—he was drafted by the Republican Party to run for President—it was generally agreed that he gave the university a major boost in recognition and goodwill and paved the way for a period of solid growth and expansion.

To Comstock, the visit with Gardiner and the anecdotal discussion of the Eisenhower period at Columbia highlighted one of the basic tenets of management. What is the CEO expected to do? What does the enterprise need? What are the priorities? Is it the CEO's job to develop new products, find new markets, raise funds, manage debt, recruit and train a new generation of employees, keep a growing business on an even keel? Directors look across the table at the CEO and wonder: Is he spending his energies and talents on the most pressing matters? And underneath the present priorities, what is the fundamental purpose of the organization? Is it to educate people and, if so, toward what objective? In the business world is making money for shareholders, employees, and other owners the chief reason for being? Is the enterprise one of service or protection to the community, state or nation, hospital, police department, school, museum, bank, food store, or defense industry?

Whatever the enterprise and whatever its priorities may be at the moment, does the CEO understand both the immediate needs and the long-range objectives? Do the directors share his views of the priorities? Is the leader articulating the priorities to all parties? How many times Comstock would hear from fellow directors: "Our leader doesn't know where he's going." In his own experience the academic, perhaps a bit more sensitive than most corporate directors to the importance of the written message, questioned the quality and quantity of the printed report and also questioned the adequacy and accuracy of the oral reports given by the CEO and his staff. A singular call stood out in his memory above all others. Another director of a bank, a most successful corporate lawyer, telephoned Comstock at home late in the evening preceding a board meeting.

"Say, Bill, did you get that armload of paper from the bank today?" As soon as Comstock acknowledged that he had, his friend opened up. "Did you read it? Did you understand it?" Not waiting for a reply, the upset lawyer continued. "It was the biggest pile of junk I've ever seen." Falling back on a familiar cliché, Comstock could only reply: "Read it–hell, I couldn't even lift it."

Written materials, carefully prepared agenda, brief and germane reports–all had a place in the director's view of the CEO. Some executives made good use of those aids, others such as John Baker, kept away from them. The only written materials that directors of RB&TC ever saw were the documents required by law or regulation to be shown to board members and signed by them. Even in those cases, such materials never left the room. All were numbered and carefully accounted for by the ever watchful corporate secretary.

Somewhere between the dumping of junk and providing nothing, there must be a reasonable middle ground, thought Comstock. In a sense this conscientious director served during the period in which director involvement and director liability for performance changed from practically zero to that of considerable personal risk. In his earlier board experience, which he could recall, there was no mention of company-paid insurance to protect officers and directors. Audit committees were made up solely of inside directors, and representatives of regulatory agencies appeared only before company officers. In those earlier years a directorship was another plum, distributed and accepted through the good-old-boy network, used to court favors from influential people for a business in question, or to reward friends and business associates. Financial compensation was low, directors weren't burdened with duties, and, of course, women had not yet gained entrance to the club.

During almost a half-century, Comstock would see junk bonds, unfriendly takeovers, bank failures, scandals not limited to the thrift industry, stock manipulation, Japan bashing, entry of private business into eastern Europe, and the demise of the Soviet Union. What a laboratory in which CEOs could work their skills, charms, or voodoo! No wonder that many a betrothal of director and chief executive became a rocky romance.

Comstock saw failure from a most unexpected source after he joined the board of a thriving savings and loan. The CEO was a truly distinguished gentleman and business leader recognized to be one of Washington's most astute financial managers. Still only in his mid-fifties, Thornton J. Stevens had been in his post for 15 years, and by all accounts had made the right moves in guiding his thrift institution to the number one position in the region.

It didn't take long for the honeymoon to end. Two years later, cracks began to appear in the thrift industry. In another year they had reached Royal Credit Savings and Loan, and both Comstock, the newest director, and the seasoned CEO faced a totally new and unexpected experience.

None was prepared for what was unfolding. For months senior officers and directors, young trainees, and seasoned employees appeared to be simply inept, bungling, and rudderless. It was a whole company flailing away in the darkness.

Stevens changed within weeks from a confident leader to a frightened schoolboy. Here was a CEO who had never known failure. Graduating from Ivy Wall University in the top dozen of his class, he went directly to Wall Street. After five years there, and after catching the attention of the chief financial officer of Royal Credit, young Thornton was lured to Washington. Moving through the right chairs, getting all necessary insights of the industry, Stevens, at 40 years of age, was the unanimous choice to lead RCS&L, as it was known to the greater Washington community. Timing seemed to be perfectly programmed for Stevens and for his family, too. As World War II burst on the country, Thornton, a few years beyond draft age, was already married with three young children. Fortunately, there was for Stevens not the slightest hint of shirking his duty. His two younger brothers went to war early, but he just happened to be in the age group that missed. He gave strong support to the war effort through all kinds of community service, and he raised RCS&L to a much higher place in the business world during the period of hostilities than it had ever enjoyed before.

To one who had never experienced serious difficulty, let alone failure, Stevens was overwhelmed by the crises in the thrift industry and the special problems of RCS&L.

Comstock watched—he and most other directors were essentially helpless—as Stevens lost control and Royal Credit began to break apart. First the depositors began to run away as they learned of the mounting losses from loans that had been made on commercial real estate. Developers filed for bankruptcy because they couldn't meet the interest payments of Royal Credit. Northern Virginia and suburban Maryland seemed covered with large, new office buildings sitting vacant. Even the heart of downtown Washington appeared filled with "For Rent" signs. Over-building, which swept New England and the Southwest first, had arrived in full fury in the "recession-proof" national capital. The toll on Stevens did not stop with his financial losses. Stress on family and friends proved unmanageable.

Striking out, Thornton, as he was popularly greeted by longtime employees, high public officials, and by directors and depositors, fired three of his most senior executives, those who had put many of the now defaulted loans on the books, and unashamedly put the full blame for Royal Credit's problems on their shoulders. Directors well remembered the many times over the years, in fact even in recent months, when Thornton was himself saying to the loans officers, "Get out there and make sure we get our share of the loan market. Let's not be left out when the big deals are being made."

It was a nationwide mania. Money! Money! Money! Everything the developers touched turned to profit, and the lenders were fighting over the privilege of shoveling tons of credit into their hands. One speculator, although that term wasn't applied yet, snowballed two million of borrowed money into thirty million of unencumbered cash by buying, trading, and promoting a small acreage near Dulles Airport. When the bubble burst, the final owner had an abandoned cornfield without any improvements and an overwhelming debt that left the bank holding the bag.

All members of the Stevens family became victims within a couple of years. Thornton moved out of the family mansion. He took up residence with a few personal belongings and lots of bottles in a one-bedroom apartment where mainly out-of-town lobbyists were housed on their frequent visits to town. Three teenage children, one in college and two yet in high school, were left stranded between separated parents and rapidly fading respectability. Mrs. Stevens dropped from sight, retreating from the turmoil to live with an unmarried sister a hundred miles away.

As the storm raged over Royal Credit, one of MU's trustees, a man with unusual sensitivity for trouble, suggested to Comstock that to continue as a director could possibly bring embarrassment to the university. To protect the institution from such an eventuality, perhaps he should leave the board. Recalling other such situations—presidents of universities had been clobbered frequently while serving on corporate boards during the chaotic days of the late sixties—Comstock reluctantly took his friend's advice and gracefully resigned. Looking back after Royal Credit was taken over by the government and later sold to a stronger financial institution, he was to learn that Stevens had understood his position and felt no ill will toward him. In fact, when Thornton began to put his life back together some years later, the two men were quite at ease with each other.

For Comstock, it was another first. He had seen much of CEO Stevens, much more of the company, and much, much more of the tragedy of failure for family and associates than he had wanted. It's amazing, he observed, the varied views of the CEO that a director gets. And, as he was to experience still further, there seemed to be no end to the surprises that found their way to the boardroom table.

Comstock had learned long before he became a university president how members of governing boards of educational institutions looked at—and sometimes through—their CEOs. In his first presidency what was—or should have been—an idyllic setting at New England U became an environment of disparate beliefs. Trustees held widely differing views not only of the president but also of the job itself. Some felt strongly, especially those from the business world, that a college president ought to be the boss, the foreman, the platoon leader, the one to give orders to all employees, making no distinction between faculty members and other workers. Even those with tenure—that unbelievable practice in higher education—were no different from janitors, clerical workers, or admissions counselors. All should follow the president's orders, and he would give the commands to all, that is, except to the trustees.

Some of the very people who thought faculty members should jump to the orders of the president were also the ones who demanded that the president jump through hoops set in place by the board. One trustee, a former governor, felt so strongly about hierarchical organization that he had personally changed many items in the budget of the university while serving as chairman of an important legislative committee when a former president was in office. To Comstock the situation was unbelievable. Moving on to serve a short time as governor, this same man, after leaving public office for the corporate world, was appointed to the board of New England U. Governor Robert Haskew thus became Trustee Haskew through a political payoff by his successor.

Before attending even one meeting of the board, the new trustee called NEU's president and invited himself "to help" him with the budget—the kind of help no university president would welcome! It was learned that in the past Haskew had made it a practice to come to the president's office on a Saturday morning to review and to put his imprint on the budget. The fact that various university staff members, working with the president over a period of many months, had carefully put the numbers together was of no concern to this self-appointed fiscal expert.

Sitting down at the boardroom table, Haskew would turn one page at a time of the voluminous document, proceeding to change numbers in individual salaries, supplies to be purchased, contingency funds, books for the libraries, athletics, and research. Nothing escaped his sharp pencil.

And all changes made were markdowns, decreasing every item except men's athletics. That budget got a sizable increase. The first such budget butchering, as the action came to be known, had been taken eight years before Comstock's arrival. Haskew's Saturday visit with the president had occurred each succeeding year. And here was an invitation for the ninth!

Since the former governor, now trustee, "understood the finances of the state so well," he just knew he could be helpful! The new president of NEU had already decided not to accept his help.

Some years later, as Comstock responded to the inevitable inquiry of a colleague about how he handled the situation, his reply was matter of fact.

"Within my first week on campus," said Comstock, "the budget officer and the treasurer alerted me to the problem. No one had told me of the situation before my appointment, and there was no hint of such a problem from the chairman of the board, the person primarily responsible for recruiting me. Anyway," continued Comstock, "I felt that everyone in the university knew of the practice, including all the trustees, so I decided to stop it."

"When Haskew called, I had been in office for just 90 days. I told him that I believed the budget was the responsibility of the entire board and that the finance committee of that body should be the first to see it. I added that the full board should receive the document from the committee with such recommendations as the members might see fit to make."

"Then you won't let me see it?" Haskew asked quickly.

"I will send you a copy the same day it is sent to the rest of the board, because," Comstock explained, "I don't think the budget of New England U should be the work of one trustee. However," he added, "I'll be glad to talk about the university's proposals and, of course, see you any time, Governor." Having served in the state's highest position, Haskew was not willing to give up the title of governor when he left office. As a matter of fact, he kept it the rest of his life!

But Haskew was determined. He came to Comstock's office on the following Saturday morning. "Perhaps," he told this president, "I can be of some service." Bill, Haskew continued, "the governor has a very tight budget this year. Some departments of state government are seeing unexpected jumps in costs and simply can't continue present services without new money. Raising taxes in this, an election year, would be foolhardy, so

I think we must go easy on our request for funds this time. The whole picture will be much improved two years from now. Then we can really push the university."

Not quick to respond but allowing a whole panorama of plans and commitments to run through his mind, the president decided to let Haskew go on. The trustee filled the brief silence with praise and commendation. "Bill, you are off to a terrific start. All the publicity surrounding your arrival has been most positive. A couple of years (a biennial budget was being submitted) won't make that much difference in the life of the university, and as I said, in two years we'll take the high road."

It all seemed so logical and reasonable to the politically motivated ex-governor. The playing field had changed! This trustee was now the liaison with the present governor, and he wanted to continue in that role rather than see the university president have it. Undoubtedly, budgets for both the state and the university had already been discussed since it was well known that this ex-governor, ex-state legislator, now trustee was quick with numbers. The university was again being treated as education programs at all levels had been through the years: Cut out proposed new faculty positions; put off the renovation of the chemistry laboratories—they have served for 40 years; surely another two years will not hurt—squeeze a few more freshmen into each section of the first-year course; and cut back expenditures for new technology, books for the library, and equipment for the music department. In other words, stand still for another two years.

What a disappointment it would be for the ten-member committee of faculty and students who had worked for two years to formulate a new honors program for arts and sciences to be told that it couldn't be implemented because there would be no funds available. To be sure, the program called for relatively few dollars, but Comstock quickly concluded, and correctly, from the message he had just received that with no sympathy to add new expenditures, maintaining present activities would be a struggle. Waiting two years to initiate the honors program meant that two years of work and study by a dedicated group was going down the drain. But, he thought, what could politicians know about academic arrangements such as an honors program?

This trustee knew nothing about academic freedom, a fact he had publicly acknowledged when the matter surfaced only two years earlier.

His comment had been brought to Comstock's attention: "I don't know what the fuss is all about," Haskew replied when a reporter inquired about a furor raised on one of the campuses after a professor of philosophy questioned the orthodoxy of a large religious sect. Haskew saw tenure as a way of protecting incompetents among the faculty.

Comstock reaffirmed his unspoken conclusion. It is the role of the university president to represent the institution in the highest councils of government and to make the backroom trades as well when they are required. Trustees can help. In fact, they must if they are to live up to their responsibilities, but neither one nor all can replace the president in that role.

Was it damaging to the institution for a trustee not to explain, interpret, or even demand of the governor, key legislative leaders, and perhaps business and industrial leaders the needs of the university? Comstock believed that few outside a lifetime of educational experience could speak to the many facets of learning and teaching with sufficient understanding. It was not simply bruised ego which disturbed him; it was the knowledge that this trustee—a former governor, experienced legislator, and successful corporate executive—simply did not know the nuances of university life well enough to be the liaison with state government.

Every appropriation to NEU, he knew, would be a compromise between what might be purchased with the same dollars in some other state service. A spokesperson not living with the institution on a day-to-day basis and not having the full history of educational change at his fingertips simply couldn't keep priorities in the best order. Comstock was already aware that enlarging the stadium to accommodate more alumni and boosters—taxpayers—for home games was an interest of the governor and some of the leading legislators. But a badly needed new reading room for the library was a known urgency among both students and faculty. Who would make the choice?

"Governor," Comstock began his response as he faced the most threatening crisis of his new presidency, "I feel it is necessary to present New England U's budget to the finance committee, get its assessment of timeliness, and then carry it to the full board. Who knows? They may shoot it down! In that case we won't have much to do for the next two years."

"So be it, Mr. President," and without another word Haskew turned and left the office.

The new president was fully aware of the confrontation he had just created. Knowing that Haskew would try next to bully the chairman of the board, a man who at times had difficulty in making even the most innocuous decision, Comstock promptly phoned the chairman and told him what had happened. The new president explained that he felt that Trustee Haskew had been usurping the role of the full board and that he wanted no part of perpetuating the practice. For himself, Comstock said, it was a showdown between him and a politically powerful trustee, a battle that had to be fought, so the sooner the better.

Comstock won, but throughout his successful eight years as president of New England University, "Governor" Haskew remained the cat ready to pounce. Outwardly, the two men worked together in amicable and constructive ways, but the president knew that he was working with a trustee who would cut his throat at the first opportunity. He also knew that Haskew wouldn't simply snip around the edges; he was too smart to show his hand on small matters. He would watch and wait for that moment when the situation would be ripe for the kill, when the issue would be of sufficient importance that Comstock could be fired.

More than one CEO—both in academe and in corporate America—serves or has served under similar conditions. In most cases the boardroom is marked by moves and counter moves, ideas tossed out to test the waters, baited hooks dangled in front of possible suckers, and all sorts of poker games played among two or more individuals or factions. Sometimes those games are played in the open, not often but occasionally.

As for Comstock, he was able to move on, as he said, when the handwriting reached the wall. Good timing served him well. As a new governor paid still another political debt by appointing yet another ex-governor to the board of New England University, Comstock was being pursued by Midtown University. He was able to tell all the audiences of New England University how much he and his family had enjoyed their eight years, how much he hated to leave, how privileged had been their associations, and the dozens of other compliments normally related to a friendly departure, all the time fully aware that the newly appointed trustee would join Haskew in every important decision about the university. Comstock could smile at the eight-year period in which he had been able to keep Haskew in check, but he knew that the partnership of two ex-governors on the board of the flagship institution would guarantee that political considerations, not education, would be the dominant factors in the years ahead.

Relief from problems for many high level executives in our society is usually short-lived. It was to prove true in the career of this university president. As he would soon realize, departure from New England University was perfectly timed; arrival at Midtown University was a different story.

In 1964 Berkeley had erupted with what was to be recognized as the opening salvo of a long war on the campus that would last for years and would reach around the world. Universities in Latin America, having served historically as sanctuaries of protest, took on new life as breeding grounds for revolution. Racked by dissension and confrontation, many were forced to close for weeks and months during the academic year. Radical leaders on European campuses picked up the cause and added their own tactics as Japanese, Egyptian, and Australian institutions experienced similar uprisings. In the United States, the SDS (Students for a Democratic Society) emerged as the brain trust of radical reform dedicated to the destruction of all law and order, confrontation of authority, and the delivery of our society to complete anarchy.

Midtown University was located only a few blocks from the White House with the State Department in close proximity and headquarters of the Selective Service a few doors away. Comstock saw his new location become the staging area for numerous, massive confrontations. Radicalized students from Berkeley, Wisconsin, Yale, Columbia, and dozens of other campuses joined forces with revolutionaries from all walks of life to test the backbone of American democracy. Comstock would see the new campus over which he was presiding invaded several times during the following five-year period by fifty- to one-hundred thousand visitors from the rest of the country, often occupying buildings, destroying property, and interrupting educational activities.

Participating in well-orchestrated protests against the Vietnam War, the draft, the Pentagon, ROTC, and many other targets, protesters seeking to shut down the government attracted a half-million participants on a number of occasions. Trustees of Midtown University would have many opportunities to observe their president during this period of almost constant crisis.

Whenever Comstock later recounted “the five years of campus hell,” the behavior of two trustees always stood out. The chairman of the board, outwardly slow and bumbling, proved under stress to be shrewd, calculating, and calm. More than once he told the worried and discouraged president, "This too will pass." Comstock wasn't so sure. Confessing his qualms to friends, he was known to have said more than once, "Why don't I resign? I fought and survived World War II and a number of my friends, among the country's finest men, didn't come back. Why am I giving my life trying to educate these little monsters?" The thing that always reversed that kind of thinking, as Bill reminisced later, was the realization that the destruction of the university, Midtown and all the others in the world, was the first objective of the revolution. That institution was the linchpin of civilization, and whenever doubts began to flood over him, he would resolutely conclude, "There is no way I will let the little bastards win."

A true watershed came when the grand old chairman played a masterful poker game with the most radical leaders of the campus.

Having confronted the president with every possible demand and having been outmaneuvered by him or his staff at every turn, the protesters decided to carry their cause directly to the chairman of the board. They would go over the president's head, bypass the CEO, and put the pressure on the trustees.

They did not quite know how best to present their demands, and they did not clearly understand the role of the board. But they knew that in some way that body held the final authority over the university. The six representatives chosen by the protesters to meet with the chairman presented themselves for the appointment acceptably dressed, all wearing shoes, and all having showered. They had also concluded that to be polite to the old codger, as they called him, might be the best way to influence him.

As pieced together later by Comstock's informants, the chairman had not gone unprepared. Listening attentively for the first hour of the session to all their comments and carefully making notes, he interrupted frequently to get further clarification of a complaint or to express sympathy for misunderstandings among various campus constituents. The old chairman set them up for his reply, which filled the second hour of the meeting.

Rambling and incoherent, EK led his visitors through issues, traditions, ideals, behavior, and values with unbelievable crooks and turns in apparent response to their complaints. It was such a display of confused thinking and jumbled rhetoric that, when he finished and asked for any further comments which anyone might wish to make, there was only silence.

Six young college students, four men and two women, who were all experienced with bull horns and protest messages, were rendered speechless. They only looked at each other in confusion as they slowly got up to leave. Not moving from behind his big desk, EK said, just barely loud enough for them all to hear, "I don't see any problems here that can't be amicably resolved." With that six fiery revolutionists were rendered impotent. It was the most beautiful display of double talk since the first politicians honed their skills. For Comstock, who would continue to work with the shrewd old chairman for several more years, the performance was so convincing that never again did he doubt his friend's support—or his talents. Many times thereafter the president was to smile inwardly as issues were faced, and muse, "Do I want to clarify the matter, or do I want to obfuscate it." What a distinction and, in Washington, how useful!

One of Midtown University's most powerful, not always constructive, but nonetheless highly respected trustees drew his sights on the president, and there was no misunderstanding about its meaning. Everett Thompson said the president was wrong.

It happened as a result of an action the president took in the heat of the long period of campus turmoil. Protesters had made a major issue of the long-held practice of the armed forces' sending military recruiters to campus to talk with college men and women about the various branches, specialties, and opportunities the services offered. Some campuses simply banned recruiters, and anti-Vietnam forces soon realized they had a made-to-order divisive issue—a good reason to push it all the harder.

With the help of a half-dozen professors, a radical student group succeeded in persuading the faculty senate to pass a resolution calling for the suspension of military recruitment on the Midtown campus.

Faced with the explosive issue and the threat of immediate violence on campus, Comstock chose to suspend recruiter visits until the situation cooled off. It was the drama of the day. The media made the most of the change in policy at Midtown, blowing up the news in the most frightening, misleading way.

Everett Thompson, "EV," as the whole city knew him, would have none of it. He was a fifth generation Washingtonian, coming from a family about as well known in the Mid-Atlantic region as the Potomac River and the Chesapeake Bay. Numerous brothers, sisters, cousins, and other relatives were scattered over the city and its suburbs, and EV was the spokesman for the entire clan. What he had to say carried weight with the Congress, business leaders, and the press. Cliff dweller, blue blood, aristocrat—each was a common term heard whenever conversation included a reference to one of the Thompsons.

Everett had allowed himself to become a trustee of Midtown as a kind of local, civic duty. A Princeton graduate in fine arts, he prepared further for the management of his inheritance with an MBA from Wharton, all preliminary to heading the family publishing empire. Skillful, wealthy, patriotic, and conservative, he considered it unthinkable that military recruiters would ever be impeded in any way from carrying out their mission.

In the privacy of the president's office of Midtown University, Thompson came to register his strong disagreement. The debate, argument, heated discussion—few CEOs have been able to avoid such showdowns—lasted only one hour. But it was a collision never to be forgotten by either man.

Demanding that Comstock either change the previous day's decision or resign, Thompson entered the fray with the conviction of a fanatic. Mentally questioning the other man's good sense, patriotism, and courage, Midtown's president fell back on one of his long-practiced but seldom uttered techniques. Use whatever force is necessary—if one can muster it—to meet the occasion. In this case don't give an inch!

Feeling it necessary to hit his accuser squarely in the face—the mule and the two-by-four anecdote came to mind—Comstock fired back.

A full hour, but only an hour, and it was over. Without question, it was the most confrontational encounter Comstock ever had with a member of a governing board. What next? It was only mid-morning, but undoubtedly a long day lay ahead.

Following still another of his tenets in conducting the affairs of the university, Midtown's president called the board chairman. Always give board members the news, especially bad news, before it reaches them through the media. It was a practice he always tried to follow. In this case it was the chairman who must be told.

"Well, Bill," the old chairman said, after Comstock reported his visit from Thompson, "you go ahead and work the problem out, and I'll try to keep Ev off your back."

Few decisions caused Comstock more grief than banning recruiters—"suspension" was the word used in the faculty's resolution—but banning was the glaring reality in newspaper stories. Deep down, Midtown's president felt exactly as Ev Thompson. Both were hard-liners who believed the opportunity to attend college was a privilege, that instead of protesting, students should be studying, and if they had other interests, in this case political, they should leave the campus—leave the campus to those who would benefit from its educational programs.

What did these young anarchists know about freedom? It was too bad, Comstock thought, that they were too young to remember World War II. Only Vietnam, the here and now. It was America's military might, backed up by the resolve of an entire nation, that saved freedom for the whole world. It was that same freedom, paid for with so much death and suffering, that was now making possible the flaunting of authority. What irony, thought Comstock.

More than anything else, the calendar rescued Midtown U and its president from the divisiveness of the faculty resolution. The spring semester was coming to an end. Exams took the place of demonstrations, and graduation exercises separated students from classrooms and dormitories for a full summer.

It was time which Midtown's president used to full advantage.

One month before registration began for the fall semester, Comstock announced that military recruiters would be welcomed at Midtown U in the coming academic year. He took the action following a meeting with the five-member executive committee of the faculty senate. He made no attempt to assemble the full senate, an impossible task anyway at that time of year. And he didn't ask the executive committee for a vote on the matter. As he explained, he didn't want the committee to be put in the position of action contrary to the full body which earlier had passed a resolution banning recruitment. Comstock wanted to be able to say that he had conferred with the group but that he alone was responsible for changing the university's position.

Academic politics had long since become a game to Comstock, and he could play with the best. In fact, he loved the contest, winning some and losing some. He never tried to balance the scorecard; it was unlike the typical won-lost record in sports. He simply wanted to win the big ones; others could win the many little skirmishes in between the knock-out events.

Students and most faculty members were away from campus in August. When they returned for the new academic year, many of them hurled their full wrath at the president, accusing him of arbitrary abuse of power and acting under the cover of darkness. Like a March windstorm, however, the swish of protests quickly blew itself out. The summer had allowed the whole university community to reflect on the ban of recruiters. Dramatic, even sensational in June, it failed now to convey the message to the country that many under the Midtown umbrella wanted to see. Only one member of the faculty's executive committee had really opposed lifting the ban. The other four were pleased that Comstock had taken the shadow off the institution, and defended the action to their colleagues. By mid-October the ban was gone as an issue. The sole source of faculty opposition on the executive committee, a man who had from time to time attracted considerable support, found himself to be a lonely voice.

Later, glancing across the board table at Trustee Thompson, the chairman and the president turned and viewed each other with unquestioned respect and mutual support. Although it was a period of great stress for the institution, it was a time of testing for the president and the governing board. The CEO emerged from the several years of crises—there seemed to be one confrontation fast on the heels of another for half a decade—with the unequivocal support of the board and the respect of all other constituencies. There were always one or two dissatisfied voices within the board of 49 members, but the occasional trustee who aired opposition was seldom heard. None ever got in a position to challenge Comstock's leadership, and while he would serve the institution as CEO for many years, substantive opposition to him or to his policies would never materialize. When he finally retired as age inevitably caught up with him, he was the most senior of all university presidents in the country.

Furor subsided on the campus in the seventies, but it then became grounded on the rocks of profit-making corporations forced to deal with unfriendly takeovers, leveraged buyouts, and junk bonds. Greedy marketplace gamblers parlayed credit upon credit to build paper tigers. Comstock still believed that corporate America and academe were so strongly interdependent that they had to understand each other more clearly and work together more closely. He felt himself squarely in the middle, trying to retain his integrity with academicians.

Still following the role of ambassador to private enterprise, Bill Comstock joined the board of Multiple Products, Inc., a company with about one billion dollars in annual sales. MPI, as it was listed on the stock exchange, operated some 50 outlets, ranging in size from a few specialty shops to a half-dozen sizable department stores in the large cities and suburban areas of the East Coast. Edwin K. Jones, the CEO and the person who invited Midtown's president to become a director, was highly respected in the business community. He also was known as a community leader, giving generously of his time and money to charities and to volunteer work. As politicians were quick to point out, MPI could always be counted on to lead the business community in trying to alleviate the city's ills. Jones himself divided his time among three attractions—helping the communities in which his stores were located, managing the corporation, and playing as many of the golf courses in the region as possible

A large, husky, and handsome man, Ed Jones cut a convincing swath throughout the East Coast. In the capital city his advice, participation, and support were considered essential to the success of any worthwhile endeavor. Bill Comstock had been quick to accept when Ed issued the invitation to join the board of MPI. These men, having worked together in a number of community activities, were comfortable with each other.

Welcomed to the board by the other directors and by the senior officers of the company, Comstock quickly realized that his opinions, although voiced sparingly as properly characterizing a new director and by one who must yet become familiar with that particular business, were both sought and respected. The honeymoon would be brief.

Ed sounded the alarm at a hastily called directors meeting. A telephone call had come unexpectedly from a Wall Street trader who said he represented stockholders controlling 20 percent of the company's stock. He wished to meet with Jones to arrange proper representation on the MPI board for these owners, some new and some old as he described them. Jones saw in a flash that the kind of furor in the business world being reported by the media had finally reached MPI: clandestine acquisition of stock, one case of "greenmail" after another, gyrations in stock prices, and all the threats that accompanied the maneuvers. The 14 percent of stock still owned by descendants of the founders—MPI had been around for more than a century—and the loyalty of friendly bankers who carried small holdings in client portfolios simply fell short of the ownership necessary to control the company.

Jones, while scurrying for legal advice, received his first offer for settlement: "Buy our 20 percent interest at 40 dollars per share, and we will walk away." The speculators, it was learned, had acquired all of their holdings before the market carried the price of the stock above 20 dollars. So, Ed concluded, they were simply looking for the fast buck—another case of greenmail—and these corporate robbers were trying to use the technique to make millions for themselves.

It was a long, hot summer for Comstock. He found himself in the middle of a crisis which he never envisioned and for which he was totally unprepared. He was the only director on whom all parties could agree to serve as chairman of what was to become the Special Committee. These people, all outside directors, must decide the fate of MPI.

A rescuer was found—"white knight" was the term—who agreed to pay fair market value and take the company into private ownership. In resolving the problem, Comstock was determined to be fair to all parties, to be honest in every action he took. After all, these were the attributes his colleagues accorded him when they drafted him to guide them out of the newly created wilderness. All summer a blurred parade of lawyers, appraisers, and consultants passed before the Special Committee. The former professor of history, he later related to friends, learned more about the corporate world that summer than he ever wanted to know.

Comstock had wise and talented colleagues on the Special Committee. Selecting the two additional directors who would serve the long stretch with him, he focused on an old, battle-scarred, ex-public servant and shrewd lawyer to work alongside another attorney, a brilliant but sometimes impetuous young woman. Mutual trust proved not to be difficult to establish among these three in spite of the stress that was already widespread.

Four months later the company was sold. Stockholders got more than 60 dollars per share from the new owner, and only 3 stockholders with less than 5 percent of the total shares voted against the proposed disposition. At the special meeting when the end came, a spokesman of the three dissenters told the group that the company of his forefathers "should never to sold to anyone at any price."

Comstock and his fellow committee members enjoyed a private celebration at lunch a week later. They congratulated each other on having survived a seemingly endless summer in Washington, on not being sued—not yet at least—and on having kept each other out of jail!

Years later Comstock would look back on the experience with mixed feelings. One of America's billionaires had paid too much for MPI. Within a couple of years, competition in the industry squeezed profit margins to a point at which all major merchandisers were seriously hurt. Many longtime employees lost their jobs as reorganizing and restructuring of companies took a heavy toll. Staggering through the recession of the early nineties, the whole industry was to change its face, and so, too, observed the veteran academic, was higher education. The life cycle of a company or of an industry had much in common with that of a college or university. How vital and far-reaching, thought Comstock, are some of our actions and our inactions!

What could Ed Jones and the directors have done that would have produced better results? Comstock could only guess at some answers. He would never really know. For the CEO of MPI it was the end of the road; Ed could not meet the demands by the new owner. Having called the signals as the chief executive for more than 20 years, Jones could not adjust to the frequent beck and call of the new boss. It wasn't so much the personal relationship with Jay Beckwith, the billionaire and new owner, as it was with the crew of tough lieutenants he built into his inner circle of advisers. In being retained to manage MPI, Jones had assumed he would move into the select group and be a part of Jay Beckwith's brain trust. Instead, he found himself being confronted at every step with unexpected demands from Jay's "numbers man," as the financial officer was called. He fell victim to poorly understood directions from the chief counsel and to berating bursts of outrage by Beckwith's personal assistant.

Jones had initially assumed the assistant was a combination errand boy and valet. Not until too late did he learn that the errand boy was Beckwith's nephew being groomed to take over the empire. So impossible was the new working environment that Jones retired early, sacrificing the major part of what had been worked out for him as a generous retirement. He salvaged enough for country club living and abundant golf, but he gave up his dreams of his own yacht, a London flat, and a Swiss chalet. Motivated by money and the things money could buy, here was a CEO who was forced to retire before he was ready—but too late to take up another post—with only golf to fill his days and the cocktail circuit to fill his evenings, a life devoid of interest in art, music, or books. He was to learn quickly that seven days a week on the golf cart, followed by too much time for drinking and overeating, is not enough. Broken in spirit, and, in time, broken in body, this once proud, confident, and successful business leader spent his last months in a wheelchair.

How different, thought Comstock, was Jones from that never-to-be-forgotten colleague and fellow university president, Francis J. Bilmore. Now retired after a long and tumultuous career in academe that included four presidencies—he was fired from each one—Bilmore was still feisty, combative, and argumentative on every question of educational policy that arose. Now in his late seventies he spent his time, every day of the week, grinding out articles and letters, especially letters to editors, lambasting faculty members, trustees, and especially presidents.

From his first days as a professor in one of America's most prestigious universities, Fran Bilmore had been involved in controversy. Brilliant but contemptuous, Fran was never satisfied to let well enough alone. It seemed indigenous that he find fault—with people, with ideas, with action, and with inaction.

Thrown together for seven years as presidents of neighboring institutions, Comstock and Bilmore came to know each other well. Many were the times they differed, the arguments getting sharp, spiteful, and sometimes even mean. Through it all, Bilmore kept coming back for more, and Comstock, always maintaining the advantage because he never lost his temper, was known at times to bait his colleague, and grew to enjoy the encounters. Since there were so many long, dreary, and dull meetings in academe, Comstock came to anticipate with some pleasure any session where Bilmore would be present.

Years later, Comstock could recall vividly and still smile with the memory of one such meeting. With some 20 participants, among them 6 presidents of universities bound together in a contractual consortium, the president of New England U had said nothing for the first hour. Financing medical education was the topic being considered by the group. It was a pressing subject on all institutions, thus the legislative leaders and other politicians from six states were present. Bilmore was behaving as usual, dominating the discussion, talking more than all the other participants put together.

Comstock, sitting directly across the large round table from Bilmore finally broke his silence. Looking straight at his target, he began, "I hesitate to say what I am about to say because it will be the first time I have ever disagreed with my good friend Fran Bilmore, but..." and that's as far as he got.

"Damn you, Bill," Bilmore exploded, "you never agreed with me in your life!" Having risen halfway out of his chair, he seemed ready to reach across some 12 feet of shiny table and take Comstock by the collar. "Now, now, Fran," Bill teased, "don't take it personally." Quick to anger, Bilmore was a CEO, however, who carried no grudge. By lunchtime the two were sitting together pursuing the business of their institutions.

It was at lunch that Bilmore shared an apparent personal achievement with Comstock and another colleague seated beside him. His announcement came somewhat as a surprise.

"Guess what I got out of my board," Bilmore said to his two companions. Having astounded his colleagues on many previous occasions, his listeners could only grin and wonder, what now? "Well, I got a six-month leave with full pay," Fran boasted. "I'm leaving the country–three months in London and three months in Paris–and the acting president can have all the headaches while I'm gone."

It was a coup. Professors got sabbaticals, not presidents; but Bilmore had confronted his board with a demand, not a request. Why shouldn't he too have a turn at R&R. "And they knew that I was ready to take my letter of resignation out of my pocket–you know I never go to a board meeting without it–and throw it in their faces if they refused."

After six years, one university president had demanded and had received the most coveted of all academic perks, a half-year of R&R at full pay.

Knowing university politics and the ways of governing boards, Bilmore's two friends wondered about the validity of his opportunity. Comstock offered the light touch, "I wouldn't leave for six months under any condition," he volunteered. "I'd be scared to death of what my trustees would do if I weren't there to watch them."

Not too surprising, soon after Bilmore's return from his sojourn, the trustees informed him that his contract, which had another 12 months to run, would not be renewed. This was only his second forced separation; there would be two more before he reached full retirement from higher education, still 20 years away.

The way Bilmore viewed trustees was becoming clear: They were the enemy, and the president must constantly do battle with them—not a pretty sight for any campus. Comstock could recall only one other president who seemed to share Bilmore's outlook, and he was gone from academe after brief periods as president in two highly respected institutions. Ironically he spent the last 25 years of his career as a professor-consultant, collecting generous fees for advising presidents and governing boards on how to manage their institutions. Somehow he never accepted the proposition that he had been fired from both presidencies. To him each was an agreed upon separation—and friendly—brought about by burnout and exhaustion. The message which flashed the full length of the academic grapevine was unmistakable—Eldon K. White was both times being "let go."

Those who followed Eldon's career carefully—and he seemed masterful at getting flattering publicity for himself—concluded that in his later role as a consultant he was especially skillful in advising boards on how to separate unsatisfactory presidents from their posts with minimum embarrassment to the institution. Given the often rocky paths of such actions, White may have ended his career with a significant contribution.

As Comstock pondered the many different people who won the CEO's hat, none was quite so memorable as Watson W. Wisehart. Just the mention of his name brought forth a rush of flashing images for this academic as he recalled four tumultuous years.

Wisehart served as "Chairman, President, and CEO"—the title he insisted upon when he was appointed—of the Reliable Bank of Credit and Commerce International (RBCCI). For years to come the very mention of his name evoked responses of disgust, nausea, anger, and raucous humor among those who had been so unfortunate to be involved with RBCCI during that period. "Wat," as he asked everyone to address him, "was out of another world," a description one director used in referring to the bank's new leader.

Coming from a blazing career in one of London's most prestigious financial institutions, Wat had moved rapidly from his first years in the home office. An American, he sought his career by way of graduate work at the London School of Economics, serving in posts of increasing responsibility in Bonn, Hong Kong, and Tokyo. The headhunter who brought Wisehart to the attention of the retiring chairman of RBCCI pictured the now 50-year-old banker as brilliant, experienced, dynamic, and sophisticated. He was at ease in the world's financial markets, well able to hold his own with the best traders in Zurich, the Far East, and, of course, New York and London. He was "available," a term used by headhunters to cover a multitude of situations. For Wisehart and his wife, it meant they were ready to come home, provided the right opportunity could be found. The nation's capital, with a view of the White House and U.S. Treasury from his would-be office, turned out to be the opportunity waiting to be fulfilled. All that remained was the negotiation of details—salary, bonuses, perks, and other trappings of corporate indulgence.

By the time Wisehart was ensconced in office, a fat, long-term compensation package had been signed. He had learned to look after himself as he circumnavigated the business globe. A richly decorated suite was created for him on the top floor of the headquarters building, and a private dining room with adjacent kitchen and a capacity to seat 60 guests soon took form. Several vice presidents had to be moved in preparation for welcoming the secretary of the treasury, the chairman of the Federal Reserve, ambassadors, other government dignitaries, and, above all, as Wat explained, prospective (important) corporate clients who would be coming to Washington. Sure enough, the first function for unveiling the new "view from the top" on the 12th floor (zoning restrictions prevented builders from going any higher) was a luncheon at which the chairman of the Senate Banking Committee was the speaker and honored guest. Maybe, the thought occurred to some directors, Wat is indeed opening new horizons for the bank. He had made clear from the beginning that RBCCI should become a major player on the international scene.

Wat was moving in other ways, however, ways the directors only learned about after the fact. Advising the board, discussing matters with the board, or seeking advice from the board turned out to be foreign to Wat. In fact, several senior and veteran officers were gone, fired and ordered to clear out their desks on short order, before the directors knew anything about it. Major responsibilities were shifted while directors listened in regular meetings to lengthy presentations of plans from Wisehart for expanding the outreach of the bank—reaching out for new capital, for new sources of money, and for new places to put it to work.

When loan offices were opened in several new, major cities, Comstock, already swimming in a sea of uncertainty because of his limited knowledge of the financial world, was compelled to voice his concern.

Still on the executive committee from appointment by the previous chairman, Comstock said he just couldn't understand why RBCCI would venture into new markets since competition among lendors was at that time so fierce.

"If I were in business in Boston, using that only to illustrate my point, and I had a satisfactory on-going relationship with a local bank, there would seem to be only two reasons for taking my banking needs to RBCCI, which had recently come to town," Comstock told the committee. He apologized for being so poorly informed about current banking practices and added, "I would seek out the new office if my regular banker refused me further credit, or if I could get a new loan at a lower rate. Are we then proposing to place loans to people who are poor risks, or are we going to lend money at less than market rates in the new regions?"

The look that Wat directed to Bill Comstock needed no words of explanation. It was full of condescension, pity, and even empathy. There was no trace of anger. This widely experienced financial genius could understand why a poor, protected academic—after all, he believed the campus was as far from the real world as one could get—would have no understanding of today's fast-moving banking world. It was a classic case of a learned man decorated with the highest degrees, scholarly honors, and supporting paraphernalia not being able to appreciate a simple market condition. Wisehart let him down gently with a matter-of-fact explanation. "We must continue to grow our loans," he said. No point in antagonizing this director, thought Wisehart. I may need his vote sometime, and since he knows nothing about banking, he will be content just to sit and watch.

Although he voiced no reply and certainly exhibited no disagreement with Wisehart's statement, it was not a satisfactory answer for Comstock. His doubts lingered and became increasingly troublesome. The bank—he could never quite bring himself to refer to RBCCI as "my" bank as Wat did from his first day on the job—had been fortunate historically. Few loans had proved worthless, and the record of repayment and the satisfactory workouts of the few problems that did arise constituted a remarkable record. Comstock wondered, would the bank always be so lucky?

Other directors were having doubts, too. New loan offices didn't alone make up the concerns. Ambassadors and finance officers from several countries were appearing frequently in Wat's dining room. Directors, World Bank officials, and friends in Congress were all brought together in what appeared to be a constant public relations parade. A few new accounts from foreign governments had been opened after Wisehart designated one of the bank's branches to specialize in international business relations. He had appointed retired foreign service officer James R. Stapleton as senior vice president to direct and promote the effort, and several frontiers were being explored. Did these efforts make sense? Were they financially sound? Was RBCCI ready to assume such additional risk? When two directors expressed doubt, they learned their concerns were widely shared.

Not accustomed to bad news, the board took the first reports from the new loan offices in stride. Loan volume was growing at more than a satisfactory rate, new markets were being penetrated, and well-known, solid businesses were making the list of new clients. But the second round of reports, coming just two years after the brave new strategy was initiated, contained no good news and at least one alarm—offshore drilling in the Gulf of Mexico, in which several sizable loans had been made, was in trouble. Domestic oil was too expensive. World markets were swimming in excess, U.S. companies were quickly putting drilling equipment in mothballs, and the marginal companies, those that had been attracted to RBCCI because they were already overextended with their older lenders, were defaulting.

Wisehart's Waterloo came with surprising suddenness. It was the VP for international affairs—the same seasoned ex-diplomat whom Wat had counted on to open the world's doors—who blew the whistle.

Early in the day, long before most employees had yet arrived, Wat burst into Jim Stapleton's office to announce his latest great idea. He would charter a 747 and fill it with CEOs who did business in Asia and Africa or hoped to in the future. He would fly the whole gang to a dozen key spots on those continents where they would meet leaders of government, industrialists, and investors. "Then," Wisehart gleefully announced, "we will be the banker to these new enterprises!" It didn't take the old diplomat, one who had spent endless hours, even years, negotiating agreements, understandings, and all sorts of arrangements to see how futile such a junket would be. Wisehart was dead set on putting his plan into action and the sooner the better.

Here were two men who had spent their early careers in foreign lands and yet had acquired widely differing views about how best to do business with those who had similar interests and ambitions around the world. Stapleton, who was ten years senior, enjoyed a more formal education—a PhD. in international relations from Johns Hopkins University, plus a lifelong scholarly interest in the languages, customs, history, and traditions of the peoples in the countries where he had served. Wisehart was a brilliant, incisive, yet impulsive banker who had learned to make deals involving millions of dollars over a single luncheon.

Jim could only conclude, unequivocally, that Wat was about to launch an expedition that would be viewed by those on the receiving end—the leaders in the countries to be visited—as a gaudy, swashbuckling, high-pressure sales display that would be insulting and costly and would accomplish nothing. Had Wat learned anything during his years overseas? Stapleton wondered, and the fact that he had seen all too many whirlwind trips by American businessmen to foreign countries achieve nothing, only confirmed the misgivings he felt.

But Wisehart could not be dissuaded. As Jim began to voice doubts, raising questions and attempting to discuss some of the possible pitfalls, Wat wouldn't listen. He was adamant, and Stapleton quickly saw that to disagree would only end their brief relationship. Unfolding, far sooner than this former diplomat could have foreseen, was a disaster of the very kind he felt he had been hired by RBCCI to prevent. And yet his own career, his second one to be sure, was tied directly and solely to his new boss, or was it? He would soon learn.

Now, as a senior vice president of a sizable bank, breathing in the fresh air of a unique personal opportunity while most of his former associates in the foreign service were struggling to adjust to retirement and escape utter boredom, this new banker had no difficulty in deciding what he must do.

He voiced no further objection to Wisehart's pronouncement—a declaration of "what we will do," not "what do you think of this idea"—and left the room. Hired by the bank to give advice on what he had learned from an active, distinguished career at the highest levels of international diplomacy, James Stapleton realized it was only a matter of time before he would face a major confrontation with Wisehart. To him, the CEO of RBCCI exhibited all the traits of the autocratic, ruthless business tycoon—a stereotype of the kind that Stapleton had only heard about and in his naiveté could not believe really existed. Having witnessed the brief but explosive early morning display by Wat and the series over previous months of dismissals, reassignments, demotions, and admonishments of employees at every level, Jim clearly realized that his premonitions about Wisehart unfortunately were all true. He would not be a party to this latest wild, silly extravaganza.

Back in his office, Stapleton called the former chairman at his residence, and after conveying a tone of urgency on the telephone, scurried out to the suburban home to join the newly retired veteran banker at the breakfast table. Having eaten much earlier, he accepted a cup of coffee from the housekeeper, then signaled for the privacy he required to lay out the problem.

No lengthy explanation was necessary. To the retired CEO, who had built the bank over a long career and who thought his last few years could be spent in relaxed retirement, the news was not surprising. Rumors had already reached him, enough to raise serious doubts. Wanting badly to see Wisehart succeed, and feeling tired from his own long battles with corporate raiders, government regulators, and city officials, Chairman Barker, as he was still respectfully addressed, now knew the transition to new management would not succeed.

"Well," said John Barker, the gruff but friendly old warrior directed, "go back to your office. I'll make some phone calls this morning and see where we go from here." Almost as an afterthought, he thanked Stapleton and asked him to keep in touch and to mention his visit to no one.

Things were already humming when Jim returned to the office. Wisehart had called a management committee meeting of senior officers for eleven o'clock, now only a few minutes away. The committee was made up of senior managers in name only. They didn't manage anything; they all had learned long ago that only Wisehart managed. Soon they would hear all about the CEO's world-shattering idea, a concept that was accepted with enthusiasm by the VP for public relations, one of several new faces brought in by Wat. The group listened, amazed and surprised, as the boss expounded. Each manager left with new assignments, jobs to be done now—"not tomorrow or next week," to use the chairman's directive. That meant setting all else aside—appointments with clients, travel plans, and staff meetings—to embark on a kind of modern-day Marco Polo expedition to see what could be found in the rest of the world.

It was late in the day before Stapleton got back to Barker. Both had been busy, and while Jim had been calling ambassadors to try to persuade them to come to a special meeting which Wisehart insisted was the way to enlist their help, the old chairman was pursuing the matter in a different way. Calling two directors, one a calm and astute lawyer and the other a longtime friend from the financial world of Wall Street and the U.S. Treasury, Barker quickly set the wheels in motion for a showdown with Wisehart. Through his two fellow directors—Barker still remained on the board but with no other official title—the wily old banker, known as a curmudgeon to those who had battled him over the years, had quickly lined up the entire executive committee, with the exception of Wisehart, to fire the new CEO.

It took only one more day for the ax to find its victim.

Barker sat down in Wisehart's new office. The plush surroundings rivaled those of the headquarters of a late nineties dot.com, and it made Barker's blood boil to think of how arrogantly his successor had destroyed the old digs. He moved right to the point.

"It isn't working out, Wat," Barker began. "And so we have decided," giving Wat no chance to interrupt, "to ask for your resignation. It isn't one thing but several. They have been adding up now for two years, so there must be a change. Let's just say you don't fit into our way of doing business. We're really a small town bank, and your ideas are too big for us."

When Wisehart attempted to speak, he was immediately rebuffed—

summarily dismissed. A technique that he had used so often on others had now come home.

"I've arranged for a meeting this afternoon of the executive committee, and although you are a member and officially its chairman, I'd advise you not to come." Continuing without pause or change of expression, Barker added, "Please give me your letter of resignation before noon." "And," he paused a moment and said, "all the terms of your contract will be honored."

In spite of the gravity of the situation the meeting of the executive committee was brief. In fact, when Barker conducted them, all meetings were brief. Comstock was a member of this inner group, another carryover from the old board, but as he looked around the table, he realized he was one of the least experienced. He could hardly believe the ways of the corporate world. But, he thought, were they really so different from academe? The old chairman read the brief letter of resignation, announced that he would personally call the other directors not on the executive committee "to get them on board." The media would be informed of both the resignation and of the appointment of a veteran VP as acting CEO. An appropriate news release was being prepared, explained Barker, "and everything is in order."

As he walked back to the campus, Comstock could only compare in his mind the short time it took to fire Wisehart with the months, even years, it usually required to separate a failing university president from his post. But he knew that one of the public accusations of the campus was often true: Academics had to talk everything to death. What an ordeal it would have been, thought Comstock, to play out the complete crisis of RBCCI in public view with all the media involved! He had seen it so often in higher education. Invariably there were faculty meetings with resolutions of "no confidence" and counteractions by factions or other constituencies, most often student or alumni groups, all interspersed with special hearings of the governing board. So this academic CEO concluded there could be advantages to all parties, sometimes at least, for concealment of the gruesome details. "Washing the dirty linen for all the world to see" collided with the need to reveal "the truth, the whole truth," thought Comstock. But then, academe did have examples of "the terrible, swift sword."

Wisehart was not seen again on the Washington circuit. With his wife he quickly left for London, leaving behind an able attorney to represent his interests, to negotiate the final terms of his departure, to sell his house in the fashionable Georgetown section of the capital, and to arrange for shipment of the couple's personal belongings to Florida where the well-traveled banker had earlier acquired winter vacation property. No detail of the separation agreement was challenged. Barker, in explaining to the directors his reason for honoring every contingency in Wisehart's contract, simply said, "Think what it was costing the bank to keep him around." In his early fifties and with the generous financial settlement in his pocket, Wat was fully prepared, as his former Washington associates would learn, to begin a new, active career in retirement.

A snapshot of the deposed CEO clearly revealed that he was fully in charge of his new life. He was smiling, dressed in a natty captain's uniform, and had one hand on the wheel of his yacht. "Quite a guy," was the comment heard most often as the color photograph made its way around the boardroom table. Amusing, too, was the fact that at least six employees of the bank had received the same "greeting," signed simply, "Wat." There were no hard feelings, no bitterness, in fact, no trace of disappointment—just the announcement made clear without words, "I'm having the time of my life!"

To show just how fully the new Florida resident had entered his new world, Wat's next message was a clipping from the local paper announcing his election as mayor of the small town he now called home. A year later, giving the knife a little twist perhaps, he sent his new calling card to the same circle of former colleagues. It carried his name in bold type and in italics his new position, which some found hilarious: "Chairman, Clay County Professional Ethics Committee."

Looking back, the directors could voice only wonder at their own gullibility. On the other hand they consoled themselves by observing that the world, fortunately, harbored but a few Wiseharts. How was RBCCI so unlucky to get in the path of this one?

Comstock again compared. Was the academic arena as full of guile, mischief, and deception as the corporate world, or was human nature such that individuals simply exhibited the full range of human behavior no matter what their walk of life? Viewing religion or politics, human relations or the advance of medicine, the academic had read too much history to believe that any one area of endeavor held a corner on misbehavior.

An elderly, unschooled but wise custodian at MU, a man who left the fourth grade to spend his life in a series of low-level jobs under the umbrella of a university, when faced with an act of dishonesty or meanness by a colleague or acquaintance, said it all: "People are people." Neither management consultants nor health care experts could say it better. And so in the Comstock household it became the readily accepted explanation of the bizarre, the erratic, or the vicious—"people are people."

Turning from his experience in banking to one in the insurance industry, Comstock found a leader just the opposite of Wisehart. In the process he learned that company leaders in the world of insurance, like those in most businesses, offered both success and failure. On an insurance company board where he was to serve for many years, Comstock saw the full cycle. The CEO who built the company from almost the ground up was in charge when Comstock joined the group. He was succeeded by one who continued the same steady helmsmanship of his predecessor for another decade, to be followed by one who had to be fired after a four-year period in which he almost ruined the company. Finally a CEO was selected who proved to be the very textbook model of a corporate leader, the kind so many scholars described as the ideal. It was a pleasure for Bill Comstock to see young Snyder go to work.

From his first arrival at headquarters, Robert Snyder, a young, green, inexperienced CEO did everything right. He hit exactly the right note with the office staff and set the correct foundation with senior officers. Bob Snyder got down to business quickly in a most effective way. He promptly disposed of the obstreperous chief legal officer, demanding his early retirement. He showed the door to the chief financial officer who insisted on a new and far more generous employment contract as his price for remaining with the company. Thus, Snyder sent clear messages that previous ways of doing business were finished.

It was the most perfect textbook case of management Comstock had ever witnessed. He would not see it again until he observed a brilliant young woman following similar paths in another enterprise several years later at a time when women were just beginning to squeeze through the glass ceiling.

Within weeks, Snyder had put together his management team, inspired a nationwide field force by setting them to work alongside home office experts to design badly needed new products, and introduced the whole company to a realistic business plan for the immediate period ahead. Comstock, who was one of the directors responsible for recruiting Snyder, kept his fingers crossed.

Having found that few CEOs, including those who attended the country's best business schools, follow the fundamental principles of good management, this academic could hardly believe what he was now seeing. As Snyder forced company officers to consider philosophy, mission, ethical behavior, and value systems and brought the results to the board, directors began to see that the young manager not only knew the book on corporate leadership, but that he also believed it so strongly that he was following nothing else. Hard-nosed, company-wide evaluations at year's end completed the story; the business was again profitable. Within 12 months, in a market and in an industry in which others were still having major losses, All American Insurance Company had left its problems behind.

It was ironic, thought Comstock, that directors had to put a bridle on Synder's enthusiasm for integrity. So often it had seemed it was the CEO who had tried to skirt the legalities and ethical boundaries. Not so with this chief executive.

Bob brought a statement on ethical conduct of AAIC employees to the directors for their approval. It read, "This company stands behind all commitments, promises, or presentations of any kind that any employee representative of AAIC may make to any client or prospective client." It was far-reaching, unconditional, and all inclusive. Seasoned directors squirmed under the prospect of forthcoming litigation. The honesty of every representative of the company, they feared, could not be guaranteed.

Snyder argued: "I won't have crooks representing AAIC."

"Of course, you won't," countered one director. "But you can't find the dishonest ones until it's too late, and then the liability will be the company's because you have guaranteed that it will never happen."

Reluctantly, the new CEO agreed to review the matter in the hope of coming up with wording that would convey the high level of ethical behavior he was reaching for in an industry with widespread misrepresentation. Directors who had been down that road before knew it would not be easy.

Unfortunately, within the year an impostor representing himself as an account executive of the company made outlandish commitments to a prospective client in order to get a big deposit. He walked away with the money and left AAIC with a sizable lawsuit against it.

In spite of this untimely development, creativity, entrepreneurship, trust, and excellence were not just buzz words to Snyder; he was determined to give them meaning within the company.

Five years later when Comstock retired from the board because of age, Bob Snyder was still following the textbook, and AAIC was continuing so successfully that the university president could go back to the campus and tell the business school dean the things being taught would actually work.

Theory and practice—the debate would never cease, Comstock thought. But it was reassuring to him that the basic principles of management, when put in the hands of one who truly believed them, would stand the test of usage. Perhaps the real test of the workability of formal learning—everything from the first course in auditing to shared decision making—was found in a manager's personal view of his own needs. Did the manager, by his own arrogance, ignorance, bull-headness, or even experience, believe that he was superior to the best the experts could offer? Or did human nature hold such caution over one's actions that few managers could fully accept the conclusions and directions of campus scholars?

Comstock had weighed such factors in his own managerial roles over the years, and he concluded the answers were all around us. It was an ongoing argument with his colleagues on campus. Every student who studied the discipline could find within his own circle of acquaintances or perhaps in his own family—certainly within his community—examples of success in which the manager broke many if not all of the fundamental principles being espoused in the professional literature. Were individual human factors, therefore, more important than proven theories?

Taking one path instead of the other was not the answer, thought Comstock. An administrator with the best training and the best preparation cannot be guaranteed success without having more. The administrator must have a respect for others, a willingness to put the welfare of the organization above his own interests, a level of integrity that will not allow shoddy work, and a host of related characteristics, many of which cannot be measured.

Late in his career and in a company whose tradition suggested that it might never take place, Comstock saw one more manager who played by the book—and this one was a woman! In a previously all-male corporation this female became a senior executive with amazing speed and reached the CEO's perch, almost before either internal or external constituencies were aware of it.

After a brilliant record in one of the country's best business schools, Nancy Jane Elkins was promptly hired by Jones and Associates, an old and reputable consulting firm. Within the ten-year period of her work with Jones—she made partner in two years, another record—she personally added to the firm's reputation. It would have been easy for the company to let her go had she not made herself such a valuable part of their program.

When Nancy first went to work for Jones, the company had done only small jobs in the publishing industry. This new, energetic staff associate, a title that branded her both inexperienced and junior to all the partners, did not hesitate to move into the publishing sector. In fact, her boss, a partner whose chief interests were in financial service institutions, didn't have any real knowledge in publishing, so he was of no help to her. Nancy's challenge, as she confided to Comstock some years later, was to learn everything possible about the publishing business as quickly as she could so she could talk the language of the field. Learn the business, whether it's growing mushrooms, marketing catfish, or building bird feeders before trying to tell someone how to do it was a never-to-be-broken creed for this neophyte expert.

Timing could not have been better. Bankruptcies, mergers, buy-outs, strikes, revolutionary technical changes were all descending on the publishing industry at the same moment. Fortunes were being made and lost almost day by day. And for Nancy Elkins it was to be a decade of unprecedented activity. Here was a management consultant who had sound advice to offer, and Nancy soon became the most sought after in the field. Hers was a heady experience. It was only logical that Sanders Kaufman, just a couple of rungs below the top of the ladder among the country's largest publishers, would be among Nancy's clients.

Her change of career came in the most routine, yet unexpected fashion.

The CEO of Sanders Kaufman Publishing Company advised his board that a consultant had been hired to look at its magazine division.

Then Ms. Elkins was introduced to make a report of her findings to the directors. It was such a common occurrence that few directors bothered to turn their chairs around to get a better view of the few charts the consultant used in her presentation.

Following her 30-minute report, Nancy was kept for another hour, responding to questions from the board members. They wouldn't let her go. She was giving this group of leaders from various walks of life, some of them professional publishers, more information on the world of magazines than they had ever heard. Although some had planes to catch, no one moved. The CEO finally adjourned the meeting since the consultant's report was the last item on the agenda.

At that point most of the group surrounded Ms. Elkins and continued the discussion. Comstock went to the CEO. His message, whispered since others were not far away, was direct. "Get that lady," he said, "Sanders Kauffman needs her." Just to emphasize further, he called the next day to make sure his message was not forgotten. But he was not the only director so favorably impressed. The CEO reported two others had delivered the same message!

One year later Nancy Jane Elkins joined Sanders Kaufman as vice president for marketing. It proved to be a hand-in-glove fit. Within another two years she became one of three executive VPs, and not many years later, she was given the CEO's mantle. It was a first in the field.

Women had come a long way in the corporate world, Comstock would write, as he tried to piece together the two decades in which a glass ceiling, while not being removed, had perhaps been cracked.

Seeing how the business world evolved gave Midtown's president an unusual opportunity to compare, as he was always doing, the business and the campus communities. On some measures he knew that university boards came up short when viewed alongside their counterparts from business and industry, but in the case of Midtown University, the president could only give thanks and a sigh of relief for the chairmen, all of them, with whom he had worked.

Glen Parkinson, the present chairman, "Parkey" to those who could be persuaded to be so informal with this quiet, solid, sensible lawyer, was especially competent. Undoubtedly, he had learned much from an older brother who had served ably as a university president for almost 20 years, but Glen's broad understanding of even the most subtle undertones of an academic question never ceased to amaze Comstock. In private discussions the two found mutual appreciation for positions on forthcoming actions. Often, surprisingly, Bill got observations from Glen about situations that had not occurred to him. Parkinson was judicious without having a trace of the imperious, and most of his comments were offered with modesty. Here was a master at influencing others, never threatening an individual's knowledge, action, or judgment.

Just a couple of years earlier, Comstock had worried about a successor to Mr. Vann who was forced to step down as chairman because of age. Charles E. "Chuck" Vann—few, including Bill Comstock, ever addressed him as "Chuck"—had been an excellent chairman. Not only was he skillful, but he was also shrewd. Pretending not to know the intricacies of academe, he refused to be drawn into any preliminary discussion of educational matters with either faculty members or students. All such inquiries were referred to the president and to the chairman of the board's committee on academic affairs. Chuck Vann was an unusual trustee, one whom Midtown U's president was especially fortunate to have. In staying out of academic affairs Mr. Vann saved himself for the things in which he could be of real help to the institution. That area was finance, and the chairman was an expert.

When Bill Comstock was faced with a money crunch at one point early in his years at Midtown U, he went with his trusted friend, the university treasurer, to get Mr. Vann's advice. In less than an hour the two left with the problem solved. It took five million dollars of new credit to weather the storm, but the chairman had made all arrangements with a couple of short telephone calls and a five-minute interlude with an assistant. He also got better terms than the university treasurer had been quoted by any source. Trustees who served on the finance committee learned of the matter at their next meeting, and undoubtedly others got the substance by grapevine, but the rest of the university community remained unaware of Mr. Vann's unselfish action. Although some trustees—and there were times when Comstock felt MU had too many—seemed to do nothing constructive for the institution, here was a chairman whose loyalty and support were simply magnanimous but who would never allow himself to be adequately recognized.

The elaborate and generous plans that Charles E. Vann and his equally able and active wife Laura Thompkins Vann made for MU in their wills would take years to materialize, but the imprint of their gifts fortunately would be permanently recognized.

After Vann's retirement, the immediate problem for an always concerned university president was the necessity of learning the ways of a new chairman. Worrying about Glen "Parky" Parkinson proved unnecessary. So smoothly did the change occur that it was months before many realized the board was now headed by a new name and a new face. Taken together, the years when Vann and Parkinson served as chairmen would be viewed, as the president-historian looked back, as the best period in the 20th century for the institution. MU emerged as a leading academic and intellectual center; the dreams of its founders were at last being realized.

But campuses are fraught with controversy, and the collision of ideas all too often brings physical confrontation and challenges. Governing boards can seldom steer clear of the fray, and for "Parky" there was no inclination to sidestep the chairman's responsibility as he saw it. Small skirmishes came and went—a librarian stole some rare books, students demonstrated against tuition increases, and a popular football coach had to be fired for slapping one of his players—but the gravest challenge to serenity and academic achievement came from an unlikely source, Midtown's medical center.

Caught between what was viewed as a university effort to control the income of physicians and uncertain government policies on health care and insurance, the university faced a tide of discontent and confusion that rolled over the entire faculty, carrying with it students, nurses, other health care workers, and alumni. Before the problem was finally resolved, it divided the board itself. So grave was the crisis that at one point it threatened the very existence of the institution.

It took a full three years for the difficulties to be resolved. Using all of his professional legal skills, Parky masterminded a campaign that delivered a university, as some would observe, "still in one piece" and stronger than ever. Spending hours in the study of health care and its attendant problems, Glen became an expert in a fraction of the time it usually takes most professionals to feel comfortable with the issues.

As president of the University, Comstock marveled at the skill with which Parkinson brought out the hopes and fears of medical students, leaders of the faculty—men and women in many cases recognized nationally and internationally in their specialties—and the entire staff of the complex health center. As Parky questioned various individuals and listened to their complaints, he pieced together the fragile parts of an often unseen mosaic, something many of those who had spent their entire careers in medical service did not themselves see or understand. At first their fears and suspicions were only further aroused. How could this quiet, unassuming lawyer, a stranger to the medical world, bring order to the chaos surrounding a medical center confronted daily with all the problems of urban America?

Working closely together, MU's president and the chairman fashioned a solution that tucked all of the loose ends of the seemingly endless components of the medical center into a workable, manageable, and acceptable unity. Patient care, education and training, compensation, and income and expense were all put together in a package which, contrary to the dire predictions of a few and the genuine concern of many, would serve the Midtown University and all its constituencies well for more than a decade.

Bill Comstock and Glen Parkinson became close personal friends as the demands of the university brought them together more and more. For one of the few times in his career, the university leader was partner with another, a leading Washington lawyer, who was as dedicated to the university and to the whole of education as was he.

Unfortunately the genius of Parkinson would not be available to Midtown for long.

Returning from a brief holiday in Europe in early summer, Comstock found his secretary with a message from Parkinson that he would like a brief call. Comstock contacted the chairman promptly, and Glen said that he'd walk to the president's office, only a few blocks away, to "bring him up to date" on a personal matter. Detecting no urgency in the chairman's voice, Comstock spent the next few minutes scanning the stack of "first-reading" arranged on the center of his desk.

Glen arrived promptly, showing his usual calmness, but after the routine "Welcome back. I hope you and Betty had a good trip," he walked over and closed the office door. Since these two men talked quietly enough to make a closed door unnecessary, Comstock was already uncomfortable about the news he was to hear.

"I have been diagnosed as having cancer," Glen stated simply, matter-of-factly, and almost passively. Before Bill could respond—actually he was groping for the right words—the chairman continued: "Unfortunately, I'm told it's a fast-moving malignancy of the pancreas and it has already spread to other organs." Still serene after revealing his own death sentence to his friend, the Washington lawyer added with equal tranquillity, "I'm afraid you will have to look for a new chairman."

Shocked, stunned, speechless, the academic who was so articulate on other occasions couldn't find appropriate words. Every phrase or possible comment that came to mind was inadequate, shallow, and superficial. In this office where two friends had come together, the English language proved faint and hollow.

Still groping, but instantly realizing the terrible loss he and the university were about to face, the president could only come up with something about Glen's treatment.

"Yes," confirmed Parkinson, "I'm already into chemotherapy and radiation, and so far I'm relatively free of the side effects."

Just two months from the day of the diagnosis, Chairman Parkinson was dead, his tenure lasting less than five years. What irony, Comstock thought, as he recalled the service of two previous chairmen—a leading banker who kept the position for twenty years and a career diplomat who stayed for fifteen. Yet this quiet lawyer who had given such vital leadership at a most critical period was cut short in life and in recognition. He was so gentle that few outside the medical center were aware of his term as chairman, a term that normally would have continued for another ten years before he reached the age of mandatory retirement.

As summer faded and fall approached, Bill Comstock could think of little else.

Working with the board—the trustees of a university or the directors of a for-profit corporation—was vital to the well-being of the enterprise. In both cases the leader of the board, whether he carried the title of chairman or not, was usually the CEO's pathway to the other members. Sadly, for Midtown U and for its president, it would be decades before another Glen Parkinson would come along.

While he faced no substantive opposition from members of Midtown's board, Comstock soberly realized that he must continue without the help of a strong chairman. His own heavy load would become more burdensome. Although he knew well how to work with trustees, he needed a chairman. Unfortunately, there was simply no one in line for the position who knew enough about a university to provide the support and the leadership required. The three giants were gone.

But Comstock was not one to embrace self-pity. He well understood that his colleagues in public colleges and universities served while regents and trustees battled openly for political, ideological, economic, or personal advantage, often embroiling the institutional president in their disputes. He knew, too, that harmony between the CEO and the governing board did not guarantee effectiveness of the organization but that the opposite certainly made success much less likely.

Comstock recognized that few university presidents in either public or private institutions had been blessed with such board chairmen as the first three who worked at Midtown with him. He looked back nostalgically to the first. E.K. Linstrom was ideally suited for the years of campus unrest that marked the late sixties; then came Charles E. Vann who seemed equally fit to the seventies. Now the third, Glen Parkinson was gone. When EK's retirement arrived, other trustees turned to Vann, a man who had served quietly but effectively as vice chairman, supporting every board decision and contributing most directly as a key member of the finance committee. The transition was smooth

Hard work and brains had marked Vann's career—all the way. First in his class as an undergraduate and first in his class in law school, Charles married the young woman who was also first in her class the same year that Vann finished his law degree. Both of them were Midtown U loyalists from the very start.

Going to work for a small company immediately upon his graduation, Vann pursued a business career that led directly to success. Joining the legal department of a firm, he quickly became the most knowledgeable and the most articulate lawyer on the staff. He was the one to whom the CEO always turned for guidance when his most difficult legal problems arose. In the meantime Mrs. Vann had joined the accounting department of the same company immediately after her completion of a commercial school cram course that had followed her bachelors degree in English from Midtown.

When Charles Vann became chairman of MU's board, he had already been CEO of his company for several years and had skillfully grown the enterprise far beyond the expectations of financial analysts or business-page columnists.

Equally successful was Mrs. Vann, having risen to the chief financial officer's position even before Charles was given the CEO's hat. It was said that the Vanns owned a trunk full of stock, the result of years of options and other compensation, but since it was not a publicly traded company, no one knew for sure.

For Bill Comstock it was to be five years of bliss as far as work with the chairman was concerned. In fact, he didn't really know how Charles E. Vann viewed his relationship with the university president until after Vann passed the office along to his successor.

Vann was meticulous with protocol and formal in all personal relationships. Comstock made an appointment for some days in advance after Vann's departure from the chairman's seat to thank him for the many years of service to Midtown U.

Looking across his desk at Comstock—there were no lounge chairs or conversation corners in Vann's office—the former chairman allowed himself a smile as he explained his view of the way he behaved as chairman.

"Dr. Comstock," he began in his customary way, "when I became chairman of the university's board, I had already concluded that you were capable in every way of running the institution. I not only approved of the way you handled the problems of campus unrest, the financial affairs, alumni, faculty, student matters, all the rest, but I also thought I could be of greatest help if I stayed out of your way."

"In my own company," he continued, "I want directors who will help me solve problems when I can't do it myself. When things are running smoothly, I don't want them getting in my way."

What a statement, thought Comstock, and what a compliment. He recalled that Vann had done everything he asked of him over the years. But he had volunteered nothing more. Even his contributions, and they were substantial, went directly to the treasurer of the university; this donor seemed not to wish to bother the president. Most other supporters, whether they were giving five dollars or five hundred thousand, wanted the president to know about it.

Comstock wondered what business school professors would have to say about Charles Vann's management style.

Now, Lindstom, Vann, and Parkinson were gone! And few would ever know of their help to Midtown U. Such were the vagaries of history.

V

Compensation—What a Fuss

The president of Midtown U witnessed money grabbing in a hundred different forms. It was usually a man but once in a while a woman, too, who was always asking for or demanding more money. The level of compensation seemed not to matter; it was the person and whatever it might be inside that person that kept pushing and pushing for more pay.

It took a veteran trustee of the university, however, to put the real label on the condition. He had held high posts in government, had served as special representative of more than one President of the United States to foreign lands, and had become well acquainted with the corporate world. His label for those people seemingly blinded by money was a simple one—it was just plain greed.

Comstock realized his own hesitance to brand anyone—a professor, a corporate director, a CEO of a major business enterprise, or others—individuals or groups—as being greedy, yet he had seen it from so many.

And then it came home. His successor at Midtown was only weeks away from taking office. Nothing could have dismayed Comstock more.

The trustee put it bluntly: "No, I won't continue as a trustee of the university. The new president is too greedy. I've checked him out in his previous posts, and he is simply too greedy." Comstock, while a bit shocked at the statement made to ten other trustees, nonetheless felt a sense of admiration for his friend's candor.

Running through his mind were all those directors' meetings in which compensation appeared on the agenda—the agenda of meetings of compensation committees, of executive committees, of special committees, and of other committees whose primary responsibility was, in the vernacular, the care and feeding of the CEO.

A whole army of consultants exists over the country, he knew, to help senior managers with their greed. They move from one company to another, carrying the word on the latest bonus plans, perks, or fringes that the organization must compete against. Always present is the threat that your senior executives are in danger of being lured away unless you not only match the total income packages of the other company but also go well beyond. After all, isn't your CEO and his management team really better than the leadership of the competition? And don't you want to express your confidence in your company and its management by approving the consultant's recommendations? To do otherwise would send the wrong message.

Can a director, sitting at the table with fellow directors, including the CEO, turn into the villain? All the pressures of group interaction, the driving force of American business and of other sectors dedicated to growth and progress, all converge to win unanimous approval of the proposal. Management may now go back to work with renewed faith in the enterprise, newly energized for the increased competition and proud to be a part of the company whose directors understand the challenges facing the CEO and his team and are not afraid to take the bit in their teeth!

On the way home from another bank directors' meeting and before getting back to the office to face his own problems, Comstock wondered if he had been too timid to point out what seemed to him to be a poor decision made last month by a CEO in opening new offices in four additional cities. Then, too, the new investment by the company in yet another smaller corporation made him question the compatibility or synergism, as the CEO called it, of their combined business activities. Stretching his imagination, he simply couldn't see any connection between the two.

These were all special concerns for Comstock, but the overriding one that would not go away was greed. The university president had too much of it passing before him everyday, and he knew that it wasn't just his imagination.

Only yesterday Sam Houston, the director of the university's surplus property program, had pleaded with Comstock for a sizable salary increase. He was already among the highest paid people in the university, but Houston sounded destitute as he sat on the couch opposite the president and argued his case.

If it had been the first time, Comstock might have been more sympathetic, but Sam was in his fifth year as the director of the program, which was certainly not central to the university's mission. True, it brought some dividends to the institution; it paid its own way, and Sam knew how to prowl around government agencies and find supplies and equipment of value to several academic departments. Having held a high-level post because of his hard work in putting his party in the White House, he brought away extensive knowledge of the bureaucracy, which he was now putting to good use for the university. He was hired when his party lost the last election, and Houston, out of a job, did not want to return to his home in the cold, upper Midwest. Washington proved to be an attractive place in Sam's view, and the job at Midtown University was the best he could get. After five years, Houston was being paid well above his salary in government where he had been an assistant secretary to a cabinet officer; his wife was a partner in one of Washington's most respected law firms; and his two children had finished college.

Sam appeared to be pleading poverty, with arrogance, as tears rolled down his cheeks. Comstock had grown accustomed to Houston's act. Each year, after letters with salary information were sent out, Sam came to protest and to perform—in precisely the same way!

Houston's efforts were certainly helpful to the university, but when placed alongside the chief development officer's benefit to the institution, and he was being paid far less than Sam, there was no comparison. Comstock decided he had seen enough.

"Sam," he said, "you and I have worked very well together for these five years. You have been helpful to the institution, but a university is not a General Motors. You are being paid well. In my mind your salary, your exceptional retirement benefits, and the other fringes that come to you and your family (both children had received free tuition, one for four years, the other for two) are more than generous. So now I must ask you to take it or leave it. This may sound harsh, but if making money, and then making still more money, is your driving force in life, you should leave academe and labor elsewhere."

The tone of Comstock's voice was not to be mistaken, and Houston knew it. Within moments Sam began a diplomatic retreat. He loved the university, he said. "And my relations with you, Mr. President, have always been most cordial and professional. You make my work here a pleasure, and I assure you," he added, as though his services were so important that the institution could not survive without them, "I won't desert the ship."

The president, not one to spend much time examining the other's motives, thought to himself as Sam left the office that he was already looking for another job and as soon as he found one with higher pay, he'd leave. Smart, aggressive—and greedy—"Dr. Houston," as he preferred to be called, put together a consulting business, left the university when the firm's success was assured, and within two years had doubled his income.

Encounters such as this one with Sam came far more often than the president could believe. Comstock had worked hard at improving salaries and benefits for everyone at Midtown University. In fact, he made the strengthening of faculty salaries his first priority when he assumed the presidency. That he succeeded beyond his own expectations was simply a stroke of fortunate timing and not the result of any special genius on his part. This he knew very clearly!

Before the week was out, the university president again met greed face-to-face, and, once again, he didn't even have to leave his office.

It centered on the appointment of a new law school dean. One of the three finalists who had been offered the job declined at the eleventh hour; another simply withdrew when it was made clear that he had considerable opposition to his appointment among the faculty. Actually, his name had been added to the list of two choices just to meet the technical requirement of the faculty code that the search committee present at least three names to the president. All of this with full details was known to the remaining candidate who came before Comstock, knowing that he was the first choice of the search committee, the preferred candidate of the law school faculty, and now the only remaining choice for the deanship.

He was in a position to write his own ticket, or so he thought. A full year of work had gone into the process. A thorough nationwide search had been conducted by the seven-member committee, and the ablest candidates were screened from an initial list of more than a hundred prospects.

The importance of the law school to Midtown University was also well known in the academic community. Even Comstock himself on several occasions had pointed to this professional school as one of the crown jewels of "our university." The comparative standing of the entire institution was directly tied to the structure and strength of the law school. Rarely could an applicant for any position be in a stronger position—a position to demand and to get from the quiet, seemingly easygoing, not-too-assertive president of MU exactly what he wanted.

And what the candidate wanted was not camouflaged in any way.

"I would like to be dean of your distinguished law school," said William H. Kirkpatrick after the normal amenities had transpired. Each felt fairly well acquainted with the other, having met on two previous occasions as the search process moved its unhurried way through the year. Recounting the conversation later, Comstock conceded that he had not been prepared for what came next.

"In order to assume the responsibility of the deanship," Kirkpatrick continued, "and to make the move from my present position, I will require the highest salary of any dean of any law school in the United States."

Salary information was available from the Association of Law Schools, which updated changes each year, and Comstock could guess that Kirkpatrick could readily quote them. Also known to both men, undoubtedly, was the fact that two or three of the most noted law schools in the country, including Harvard, refused to report the salary of the dean, or any other person on the grounds that to do so would be an invasion of privacy. And unlike less known law schools, Harvard could prevail in such a confrontation with the Association. Schools at the lower end of the academic pecking order succumbed to the pressure and readily complied with all requests from the central office.

As the conversation then shifted to the Association, Comstock used the few moments to frame his response to Kirkpatrick's demand. The president was being blackmailed, and he would under no circumstances knuckle under.

"I believe," Comstock began, calmly and earnestly, "Midtown University is in a position to pay the highest salary in the country to the dean of its law school (the president carefully avoided, as was his habit, referring to any part of the university as "mine"). This institution is rapidly gaining financial strength, and nowhere is that progress more pronounced than in the law school. The annual fund has been growing at the rate of some 30 percent for the past five years; two sizable bequests, which will be used to endow five new professorships, have come in the last 18 months. Yes," the president concluded, "the new dean could be paid the highest salary of any dean in the country." Having made up his mind quickly and firmly that he would not allow the institution to be made hostage to this extortionist, the president gave his reply.

"How do I know you are the best of some 500 deans of law in the country? Are you now dean of the best school of law? Have you recruited the best faculty during your six years in your present post? No! Have you raised the most money of any law school? No! As you can see," Comstock concluded, "you are in no position to demand the highest compensation because you haven't proved yourself to be the best. Your cart is before your horse." The president was already on his feet as he finished, and the candidate needed no further cue as he headed for the door.

Irony, thought Comstock, as he went back to his desk. What irony. And we look to our law schools to teach young men and women about fairness, reasonableness, justice, and right and wrong. What would this man Kirkpatrick advise a student or faculty member to do when faced with similar decisions? No wonder we have become a land of litigation. Graduates of America's law schools could enter practice prepared only for hand-to-hand combat if all the professors were like this one.

He fell back on a cliché to sum up the situation: It's back to the drawing board! The consequences of the whole futile affair raced through his mind—a year lost; the time of members of the search committee; the emotional let down that would come with the saddening disappointment; the frustration that now must be somehow overcome; and the nauseating feeling that greed, pride, image, and ego somehow interact to bring out the worst in people.

Are such things as humility, a spirit of service, sympathy, understanding, and concern no longer a part of humankind? Here Comstock seemed always to come to a roadblock. With the problems facing the world, how could anyone, no matter how talented, be so arrogant. "If I am paid the highest salary of any dean, then I will be recognized as the best," the spurned candidate somehow reasoned.

Several months later in a chance meeting with the president of Kirkpatrick's institution, Comstock was brought up to date.

"In a way I'm glad Kirkpatrick didn't come to Midtown," said the colleague whom he had known for many years and one for whom respect was widespread in both the university and corporate worlds. "Why do you say that?" Comstock inquired. "I thought you were quite high on the fellow."

"To make it brief," the friend explained, "Kirkpatrick has decided to go into private practice. Upon his return from his final visit with you, he left his wife and moved in with a girlfriend, a young woman who graduated just last year from our law school. Mrs. Kirkpatrick apparently was aware of the affair that had begun at least a year earlier. Gossip has it that she kicked him out and filed for divorce the next day. Now we, too, are looking for a new dean," the rather exasperated president concluded.

Comstock felt that both he and Midtown U had dodged a bullet. In fact, after Kirkpatrick was abruptly rejected, the deanship was filled with the appointment of a very able in-house faculty member. What might have happened, thought the president, if Kirkpatrick had been appointed?

Turning to athletics Comstock witnessed another case of greed with its own irony, but it was one that exemplified thousands.

He saw the high stakes drama played out in the person of John Smith, a high school basketball star who entered Chesapeake U with the publicity usually reserved for a popular governor or mayor. Midtown's president, quite serendipitously, rejected the chance (some of his critics called it a missed opportunity) to be a central player. Instead, he became one of many observers. Only a few people were aware of Midtown's possible role.

"We can get John Smith at Midtown," Grover Stonefield, the veteran athletic director, said enthusiastically, as he sat down with Comstock, along with Bob Tuttle, the basketball coach. "You see, we have an alum who is a car dealer in Johnny's home county (the nickname had long since replaced the more formal John), and he knows the father. In fact, one of Johnny's older brothers works as a mechanic for our alumnus."

"Well, what stands in the way?" Comstock guessed the problem, but he wanted to hear it from his two callers.

"We have talked to the people in admissions, and they tell us Smith doesn't meet our standards." Stonefield did all the talking as Tuttle, sensing the inevitable, listened glumly.

"How weak is he as a student?" No point in ignoring the facts, thought the president.

"He is 200 points below our cut off on the SATS," Stonefield replied. "But two very good universities have already admitted him," the AD quickly added, hoping to take some of the sting out of a devastating fact.

They were indeed, Comstock learned, two of America's most prestigious institutions. Both fielded winning teams, often placed among the nationally ranked, and both were first-rate academically. It was the kind of competition that caused presidents like Comstock to squirm when confronted by the reasoning of gung-ho alumni: "If great universities like Michigan, Duke, Virginia, Notre Dame, Wisconsin, USC, and UCLA can be strong in both athletics and academics, then why can't Midtown?"

Comstock felt he knew the way these institutions succeeded in both, and he didn't like it. No point, however, in arguing with Stonefield and Tuttle. He had been over that ground with them on previous occasions.

"I'm afraid my answer is not one you want to hear," the president said. "If we bring him in, everyone will know, including the young man himself, that the bars were let down so he could step across. We know from bitter experience that he's not ready for our academic program. Oh yes, a tutor could write his papers, hold his hand, pick out all the gut courses, and keep him eligible; but we know that every step of the way he will expect whatever accommodations necessary for his convenience and well being."

"I don't believe the integrity of Midtown should be sacrificed to the basketball program." With that, Comstock dashed whatever dreams his two visitors might have carried for greater visibility, perhaps even a national championship.

While the three never again mentioned the subject, they watched from the sidelines as Johnny Smith had his run at fame and fortune. By the time he enrolled at Chesapeake (and that came only after a long courtship which lasted well into the summer), few details of his life or that of his family had missed the pages of newspapers or magazines.

Driving an 18-wheeler from coast to coast, Jasper Smith, Johnny's father, had supported a wife and seven children on a small hillside farm on the border between Virginia and West Virginia. Neighbors knew whether or not Jasper was home by noting whether his rig was parked at the turnoff where the dirt road up to his house crossed the little mountain stream just off the hard-topped road that cut through the hills. He never stayed home long; his company required both truck and driver to be on the move.

Suddenly, it seemed, Jasper Smith quit the work he had seemed so proud to be doing for 20 years. How did he continue to earn a living? No one quite knew. Neither did anyone have the effrontery to ask. A large new sedan took the place of the truck in the usual parking place. The family had entered a new world.

But neighbors also saw a change in Jasper Smith. While big and brawny, confident of his ability to make his way in the world, not afraid of night deliveries in the warehouse districts of the inner city, and never hesitant to take his rig into new territory, he was also considerate of his neighbors, always ready to offer a hand to the downtrodden and to pull a friend or stranger out of a ditch. Within the period of a few months, he began to act like a bully, strident in his manner, demanding of everyone around him. He asked for something more each time university officials came to call; his son had become a valuable commodity, and he knew he held the purse strings.

"We can give your son the highest quality four years of college education to be found anywhere in the country," was a refrain which Jasper heard from a chorus of recruiters. Cars appeared with license tags from as far away as Kansas and Indiana, as well as from nearby states, including North Carolina.

While listening politely to the fancy talk, this father from the hill country waited patiently for dollars to be put on the table. But recruiters, at least those who came in an official capacity, invariably stopped short of making any specific financial commitments; those came from visitors who always introduced themselves as "friends" or "boosters" of such and such institutions.

Long before Johnny enrolled at Chesapeake, Jasper's demands had been met. Title to his new car had been delivered, and enough money had been moved under the table to assure all parties of the young man's future.

Registration in September brought a flurry of publicity to both Chesapeake U and to Johnny, but it was nothing compared with the official opening of the basketball season. More season tickets had been sold than ever in the history of CU. With a dozen NBA scouts in the stands for the first game, fans opened their high-gloss programs to find a full-page picture of the campus president shaking hands with and looking up to Johnny Smith, standing seven feet tall and weighing some three hundred pounds.

No one was disappointed. Chesapeake never quite made the top ten on any poll during the long season, and the team didn't get to the Final

Four, but Johnny Smith established himself as one of the best college players in the country. Announcers, writers, and opposition coaches were unanimous in their praise. His skill, maturity, quickness, and strength all combined to make him a surefire, first-round draft choice when he finished college.

But Johnny didn't finish college. One more year, his second, turned out to be his last. Helped along by a bunch of new recruits—the coaches found it much easier to persuade prospects to come to Chesapeake when they saw the chance to join an already established star—the team made it to the top, almost. Playing before 35,000 fans in the Superdome, Chesapeake lost the NCAA championship by just three points.

Player of the year, first pick All-American and other individual honors came to Johnny. Just as they had done in high school, all members of the Smith family went to every game and shared in the glory.

And Jasper was just as gung-ho as all the rest of the family, outwardly at least. Most importantly, Johnny always deferred to his father. In the most important decision in his life, something he was soon to face, that trust was not misplaced.

In the two years, plus a few months, which had passed since Jasper walked away from his rig with its regular paydays, he had crossed paths with agents, chiselers, clergymen, bankers, mobsters, lawyers—an equal number, it seemed, of those who wanted to help and those who wanted to defraud. Jasper listened, questioned, and learned, stopping short of signing any contracts or other firm commitments.

Should Johnny leave college and join the professionals? That was the question. Another year and an almost certain national title or jump now to a fat paycheck? Jasper knew all the numbers. Sports was the common language of truckers, and contract bargaining was a piece of their daily lives. Each route had its own risks.

As writers and commentators speculated on Johnny's future, Jasper was playing the game—high stakes, to be sure—with prospective agents, general managers, and those ever-surfacing emissaries who claimed to be any number of things. Since both father and son delayed a definitive reply, the number of callers continued to grow.

With Johnny, things were more personal, more intimate. "Have you had any swelling in the knee since the Superdome?" his trainer asked. The knee was the right one, and both father and son were concerned. Back in January, after a busy week—three road games with double overtime in one—the trainer had warned Johnny of possible trouble. Ice packs were present for the rest of the season, not an uncommon sight however, among basketball or football teams. Ankles and knees were vulnerable joints to big men, heavy men, those who had to run and jump, putting maximum stress on muscles and tendons. Jasper Smith, well aware of the dangers, decided to test the market.

"You say he could sign for big money," he said to Joe Mahoney, a respected super agent whose two partners had already made more than one trip to the Smith household.

"Tell me what that means." It was more like a command than an innocent inquiry. Mahoney knew his answer had to be real. No pipe dreams.

"Jasper, I believer Johnny could sign for a minimum of 25, and possibly as much as 50 million dollars if he were to join the pros this year. That would be for a multi-year contract, of course."

"And if he stays in school another year?" Jasper followed.

"If he keeps healthy, and if he has a good year, he could probably sweeten his contract. That assumes, of course, that we don't have a strike or other unexpected development."

Signing bonus, cash advance, length of contract, insurance against injury, and, of course, taxes were all addressed. Mahoney, having been through it many times, was careful not to raise false hopes. But expectations, whether minimum or maximum, all sounded more than adequate to the former truck driver. A world that he had only read about, athletes and their rich contracts, was now within his reach. From his service in the army, most of it spent as a military policeman, from his seat at the poker table, and from his miles on the road, Jasper Smith had become wise in the ways of humankind. He brought it all to bear in Johnny's behalf.

Young Smith was drafted by an NBA contender, a team whose center was reaching the end of a dominating career. Even in his first year, Johnny could expect to get considerable playing time while learning the inside of the game from a master. It was an ideal setting, and the contract which Joe Mahoney put together wasn't far from the maximum that he had outlined for Jasper months earlier.

Forty-five million dollars! What a message for the neighbors back home, most of whom could not comprehend that much money. And for Chesapeake U? A mixed message. There went the championship; but after Johnny Smith, basketball would never be the same.

Up front was five million as a signing bonus, and the rest would be paid out over seven years with half safely tucked into a trust fund, providing life income to a young man who was now a rich man.

Early in his third season, just as Johnny became the first string starter and his mentor became the backup, he had to leave the team for corrective surgery. The sore knee had to be rebuilt. Recovery and rehabilitation took his entire off-season, and Johnny's return was less than satisfactory. With another operation in the next off-season, this time on the other knee, the young man who showed so much promise never got back to his peak playing performance.

Complete retirement from basketball came after five years; only the first two had met expectations. It brought great disappointment to everyone concerned, especially to Johnny. But his father had foreseen the possibility—or was it genealogy? Jasper remembered his own discomfort from his knees. Gimpy, he described them. Troublesome almost from his first weeks behind the wheel of his truck the aching simply got worse as the years passed.

No, the Smiths did not go back to their home in the hills; they bought a sizable farm in the horse country of northern Virginia, settling into the breeding and racing business. With an Olympic size pool, Johnny continued therapy on his knees, swimming being the only exercise he could still endure.

Back at Chesapeake U appetites had been whetted. Coming so close to a national championship only convinced the AD, coaches, and rah-rah boosters that it would soon be theirs. A bigger share of the institutional budget was only logical; a new infection had spread through the campus.

Poetic justice? Some other kind? Comstock could only muse. In the greedy world of athletics, and few other circles could match that level of deceit and chicanery, a truck driver walked away with a fortune.

Just how greedy humankind can become was not yet fully clear to Comstock. A further awakening came when he was introduced to incentive compensation, an idea whose time had surely arrived in the corporate world. When a new plant, discovery, invention, or procedure burst like wildfire onto the scientific or economic scene, "pay-for-performance" spread quickly through corporate America in the seventies and eighties. It took the form of "a bonus for outstanding performance" and was reflected in short-term incentive plans and long-term payoffs.

Again, a unique brand of consultant appeared. CEOs in American business seemed always to have their telephone numbers. Perhaps, "pay-for-performance" was just their most recent product, created especially for a ready market and guaranteed to command attention.

"If your company has a good year, you want to reward the leaders who made it possible...Well, don't you?" It was a question asked freely by the experts who were not hesitant to point it out to reluctant directors. Unfortunately, the bonus for a good year was only the first step.

"You want that success to go beyond 12 months," the consultants advised. "To do that you should have a short-term incentive plan, say three years. That will spur your senior officers to repeat or even to surpass that first good year."

It was the same story across each boardroom table, and Comstock quickly learned that a third leg would be added to the compensation stool. It was called "long-term" payout."

Most CEOs developed a strategy for the three-step process as the program was broadened to include compensation of all senior officers. National meetings of executives provided the common ground for exchange of information on pay levels, stock options, bonuses, and other goodies for corporate leaders. The consultants were always present, spreading the word that executives wanted to hear.

Often a special committee chaired by a director who was himself the CEO of another company, usually in another field of endeavor, was the first to hear about the consultant's report—first, that is, after the recipient CEO had himself, perhaps tacitly, blessed the general content. By such tactics the chairman of the committee then became the spokesman for the proposal before the full board. A conspiracy of CEOs at work? Probably not. It was simply a matter of consultants advising business leaders of the best way to achieve a desired objective. The fact that the process was repeated from company to company and from industry to industry was only proof of its reliability.

Bill Comstock remembered the first time he had heard of the practice.

"In comparison with the industry," the chairman of the compensation committee began, "our leader is greatly underpaid, and he has been for years. We know he is doing an outstanding job, and we can't afford to lose him," continued the spokesman. "By adopting that short-term plan, which you have all had a chance to study," a statement that was not always true, "we can reward our chairman immediately for some of the shortfall, and by approving the long-term plan, we can build in real protection against his being lured away by one of our competitors"

Many directors were simply awestruck when they heard the presentation. While having doubts, Comstock wasn't aware of or up to date on the matter, and he willingly admitted his ignorance. He believed that the chairman was already well paid, but faced with what appeared to be overwhelming evidence to the contrary, he was in no position to protest. Was the CEO really all that great, as the committee chairman said? Just a few months earlier the company had suffered a sizable loss from one of the acquisitions that had been pursued so vigorously by the man whose compensation was now being raised so dramatically.

What was a university president to do in such circumstances? Challenge the facts? Object to the recommendations? Point out the situations—and there were several that Comstock could readily recall—in which the chairman had clearly steered the enterprise down the wrong road? Why not resign and let the other directors take the responsibility? After all, his life was busy enough with problems of the campus.

No, Comstock realized, he couldn't resign.

Across the table was the senior statesman of the board. Fortunately, most boards included at least one, and this man was personally responsible for the selection of Comstock in the first place. Not only was he a friend and in earlier years a mentor as well, but he also was a major donor to the university. Though doubtful about the proposed action and not satisfied with the rewards that were to go to the company president, Comstock retreated to the uneasy comfort of the senior director and joined the others in the unanimous vote to approve.

In due time the revolution in compensation for CEOs reached every major segment of American business, and Comstock, serving on several boards over a period of many years, witnessed a similar scenario time after time. He saw and helped in each case as three chief executives were dethroned for their inability to separate greed from performance. One of those CEOs would never be forgotten. After three straight years of gross ineptitude, the company leader insisted that he be paid the maximum bonuses because "conditions" over which he had no control "had caused the difficulties, not his actions." A pyrrhic victory! Not quite. His successor turned the business around almost immediately, making the director proud of both the firing of the one and the selection of the other. Comstock had played a leading role, a fact that did not go unnoticed by his fellow directors, for it was something unexpected of the man from a university campus.

As it turned out, something resembling a hyena—neither a bull nor a bear—had been turned loose to prey on shareholders and other innocent investors in business and industry. Bonus plans were brought forth to cover every conceivable eventuality. One major corporation decided that its senior officers should have their salaries doubled if the price of the company's stock went up by ten points and held at that level for a few days. If that weren't enough, the salaries would be doubled again for a repeat of the ten-point rise. As might be guessed, human nature—greed—took over, and the executives drove up the price by concentrating on quick pay off, collected their fat bonuses, and then went fishing as the stock settled back to new lows.

Executives broke through like race horses leaving the gate. Men and women—few of the latter to be sure—maneuvered themselves into bonuses that represented 20 to 40 times their salaries. Traders on Wall Street earned (a curious term to some investors) hundreds of millions in a single year. Greed had no bounds in those high-flying days. Some who made many millions walked away with their loot, having their wrists slapped but not enough to loosen their grip on the bankroll they carried away. A few paid fines, one or two went to jail, and businesses "restructured" in an effort to prevent such things from happening again.

As the bubble burst in real estate in the late eighties, Comstock could not forget his own ghostly memory of the mistakes he had witnessed and his own stupidity in failing to question an action at Middle Atlantic Bank. The bank began to slide toward insolvency, and he would relive for years to come the single, defining moment that marked the point of no return.

Ten directors of the bank, assembled around the conference table at corporate headquarters, were called to order for a regular and for what all assumed would be a routine meeting of the executive committee. Meeting monthly, usually the day before the meetings of the full board, this committee heard reports from senior officers, resolved differences on matters that were to be presented to the board, and in all except rare instances, controlled the agenda of the next day's meeting.

Middle Atlantic's CEO on this occasion raised eyebrows, however, when he reported that a loan of 30 million dollars had been made the previous week to the Henry James Company on unimproved land near Dulles Airport. Two directors, both experienced developers and property managers, questioned the CEO, expressing their concerns that Henry James was over extended. Even though the business still carried the founder's name, none of the James family was now associated with the once highly regarded 90-year-old company. Rumors were afloat that some of the firm's other loans were in default, and as these two directors put it, here was a loan that meant trouble.

"Is the bank committed? Can we still get out of it?" Hard questions were put to the CEO.

A long explanation by the chairman and CEO, strongly supported by the president and chief operating officer, ensued. Yes, it would be possible for the bank to back out of the loan. However, it would send the wrong message to the loan committee, those other directors whose job it was not just to approve loans but to promote them as well. Loan officers of the bank would be demoralized since they had spent weeks cultivating the borrower, and the chairman concluded, "As we all know, we don't make money unless we lend money."

The two senior officers, no doubt, thought their explanation was thorough and complete, but it failed to stop the questions. "Don't forget," the chairman said, "we get a big, fat fee up front for this loan!"

Were the loan officers looking at their year-end bonus when they negotiated with a risky borrower? Was the CEO looking at the year's bottom line as well? How about his own bonus? Short-term incentive? Was American business caught in a vicious cycle—get everything you can and take everything you can? Where was the end? Where was rationality?

Greed and the bottom line! A frightening partnership to this man from the campus.

As the tragic drama played out over the next few years, as scandal after scandal became public, as loss piled upon loss, and as culprit after culprit was exposed in the press, Comstock kept mentally returning to the meeting of those ten directors of Middle Atlantic Bank and the thirty-million-dollar loan. Billions and billions followed the same pattern. Loan officers, whose jobs depended upon their finding borrowers, searched high and low for them. Any borrower, it seemed, even those who knew full well that their circumstances would not make repayment possible, became targets. Banks, savings and loans, insurance companies, all lenders, it seemed, raced to see which could be first in putting a loan in another's pocket.

Middle Atlantic had to be rescued by a stronger financial institution. The Henry James Company was not able to repay. The loan was restructured and then restructured again.

Proud of many of his activities, satisfied with most of the results of his various efforts, Comstock would forever recall and regret his timidity as a director of Middle Atlantic. In hindsight he felt that he could have made a difference in the practices of at least one bank during those critical years if he had only been willing to stand against the tide—a position which both intuition and integrity supported. As a bank director, he let down his guard, and as a result, was carried along, failing to meet his responsibility. It was an experience never to be forgotten.

What should the CEO be paid? In the big corporations, in the big universities, in big or little? A silly question, Comstock thought. But here he was, like so many other leaders in the nation's various enterprises, trying to make sense of a changing landscape where few of the players remained the same from one day to the next.

After that eventful Middle Atlantic meeting, the president had returned to academe for what he thought would be an evening of relaxation and good feeling.

A fellow president for whom Comstock had developed a high regard was being honored. Strangely, even here greed surfaced, this time far away from the much maligned cutthroat world of industrial competition. Midtown U's president found unbelievable, selfish power-grabbing; sadly, it came in the person of his friend, the honoree.

To mark ten years of his colleague's service in the presidency, the trustees had invited a few heads of neighboring institutions, plus national and local leaders in the Washington area, to attend the black-tie dinner. Rarely could Comstock attend such a carefree event—no speech to make, no heavy hitter to cultivate. He expected to congratulate his friend and go home early.

Comstock found himself seated next to Lamar "Bud" Braddock, a leading trustee of the sister institution headed by the honoree, and a long-time friend. The two served together on one of the city's charity boards for years. As they chatted, Comstock learned that Braddock was also chairman of Chesapeake University's trustee committee on compensation.

Bill and Bud, as they had come to know each other, had always been comfortable exchanging trade secrets, seeking each other's advice, and sharing confidences without fear of misuse. Theirs was a relationship of mutual trust, a rarity in Washington.

The two men had come together from widely different interests. Bud Braddock was a hard-bargaining chain store executive; Bill Comstock, aside from four years of military service, had spent his life in the academic world. If he were to examine carefully the comfort he felt in the presence of his friend, it would be attributed to Bud's inherent belief in honesty and fairness.

Here was a successful business leader who had a full measure of integrity. Would that he could say as much for other friends and acquaintances from banking, manufacturing, and insurance whom he had known over the years, or even associates in the world of academe. Such people as Braddock seemed all too scarce.

So when Bud began his comments, it came as no surprise that the message, whatever it turned out to be, was meant for Comstock's ears only. Within the formalities just beginning to ensue from the dignitaries at the head table, it was not difficult for the quiet, private conversation to proceed unnoticed.

"I have just come," Bud began, "from a full day of meetings on the Chesapeake campus. I thought I knew our president, but I saw a new side of him today." Comstock could see that no comment was expected, only an attentive ear. Surprised somewhat by the concern evident in Braddock's voice and expression, he had a serious interest in what was coming, for his friend of long standing obviously was worried about a turn of events at Chesapeake U. Comstock at this point had finally crossed over that invisible boundary of serious doubt about the performance of Chesapeake U's president. He now thought that Dr. Mullins, after ten often rocky and uncertain years, was on the road to becoming a very successful leader. Comstock believed, as opposed to the views of some other university presidents in the region, that all the institutions of higher education benefited as each grew in stature, a position he had made clear to many audiences over the years. He often used Boston as an illustration of a center of learning, not because it was home to one great university but because it was the site of many first-rate institutions, large and small.

With genuine concern Comstock listened as his friend continued. "Tony," as the president of Chesapeake was known to every leader of the community, "threw us a curve today. When the trustees came to celebrate his first ten years, he quickly let us know that he wasn't interested in looking back, only looking at what lies ahead." Braddock hurried on as the master of ceremonies invited guests to enjoy dinner, and waiters approached to serve the soup. "He asked us today for a whopping increase in salary, and I had thought we were already paying him well. The way Tony put it was a bit unique. He said to us that his first ten years constituted a shakedown cruise. Now, however, the tumult and chaos of the early years are past, he declared, and since the university is on a steady course of progress, he feels he should be paid accordingly.

It wasn't necessary for Comstock or Braddock to remind each other that much of the trouble for the campus had been caused, particularly in the early years, by Mullins' own blunders and that the trustees had come very close on more than one occasion to asking for his resignation.

"When did Tony spring this demand on you?" Bill asked.

"It was at a breakfast meeting of the compensation committee. We began our day with him, and he was quite adamant, giving no room for negotiation. In fact, he outlined what he wanted and then left, telling us to enjoy our breakfast."

"And did you?" Comstock teased, and they both shared an exasperated chuckle.

"He asked for a ten-year no-cut contract with built-in raises commensurate with inflation, and the first year would be just double his present salary. In addition, he asked that his wife, Connie, be put on the payroll since, as he phrased it, she works full time for the university, too. Her salary would be pegged to one-half of his, and hers would be the same ten-year commitment as his." Almost as an afterthought, Bud added, "Needless to say, the trustees were shaken up."

Someone from across the table raised a glass in an informal toast to Chesapeake U, and the two friends didn't get back to their conversation until the salad course.

"What was the committee's response?" Bill inquired when others at the table turned their attention to examining the wines being served

"Well, the first thing we had was a long and loud discussion. Some trustees were mad, others were in shock, and it was mid-morning before we were settled down to a rational group. Three other committees of the board had breakfast meetings also, and they had concluded their business while we were still wrangling. The chairman of the board joined us, and others stuck their head in the door from time to time to see if we were still alive. Pretty soon the grapevine was buzzing as word spread that our committee couldn't reach a decision"

"I think all the trustees expected us to meet, give Tony a generous raise, extend his contract for three years, and then we would congratulate ourselves and begin the celebration. Instead, it took the compensation committee until lunch time to reach agreement. We knew it would not be easy to persuade the full board to agree with our decision. And it wasn't. The board spent the whole afternoon replaying every detail of Tony's ten years. Not one of his mistakes was missed, even though some trustees were quick to acknowledge his achievements."

Bill waited for more. No prying or pushing was necessary, for he knew Bud was in a real sense unburdening himself to a trusted friend. Comstock had come to appreciate such relationships over the years, in part because they were so rare.

"I said, finally, first to the committee and then to the full board after I saw the crisis that was brewing, that we should meet Tony's demand. If this is what it takes to nail him down for ten years, let's do it. Let's look at the situation as though we have invested the first decade in training him for the second term and now the university will make real progress with Tony at the helm. We know that the last couple of years have been his best. In fact, he gives every indication of having reached the level of experience and maturity necessary to give him a statesmanlike position among university leaders in the country. Yes, I agree, I told the trustees," continued Bud. "His price is high, but I believe he will earn it, and if meeting his contract demands is what he wants, I'm in favor of agreement, and then we can all get on with the job." That was Bud's report of a frenetic day in the life of a university board of trustees.

President Mullins responded to the accolades and messages read by the master of ceremonies, including one from the President of the United States, with enthusiasm coupled with the right balance of dignity.

Those among the more than 500 assembled who knew nothing of the harangues earlier in the day went home with renewed pride in their institution. That three trustees resigned within the next 30 days was known only to a few within the university and caused no public embarrassment. One of the three was too well known and too highly respected, however, for his departure to go unnoticed for long.

Some 18 months later, the editor of the student newspaper learned about Mullins' demands and the board's action. He picked up information on the president's new salary level when the annual report required of non-profit organizations by the IRS was carried in the city's leading newspapers. Mullins, thinking the campus publication was consumed with reporting and editorializing on student social and athletic activities, was caught completely by surprise by the blazing headline on the front page, "Prexy Leads Pack with New Salary," and underneath in bold, glaring print, "Connie Makes Payroll Debut." These attention-getting headlines were followed with embarrassing details. Further down, a sub-head raised a question: "Maybe the highest paid university president in the country?" The story drove home the new ground of Mullins' leadership. The IRS reports on Chesapeake and other universities didn't carry the additional details that the article included. Someone had talked, and the student editor had found the voice.

More was said on the editorial page. "Is our president really the best among his peers? Is Chesapeake the highest quality, the richest, the most prestigious? Will our degrees, when we receive them, carry greater weight than those of Harvard, Yale, or Princeton? No! Our leader," the editorial concluded, "is simply greedy, and students are being ripped off again."

Mullins dug in for the attacks which he knew would follow. Fortunately for him, the campus paper didn't publish again until Monday, and with many students headed home for the weekend he had a little time to prepare for his next move.

But the student editor didn't know everything. What was to come could hardly have been programmed by even the most sinister member of the Chesapeake University family.

Before the faculty could begin its own inquiry into the president's compensation package (faculties are notoriously slow to act) an item buried in the back pages of one of the local gossip columns caught the attention of some readers. The article simply reported that Connie Mullins had gone to work for a ladies' apparel shop some weeks previously. The article quoted her as saying she would be working full time and would participate in all phases of the business—selection, buying, marketing, and management.

What did this mean for her service to Chesapeake U where her husband was into the second decade of his tenure and where she reportedly was on the university's payroll? Before the dust could settle from this development, an announcement came from the Chesapeake campus that President Mullins had requested and had been granted a leave of absence because of health problems. Bombarded with inquiries, the campus public relations office issued a second bulletin reporting that Mullins had been warned by his physician to slow down and to take things easier or suffer frightening consequences. Instead of allaying curiosity, each statement only raised more questions. Why did Mullins leave so abruptly? Where did he go? How can he be reached? Is Connie with him? The man named to be acting president during the interim either couldn't or wouldn't supply any answers. Neither would the chairman of the board.

Left with a hovering tragedy, unseemly behavior, or downright chicanery, the campus was thrown into rampant conjecture, speculation, and foreboding. Every classroom and laboratory, every extra-curricular activity was permeated with curiosity. If a professor tried to avoid the subject in his lecture, a student would raise a question; if students didn't initiate the topic, the faculty member would introduce it.

Proving that time does indeed heal, the campus slowly and painfully became somewhat rehabilitated from its paralysis. The acting president was fortunately one who had the respect of all constituencies, and he took a number of actions that helped return the university to a place of teaching and learning. Conditions were quite calm and constructive some three months later when a rather lengthy letter appeared as a special release from the campus news office. It was signed by Anthony K. Mullins and in it he apologized for leaving so abruptly, reported that he was being treated at an undisclosed medical center, was feeling much better, and looked forward to his return at the end of the year.

Too many questions were still left unanswered, however, for the message to satisfy its readers. Instead of calming and reassuring, the news reignited the fires of curiosity, giving further cause for skepticism. "If the president, after all this time," one professor told the university faculty at its regular meeting only a couple of days later, "will tell us only what appears in his letter, then we must demand that the board of trustees tell us what is really happening. This is our university, one to which we are giving our lives, and we demand answers from the trustees."

As a courtesy and for effective campus political reasons, members of the board always received copies of the minutes of faculty meetings, but they didn't have to wait to receive the record to learn about the professor's statement. The meeting had hardly been adjourned before a reporter from the student newspaper was on the phone to the chairman, passing along the gist of the faculty discussion and asking what the board would do in response.

Accustomed to conducting his company's business behind the closed doors of his own office, the chairman was still trying to understand how every faculty member and even the newest student on campus seemed to know everything about the institution and about its board members—how many meetings trustees missed, what environmental laws their companies were breaking, what political party they had supported, how much money each had given to the university, and on and on.

Somehow he had to have some time—time away from reporter's questions, time to think, time to discuss the situation with a few other trustees, time to get help. So he said to the reporter, hoping to get some of that time, "I'm having a meeting of the executive committee very shortly, and we will let you know then how the matter stands."

"Mr. Chairman," the student pushed on before the trustee had finished, "can I attend that meeting? You see, these things are pretty important to the students. After all, it is our university."

Here it was again—our university. How many times must he hear that and from how many sources! But that wasn't the point. He could take comfort in his reply, "Well, you know the policy of the board, established years ago and reaffirmed just last spring. All meetings are closed to the press and to the public, but," in a kind of sop to the student, he added, "I'll let you know what happens."

Another long, long period of inaction ensued. Apparently, the executive committee didn't meet promptly as the chairman had indicated. Members were traveling or were pulled away by private matters. It was a difficult time, and other excuses were offered as inquiries kept coming from key faculty members, leaders of student groups, and media people from the community.

Goodness knows, he thought to himself, I have had no problem in running my own business, but Chesapeake University is a totally different animal. To damage the institution with his own ineptitude, with some stupid mistake on his part, was of deep concern to him. Here was a man with all the proper credentials—independent wealth, community respect, proven leadership, and a full measure of altruism. He sincerely wanted the best possible education for Chesapeake students and the most favorable circumstances in which professors could teach and pursue their scholarship. It was neither pride nor ambition that had prompted him to accept the chairmanship. Here was a man who wanted to help make a better world, but each turn of campus events seemed to result in another frustration, another obstacle.

Would the trustees be able to work out a solution before the suspected scandal erupted? They were trying mightily to do so and to keep the whole sorry mess, if rumors were true, from exploding in their faces.

Connie Mullins had indeed left the university. She had resigned her position on the payroll and had taken the job as announced in the news item. But there was more. She had moved out of the president's house and was living on the other side of town in a small apartment listed under the lady's name who owned the apparel shop where she worked. Tony Mullins had been having an affair for at least a couple of years with one of the city's social leaders and an active alumna of Chesapeake U.

The five trustees who made up the executive committee of the board—the chairman, plus the four chairmen of the other standing committees—

dared not share the information with even the rest of the board lest it be leaked to the press. It most certainly would have been leaked since there were at least two members who were ready to fire Mullins anyway. The executive committee must somehow persuade Mullins to leave the university. It was unthinkable to these five trustees that he could ever come back, let alone return to the presidency. But the president was continuing to be as obstreperous with his continuance into a second decade as he had been with his compensation.

Lawyers, who had long been involved for both parties, succeeded, however, in reaching an agreement.

Again, it fell to the campus public information officer to release the news. His release simply said that President Mullins had requested that he not return as president but that he step down from that office and come back as professor of plant genetics, his field of scholarship and the department in which he held a tenured position.

The sigh of relief brought on by the announcement was brief. Within days the grapevine began to drip with news of the other woman, of Connie's departure, of the separation package which the trustees had agreed to give Mullins—much, much more than faculty or students found reasonable. The renewed uproar was louder than any before it.

"Greed, greed, and more greed," screamed the student paper! Special meetings of the faculty, a torchlight parade that poured into the city streets, and calls from wealthy alumni led the trustees to seek—and get—a new, less generous separation package for Mullins, plus an agreement that he not return to the university in any capacity. It all led to eventual closure of the unfortunate episode.

What is reasonable or what is unreasonable may, indeed, be hard to define when a high-ranking officer's compensation is concerned. But turmoil seems certain to follow on a campus where the president's salary and perks are out-of-line.

Adelphi University, a medium-size private university on Long Island, later became a battleground for such differences. The turmoil eventually became so serious that it attracted formal hearings by a committee of the New York State Board of Regents. Each constituency had its own interest. Students saw their tuition going to support unreasonable compensation for the president; faculty members saw their own salaries suffering because of the seeming excesses; alumni felt embarrassed at the unfavorable publicity of their alma mater; and trustees had difficulty defending their stewardship of the institution. Amid charges and countercharges, all parties seemed to lose, just as everyone had lost as a result of the Chesapeake University episode.

It was only a few weeks before Bud Braddock and Bill Comstock sat down together again. Following a regular meeting of the Community Services Board where both had served for a number of years, Braddock issued a spur-of-the-moment invitation to lunch, and Comstock accepted.

Both men knew the Chesapeake U fiasco would be the primary subject discussed.

"I still can't understand the furor over the financial package we worked out for Mullins. As I thought about it, it was generous but not outrageous. But it sure brought down a hail storm," Bud confided to his old friend.

"Hindsight is usually so clear," Comstock replied, as a gesture of comfort, "and your experience with Tony is but another good example."

"Of course," continued Braddock, "I'll never get used to the fact that everything done in a university is on the evening news that same day. We do have a lot more privacy in business."

"That's for sure," Comstock agreed. Then, backing off a bit, perhaps to gain a longer-range perspective, Midtown's president added, "In spite of those negative news reports, it seems to me that the general public does not really want to see the darker side of human nature—arrogance, greed, insolence—embroiled in an institution whose basic purpose is to civilize all of us."

"By the way, Bud, I need your help. Just yesterday I was invited to speak to a group of CEOs from private industry and a few university presidents on the topic we've been talking about. 'The Right Pay for the CEO.' With the meeting a month away I'll have time to put some thoughts on paper, and if I can impose on you, I'd like very much for you to give me your reaction."

"You bet. I'll take a look. I may learn something!"

"Can't we all," Comstock agreed.

What had begun as a meeting in which two good friends could unburden themselves over a sandwich had developed into an important follow-up activity. Mutual respect had grown over the years as these two men shared their interest in both business and education. Work in and for universities had created a special bond, essentially a sacred trust which went far beyond day-to-day living. Braddock and Comstock had already learned much from each other; both anticipated continuation of their joint search for further understanding.

Bill Comstock felt deep sorrow for Tony Mullins and Chesapeake U. He knew that all universities suffered when any one of them was stained by the misbehavior of a professor, trustee, or student, and even more by a scandal on the president. Bud Braddock, successful in business, felt he had stumbled in his responsibility as a trustee. He did not want to see another such episode—ever. Indeed, he wanted to see what his friend might have to say on the subject.

How to tackle the topic took Comstock to his desk that very evening. It was late, well after ten, following a meeting on campus with student leaders, before he could ask himself how he would approach the presentation.

Looking carefully at the faxed copy of the invitation, Midtown's president got further insight.

"The assembled leaders," it read, "will take stock of practices and trends in philanthropy in America. Since the CEO's compensation has become somewhat of a controversial issue in recent years, the planning group would like to open the conference with that topic."

What an understatement, thought Comstock as he mused about compensation, that talk of show hosts, professional athletes, Wall Street traders, CEOs in industry, leaders in certain philanthropies, and, yes, a few university presidents. Having gotten into the subject, Comstock did not put down his pencil until after midnight. But he had found his approach. Putting the meat on the bones would be routine.

Comstock decided to select two leaders, one at the top in private enterprise and the other from the non-profit sector. From big business it could be IBM, General Motors, ExxonMobil, Disney, or a host of others. He chose General Motors. From the tax-exempt area there was only one choice for this academic leader; it had to be Harvard University.

As he sat down a few days later to put on paper some of the possibilities for constructing what would turn out to be a 20-minute presentation to the conference, Comstock's first task was to place each of the selected leaders in his appropriate niche within his particular activity and in the great public arena.

Immediately upon their appointment, the CEO of General Motors and the president of Harvard achieved—it might be better described as having inherited—positions of top leadership in their respective fields. To Comstock it was easy to see that the positions brought to each appointee wide public recognition and acceptance of their individual responsibilities. One automatically received recognition as a world leader in business and industry, the other in education. Serious attention would be given, Comstock wrote, to all that they would say or write, and to whatever they would do.

Instant prestige and far-reaching influence would accompany the holder of each office. Powerful constituencies would be in place to aid, abet, or confront each leader.

Bill Comstock had no trouble drawing parallels between the two positions. He saw the GM leader having to meet the demand for high quality products, producing them more economically, keeping morale high among employees, and satisfying the desire of stockholders for higher earnings. Harvard's president, he noted, would be expected to look for new ways of learning and teaching to set the stage for breakthroughs of new knowledge and to suggest new avenues for attacking the world's ethical and moral dilemmas.

It was quickly apparent to Comstock that his audience would have no difficulty accepting the premise that Harvard's president and the CEO of GM would each carry awesome responsibility, but each, too, would be constantly surrounded by unparalleled opportunity. Furthermore, he would observe, both leaders would have tremendous but not unlimited power.

For Comstock outlining the similarities of the two positions was only stage setting for the main point he wished to make—how these two front-running offices in our society differ.

His assigned topic for the keynote spot on the program gave him the opening he wanted: "Should the CEO of General Motors and the president of Harvard be paid the same?"

"Heavens, no!"

It took no genius to anticipate that his audience would be unanimous in its response. But Comstock's plan was to go further, much further, in trying to clear up and clear out the fuzzy thinking that was causing the wrangling over compensation in so much of American life.

"Blurring is our problem," he wrote. "Too often, governing boards of colleges and universities have begun to equate the president of their institutions with the CEO in a profit-making corporation. And you men are guilty (there still were no women among the group) because you have come to dominate the debate on questions of compensation for the president. But it isn't all your fault," he continued, "the presidents themselves have remained silent as you have run up more yardage in the form of increased salary and new perks. They, too, have succumbed to the blurring of lines between the two areas of endeavor."

Aiming his next remarks at the interface between business and education, Comstock put in a few thoughts intended for the broader audiences of philanthropy and private enterprise.

"In the world of corporate business we expect the CEO of a giant company to have a giant-like compensation package It is generally accepted, too, that he will benefit further from whatever financial success the company may experience under his stewardship. We know that size of the enterprise helps significantly in creating the pecking order of its CEO among his peers. To grow or to expand the business serves to move the CEO up in that hierarchy. If he handles labor problems with skill, solves production snarls, and adopts successful marketing strategies, the leader's standing rises. Size alone often establishes the starting point, and in today's interdependent economy that pecking order encircles the globe.

"But Harvard University and the rest of the non-profit world are governed differently. What is adequate, fair, and reasonable compensation for a non-profit institution or organization cannot be compared with a business, profit-making enterprise without great risk. One depends upon stockholders—people who invest money in order to make money—for their continuance; the other must look to philanthropy—money donated for goodwill and for the advancement of human welfare, for survival."

"And pecking order among university presidents? Do factors in academe differ from those in the profit-making world? Yes, indeed." Comstock was determined to hit the greedy among his own university colleagues.

"Rank among peers is established by the prestige which the institution holds in the eyes of the world. Professional academics may apply a slightly different standard in the short term, but, generally speaking, the acclaim of the general public places universities on their respective landings of the educational staircase. A university president, by his actions or inactions, can move the institution either up or down in that empirical but highly visible order. One who drives his own compensation beyond a reasonable zone moves both himself and his institution down in the eyes of those who follow such matters.

"Therefore, what is reasonable and acceptable at GM is unthinkable for Harvard and vice versa. Which is the more important position? That too, has no reasonable answer. Why then are we having difficulty keeping the lines between non-profit and for-profit enterprises clear and precise? It could be that, like a great river, the profit-making corporate world has overflowed into the charitable arena. Unless contained, the flood waters of money-making, pushed by leaders whose objectives are of the highest order, will, unfortunately, do irreparable damage to the eleemosynary sector of our society."

Comstock had gone far enough in his first draft. He sent a copy across town by messenger so Bud Braddock could take a look. Bud wasted no time. He called for a ten-minute stop on his way to an appointment.

"Bill, I like your comments," he began, "but I don't think you went far enough."

"In what way? I thought I was rather hard-hitting," Midtown's president replied.

"You went far enough for me to see the real difference between the profit-making enterprises in our society and the philanthropic ones. Yet you stopped short of driving it home. I see in the university leader the unmistakable element of sacrifice." Not waiting for his friend to reply, Braddock plowed ahead.

"You picked the right example. Obviously, the president of Harvard sacrifices heavily in order to serve—to serve a great university and its constituencies. And for what purpose? All in order that Harvard may be of still greater service to humanity."

"Bill, in reading between the lines—your lines—I see the person's sacrifice as being the ingredient that separates one world from the other. Whether it is the Salvation Army, Red Cross, United Way, or Chesapeake University, those who choose to spend their lives in such work are expected to make sacrifices. Am I not correct?" Braddock paused a moment to invite response. While Comstock wrestled for the right comment, his friend continued.

"Tony Mullins didn't have that spirit of sacrifice. I see it now. While he wanted the prestige of being a university president, he wanted to keep the income and perks of a profit-making business. It mattered not to him that thousands before had sacrificed over decades to make Chesapeake what it is today."

"Yes, yes," now ready to respond and to round out the package, Comstock spoke.

"Bud, our major ingredient goes back to psychic income. It is present in much of our lives. Money could never compensate for the honor of serving as president of Harvard. On the other hand we see it at every level of work—the public health nurse making her rounds, the classroom teacher in the woods of rural America or the slums of the inner city. It is the fuel that makes life civilized, and it follows that such service is its own reward. Unless a person feels good about such work, understands the sacrifice being made, and is satisfied—yes, more than satisfied, proud is a better word—with his role in that particular endeavor, then it is the wrong place for him to be.

"For many, it is the honor that counts." Becoming self-conscious, Comstock paused. He felt himself mounting the soap box. That was out of line with this friend who needed no preaching.

"And then," Braddock picked up, "we look at public service. Whether it is elected office, congressman or governor, legislator or sheriff, we know that many seek the honor to serve, sacrificing income and wealth. Others seek the office only to use it to feather their own nests."

"You are so right," agreed his friend.

Then, turning back to the task before him, Comstock added, "I'm afraid the conference has a mammoth task before it. As for my part, I shall rewrite the speech. I'll focus on psychic income and honor and the satisfaction of service. I hope that some of it hits home!"

"One more word of advice," Braddock added as he rose to leave. "Tell those CEOs from business to reset their priorities; tell them to get rid of university presidents whose driving force is personal greed; and tell them, too, that sacrifice is a hundred times more rewarding than the dollar."

Compensation—What a Fuss

Bill Comstock spent many hours within the period of just a few days hammering out the final version of his speech. Seldom had he taken an assignment so seriously. Accustomed to speaking to many audiences and carrying the message of learning, teaching, and research, Midtown's president could, with ease, influence public officials, alumni, and the general public to a better understanding and appreciation of education and its many roles in our society. In Colonial Williamsburg, where the group would meet, he was determined to show, too, that the thousands of men and women who were devoting their lives to the cause of higher learning were spurred on by the spirit of sacrifice and service. If that was not the driving force, they ought to be elsewhere!

To his great surprise and delight, who should be sitting on the front row of the opening session but Bud Braddock. He had not been invited, but after he learned of the conference from his friend, Braddock had "wrangled an invitation," he later explained, "from the powers that be."

"Bill," he said, "I came for two reasons. I wanted to hear your speech, especially after our discussion in your office. Then, I wanted to be on hand to hear you enlighten this bunch." Truth was, most of the "bunch" were friends and acquaintances of Braddock.

Years later, governing boards, presidents of colleges and universities, and CEOs of business and industry far and wide were still discussing compensation, psychic income, sacrifice and honor, all of which attested to the success of a single conference which had involved only a few people. Midtown's president always remembered that it was his friend in industry, a devoted trustee of another university, who led him to put the red meat into his speech.

VI

Women, Boards, CEOs, and Discrimination

"Well, you wouldn't want to work for a woman, would you?"

It wasn't a particularly challenging remark, nothing confrontational in the tone. It was a fact of life simply stated. The academic world, insofar as Midtown University represented that world, was just not ready for a female president. And the chairman of the search committee, explaining to the old treasurer of the institution why a certain candidate had been selected, closed all further questioning by pointing out that the next name on the list was that of a woman.

Both treasurer and trustee were fully satisfied with the results of the lengthy search for a new CEO. No one knew how the female candidate might have viewed developments–or seemed to care.

The fact that a search committee, which included women, had concluded that a woman should not hold the office of president of this major American university went unchallenged. History, the long march of history, was simply continuing.

In the boardrooms and executive offices of academe, private business, and government women still remain a distant second to their male counterparts. No major world culture yet places women on an equal footing with men. Some progress is being made, but ever so slowly.

Comstock first became aware of the imbalance, "something is wrong here," while a young professor in an Ivy League university. Women students consistently won the lion's share of academic honors, led throughout their college years in grades by wide margins, and suffered only a fraction of the disciplinary casualties of their male classmates. Yet, it was the men who gained acceptance in far greater numbers year after year at the most selective schools of medicine, law, business, and other graduate study. And, as Comstock learned still later, males and females were admitted as freshman on the basis of quota; otherwise each class would have included more women.

Then came legislation calling for equal pay for equal work. Comstock would never forget its first application at Midtown U.

When directed to adjust faculty salaries to correct past inequities, Dean Land of the College of Arts and Sciences couldn't bring himself to take such a giant step. He went halfway and, as he explained, that action would give the women members of his faculty their highest raises in history! When told that such big increases only confirmed the blatant gap that had previously existed in salaries, he accepted the new numbers that the comptroller supplied. But any thought of fairness or equality escaped the dean, blinded as he was with the feeling of wasting thousands of dollars. Why pay the women as much as men? It had never been done, and there was no necessity for doing it now. And besides, using all that money to bring along the pay of women would leave less for future raises for men. To one who had scratched and scrambled to balance budgets year after year and had saved the university many thousands in the process, Dean Land thought this new policy, supported by federal legislation, was the silliest waste he could envision. The whole experience made him think about his forthcoming retirement.

Women were left behind in the corporate world as well, and Comstock would soon witness a flagrant case. It happened in plain view of all the directors of Merchandise Managers, Inc., a board which the vigorous academic had joined only a year earlier. Suzanne Brady was the woman involved. She was only 35 years of age, but she already had a decade of corporate legal experience. Ms. Brady had been handed the hottest problem facing the company—to map a strategy to stop an unfriendly takeover by a financially stronger competitor. Of course, the company's chief counsel was officially in charge, but Ms. Brady, listed in the corporate directory as assistant to the chief counsel, did all the work.

Eight months later, Merchandise Managers was still independent, the challenge had been skillfully thwarted, and top management was breathing easier. The chief counsel was still the chief, and his assistant was still the assistant. Fortunately, directors had not only witnessed the high stakes drama, but they also became major players themselves in succeeding chapters as each scene unfolded. Suzanne Brady had saved the company, and this time outside directors learned firsthand what insiders had known for a long time—the assistant was the brains of the legal department.

Through the months of study, briefings, and special meetings, directors viewed a continuous parade of experts, advisors, and authorities from the legal and financial world of mergers and acquisitions. Guiding the procession with uncanny insight was Ms. Brady always, it seemed, several steps ahead of unfolding events. Through it all, she continued to defer to her boss, never once appearing to upstage him.

After the victory, and all concerned considered it a monumental one, directors began to ask questions of the CEO about the future of Suzanne Brady. Would she get a bonus? How about a promotion? A significant raise? A new title?

Responses were fuzzy, indefinite, unclear. Obviously, the CEO had never even thought about rewarding an assistant with special recognition for making an outstanding contribution to the company. "It would be difficult," he said, "to single out the assistant for special honors without also rewarding her superior."

Comstock could hardly contain himself. Did other directors not see, as he did, the seldom-to-be-matched contribution of this young, professional woman to the enterprise? Would nothing be done to note her accomplishments? Was this corporation as blind to equity for women as the old dean back on campus?

Just how far were women behind in equal-pay-for-equal-work and equal-recognition-for-equal-achievement? Comstock learned as he informally sounded out other directors in the weeks ahead. Only one other board member was willing to express any concern whatsoever, and then only privately. These were the directors who had seen the genius of Ms. Brady with their own eyes. Pulling in his horns—he didn't want to become known as a "women's libber"—Comstock retreated to the campus, another place where women were constantly shortchanged.

A chance meeting with another director of Merchandise Managers at a local club patronized by business and professional leaders of the community (membership was restricted to men) gave the frustrated university president a slight ray of hope. Taking a seat at the community table, the friend said surprisingly, "Bill, you were right to ask how Suzanne Brady could be properly rewarded for her outstanding work at M M, Inc."

"But you saw how much of a shock it was to the CEO! It was apparent such an idea had never entered his head," Comstock replied.

Carl Burris, his fellow director and unscheduled luncheon companion, was an unusual person. A good student in his undergraduate years, he also had made a better than average record in law school. But while studying law, he was still searching for a career not necessarily limited to legal practice. Working as a student intern in the trust department of a local bank, Burris was immediately attracted to banking, and having made a good impression during the summer, he was asked to join the staff of the bank upon graduation.

Thirty-five years later Carl G. Burris was not only CEO of that bank, but he was also recognized as one of Washington's business and community leaders. Merchandise Managers was only one of the several corporate boards on which he served.

The unfair treatment of Ms. Brady was on his mind, but like many bankers, he treaded lightly on society's mores, ever fearful of rocking the boat. Heaven forbid, never irritate a customer! Courting borrowers and depositors and getting them to use your bank for their financial activities seemed to Comstock to be foremost on the minds of the bankers he knew.

For Burris to bring up the matter, for him even to remember, caused Comstock to take hope. If this conservative, never-ruffle-the-feathers banker recognized the injustice being done to this woman, there was hope others might also be sensitive to Ms. Brady's dilemma.

The academician, having trained himself to be a good listener, waited to hear more. The banker obliged.

"If the chief (another common reference to the CEO) isn't going to do anything, what should we do? I mean what should the directors do?"

Having already canvassed, casually and obliquely, other opinion leaders among the directors, Bill Comstock could not be optimistic. "Let's wait and see if there is any follow-up from either senior officers or other board members," he replied.

Months later, nothing had been done; the subject had not been raised by anyone.

After a year in which Ms. Brady was not seen at any meetings of the board or its committees, the corporate secretary reported that she had left the company to go into private practice. Twenty years later, she was still an unknown in the Washington legal community, her contribution to Merchandise Managers unheralded, and her work in her new firm unrewarded. She had gone to the back room of the firm, working entirely on the research so necessary to successful legal service to clients, out of sight and without recognition even on the company letterhead. Frustrated, disappointed, or satisfied, her former associates at Merchandise did not know or seem to care.

Comstock saw a new side of Carl Burris, however. The flickering light from Burris was one the banking world would never extinguish. Years later it burned brightly, and in a way that enlightened the whole city.

It came with the battle over admitting women to the Oxbranch Club.

Long the playground of the business elite, the club catered to and was run by the captains of industry, whether CEOs or other senior officers, by lawyers who were both legislators and lobbyists (often alternating one with the other), by diplomats, and by a non-resident membership list that read like a who's who of political and financial influence in the whole country. Sitting down to lunch in the members' dining room on any given day, you would likely have a man on your right or left or across the table who had recently returned from Russia, Saudi Arabia, China, Israel, or Capital Hill. Both metropolitan and cosmopolitan, the club, located at the center of the city's commercial life, was the meeting place for Washington's "cliff dwellers" and its traveling wheelers and dealers.

But it had no women members. Women could come, and they were graciously welcomed, as guests for dinner, but "not for lunch." It was in that historic bastion of male chauvinism that Carl Burris, the cautious banker, released his decades-long frustration over female exploitation.

At a meeting of the board of governors called to handle routine business but open to the full membership and unusually well attended, Burris could contain himself no longer.

"Gentlemen, the time has come to admit women to this establishment. Indeed, it is long overdue." Continuing before others could recover from the shock—the item was neither on the agenda nor was it anticipated—the mad old banker, as he was later branded by another governor, launched his full broadside.

"We have had our heads in the sand long enough. It is a disgrace for us to discriminate against women. They must be given the opportunity for full membership in this club—immediately. Now I know the hundred reasons why it can't be done. Why it can't be done now. Why it couldn't be done in earlier years, and why it should wait. I'm tired of waiting, and I'm not going to wait any longer."

No one at the table could remember such an outburst from Burris. He was always one of the quiet members of the board, listening courteously, seeming to weigh his words with care, hesitant to disagree with opinions of others, and at least until now not much interested in anything at the club except the finances.

The outburst was greeted with silence, a silence Burris did not wait long to break.

"For some time I thought about resigning from the board; then I considered leaving the club. But I'm staying. This is my club. I'll be a member until I'm carried out for the last time—to the cemetery, that is. To resign, leave the club, lick my wounds, drop out of sight, go elsewhere—all would leave Oxbranch the same old archaic monstrosity it is now. It's nothing but a chauvinistic mausoleum!"

What a description! What wording! Was Burris actually referring to written notes as he spoke? Yes. Those seated within view saw the scribbled sheet Carl had deftly placed on top of club reports to be reviewed. This was no instantly provoked tirade; even the pointed words had been carefully put together well before the otherwise routine meeting began.

Whether planned or not, the effect on the rest of the members was sobering. Both surprised and shocked, they were also cowed. Unease filled the air. Guilt smacked more than one of his colleagues—those who had sympathy for the odious treatment of women but didn't have the courage to voice their honest feelings, others who just didn't want to get involved, still others whose wives and children had made the problem a matter of family discussion.

There were the diehards; they had voiced their positions on many occasions. Men were put on this earth to be the leaders, to make the decisions; women were to follow, to defer, to be subservient.

Battle lines had been drawn. Carl Burris, the shrewd, often gentle banker, had thrown down the gauntlet. Each of several defenders of the status quo waited for others to take up the challenge. It didn't come.

As quiet prevailed, there was a bit of squirming, sipping from water glasses, shuffling of feet. Finally, when it became embarrassingly apparent that no member would break the silence, the chairman meekly raised the question of how the board might best proceed to consider the "request," as he termed Burris' demand. It remained for Burris to respond.

"I suggest, Mr. Chairman," he responded in such a calm and steady manner that it was hard to believe it was the same person who just a few minutes earlier had addressed the group with a reddened, angry face, "that you appoint a special committee to consider ways of bringing women into the membership of this club and that the members of that committee be instructed to expedite their work. I further suggest that the committee report each month to the board of governors as to its progress."

Results were astounding. Grumbling, griping, and backbiting dominated private conversations. An undercurrent of discontent, in spite of its being fueled by many of the old guard for several weeks, never got off the ground. Within 12 months the Oxbranch Club had voted into membership several local women from business and professional fields. Before the second year had ended, many members were speaking proudly of the change that had been made, more than one allowing himself to take some of the credit!

From a membership that numbered upwards of 3,000, one member, Carl Burris, had made a difference. To Bill Comstock the work of his friend had been heartwarming. The academic world had no corner on the vision and courage necessary to correct society's ills. He would be hard put to find a comparable victory for fair treatment of women in all of his years in academic life. Instead, the thought that the university was not yet ready for a woman president kept haunting him. It was a sad story—a particularly troubling one in the history of Midtown U.

Barbara Newcomb could only be described as brilliant, level-headed, and seasoned. After a decade as president of one of America's leading women's colleges, she served a stint as an ambassador, representing the country's interests in the world's cultural, educational, and scientific circles. Then came a period of leadership as head of a statewide system of higher education—eight universities under her supervision. Experienced? This woman had faced and resolved with phenomenal success the many and varied problems of both private and public institutions of higher learning. Yet, she could not succeed to the next campus because the chairman of the search committee put up that Berlin Wall of academe: "You wouldn't want to work for a woman!"

Protocol required Comstock to stand on the sidelines while the tragedy unfolded; it was his own successor who was being chosen. While clear of any direct responsibility, he could never forgive himself for failing to intervene. For him and for the few others who knew the full story of events, it was a chapter in the history of Midtown which would live in infamy. The story must be told, Comstock concluded, and he was the only one who would dare write down the facts.

Not wanting to work for a woman, as it turned out, was the feeble excuse that led to the appointment of a new, male president who quickly became involved in serious controversy, failed to gain the support of Midtown's several constituencies, and whose behavior threw the campus into turmoil. Members of the governing board, determined not to admit a mistake in selection, soon remained the lone supporters of the new CEO.

The selection process for the new president of Midtown University, as a few people learned later, had been cleverly rigged.

Following common procedure, trustees of the university, recognizing their need for guidance in the process of selecting a new president, secured the services of a reputable educational organization, neither knowing nor suspecting what would follow. The consulting firm engaged ranked among the top three such groups in the entire country. When one of the senior partners was chosen to handle the work at MU, the trustees had no cause for questioning. It was a perfect setting for what followed.

After months of preliminaries during which more than 200 names were screened, the final dozen candidates were tagged and the stage set for the committee to see only the best of the entire group. The consultant, Dr. Thomas McNulty, was in a position to work his mischief.

Going through the armload of paper that applicants had submitted, adding letters of recommendation from a wide range of references, carefully noting the strengths and weaknesses of the dozen survivors, McNulty fashioned the list to make sure that three particular names remained. If these were included among the finalists, the consultant then had a good chance of accomplishing his goal—placing a long-time friend in the presidency of Midtown U, an ambition the friend had many times confided to McNulty to be a lifelong desire.

With a diverse selection committee—trustees, faculty members, students, and alumni were all represented—McNulty knew the task would not be easy. But this consultant had influenced more than one such committee, and he knew all the tricks—all the ways to fool search committees! And if successful? Well, there would be long-lasting monetary and psychic rewards. He had already learned that Roger B. Gordon paid well for favors.

But he struck a snag. Ten of the twelve invited for interviews accepted. As often happens, individual situations changed from the time of the initial application to the time for campus visits—often a period of several months—so two had eliminated themselves from further consideration. With the usual scheduling problems it required another month for the committee to see each of the remaining ten. Then the all-important meeting was called for further reducing the list. Five was the agreed upon number for final review. McNulty had wanted just three, but he didn't want to come down too hard on the group at that stage, so he went along. One surprise showed up, however. Two or three members insisted on making Barbara Newcomb a member of the final five. Again, the consultant accepted the decision without alienating any of the members.

The presence of a woman among the finalists for such an important post had occurred before in other searches, but seldom when McNulty was the chief consultant.

Returning to his office, Tom McNulty went to work. Again, following normal procedure, it was his responsibility to contact the five candidates and inform them of their presence on the final roster. A less pleasant task was to inform the others they had come to the end of the road, but this presented no embarrassment. McNulty had done it many times.

In talking with each of the finalists, McNulty learned of even more recent developments. One on the list, perhaps the strongest candidate of all if McNulty were to be completely objective about the matter, was about ready to remove himself from further consideration.

"I have been advised that I should stay put. Our president is retiring in another year, and I've been given strong indications that the job is mine if I want it," explained the finalist. His was a larger institution than MU, financially stronger and perhaps more importantly for this man, he had spent his entire 30 years of professional work on the campus.

McNulty had an answer.

"Why not remain on the list at Midtown and see what the results are? You could emerge as an even stronger candidate on your home base." The finalist, not having worried through other presidential searches—he was not a job seeker—and hearing such advice from a very experienced consultant, readily accepted.

Knowing a powerful member of the governing board of the other institution, McNulty called him at home late at night, and with a little delicate questioning confirmed what he had heard earlier from the applicant.

That information made McNulty's plan much simpler. He could put the strongest candidate at the top, knowing now with certainty that he would not accept the post at MU if it were offered and thus remove the biggest obstacle to getting the presidency for his friend. But that would leave Barbara Newcomb one among four instead of one among five, improving her chances for appointment since her credentials were stronger than those of her competitors. McNulty realized he had to get her out of the running for the presidency before he could put his friend in the job.

As the committee assembled for the all-important task of ranking the final five, Roger Gordon's picture was painted much brighter. McNulty used an old device; he reworked the thick folders containing each candidate's credentials. By carefully crafting a one-page summary on each of the five from the voluminous materials which had been accumulated, the consultant was able to raise to the number-one spot a candidate he knew would turn down an offer when it came to him. He put his friend next in line in second place; and then in an effort to freeze out the rest placed a woman in the third slot. It was very clever, but would it hold together?

McNulty had read the committee like a never-fail recipe.

After number one turned down the offer, a complete surprise to the committee but precisely what McNulty anticipated, it was easy to lead the group in hot pursuit of the second name on the list, the strategically placed Gordon. When a single voice suggested another meeting of the full group in order to review the order of those remaining, the chairman, with firm advice from the consultant, turned it down. Moving promptly was even more important now than ever, it was agreed. What if the next person on the list also rejected an offer? There was no time to wait.

Fatigue had already set in. McNulty was being well paid. It mattered not to him how long the process might drag out; for the committee members, however, it was extra duty. Student members had grown impatient. (Gordon had won them early with his promise to "bring students into every phase of campus life"). Faculty members had given up precious time from research, from family, and from consulting because of late afternoon and evening meetings, interviews, cross-checking of references, and reports back to their colleagues. Squeezing time for everything that was neccessary in the search was even more difficult for trustees and alumni representatives, all business and professional people. The prospect of still further delay and the possibility of losing the next candidate were too much for them. It was not difficult for McNulty to convince the chairman, who in turn persuaded the others, to "get Gordon and get him nailed down as soon as possible."

Now in the driver's seat, Roger Gordon toyed with the chairman when the invitation came, finally agreeing to become the next president of Midtown U only after he had negotiated the most generous contract in the history of the institution.

Barbara Newcomb was forgotten in the collective sigh of relief. Committee members returned to their everyday routines, not a single one interested enough to review the credentials of the three remaining candidates. While great excitement prevailed as the search had begun almost a full year earlier, the final weeks had been drudgery. Now that it was done, let the chairman add the finishing touches, and let the new president go to work. There was a news conference at which the chairman introduced Gordon, and the president-elect emphasized a new beginning for Midtown U. With that the whole agonizing ordeal was over.

For MU it required a continuing rationalization which only a few heard, and if others had heard, they would not have understood: "You wouldn't want to work for a woman, would you!" Not a question. A simple statement of an all too commonly accepted prejudice.

Barbara Newcomb never again applied for another presidency, nor did she allow her name to be submitted by others. Her remaining years were spent in the professorship, teaching and writing, and guiding both graduate and undergraduate students through vigorous but satisfying pursuits in her special field of history. Closest associates were unanimous in reporting her brilliant success in the classroom, with never a hint of bitterness or disappointment on her part. As is sometimes the case, she didn't need the presidency of Midtown U for her personal fulfillment; it was Midtown that needed her.

That final year before retirement brought Comstock still another view of women in the world of academe. It turned out to be both hopeful and disappointing.

By her middle thirties, Cynthia Woodward had already worked her way up through the academic ranks and was serving as a dean in a medium-size public university when she was chosen for a year of internship by the American Council on Education. It was the placement officer of the council who informed Bill Comstock that Dean Woodward had chosen Midtown University as her first choice as the place to spend her year. According to her letter, she hoped to "observe Dr. Comstock (whom she had never met) and to learn from him some of the ways in which a university president could be most effective."

"Your PR must be good," chided the placement officer, as he spelled out the details of the internship program and the responsibilities of the host institution.

The request could not have come at a more difficult time for Comstock. He had served some years earlier as mentor to another intern, one who was nominated by his university president as having promise for greater administrative responsibility. While the experience was genuinely satisfying to the mentor, Comstock remembered that both he and the other senior officers of the university had devoted a lot of time to the intern. As the president of Midtown U pondered his answer, the placement officer provided the clincher.

"You see, Bill," his acquaintance continued, "Dr. Woodward is both female and black. She wants to learn from you how to run a university." The flattery was unnecessary; the president now looked toward to an even busier year.

By Thanksgiving, Cynthia Woodward was welcomed in every corner of the university. While it was true that President Comstock went the extra mile in giving her a genuine welcome to Midtown, Dr. Woodward quickly established her own credentials—genuine honesty, unusual ability, respect for confidentiality, and complete understanding of the subtleties of faculty-student-administration relationships. As a special project, a requirement by the council of all interns, Cynthia completed a review of Midtown's budgeting process, making a number of recommendations that the administration was quick to accept. Midtown's constituencies–faculty, students, administrators, and even trustees (Cynthia had been invited to attend all meetings, including those of committees)–were unanimous in their praise of this young black woman.

As was expected, Dean Woodward was offered the presidency of two different universities within the ensuing three-year period. She chose to remain in her deanship, turning down other offers, and after another few years of courtship by other colleges and universities, this very capable, by now widely recognized leader, removed herself from the ranks of would-be presidents by turning down an offer to head her own institution.

Had she learned something at Midtown U during her internship which soured her on the work of a university CEO? Still in touch with her through the years by telephone or mail, Comstock never got a satisfactory answer, although he wrote many letters in response to various inquiries. Here was a lady, a characterization which fit Dean Woodward perfectly, thought Comstock, who could have been an outstanding leader for some institution of higher education–and she chose not to be. Society was clearly the loser. Even greater losers, thought Comstock were any number of young black women who might have found further inspiration had Cynthia Woodward only taken the final step up the ladder of academe. He never quite succeeded in putting the matter to rest.

Everywhere Comstock turned, discrimination against women seemed to be the order of the day. It was his church where blatant disregard of fairness, justice, and just plain decency next cried out. Here, of all places, or so the academic reasoned, one should expect to find religion to be the home of understanding, sympathy, and brotherhood. Ah, maybe that was the problem–BROTHERHOOD! Reaching men only!

Bill Comstock simply awakened one day to find his church awash in controversy–members, deacons, elders, and professional staff. It centered on Alice Thomas McKiver-O'Brien, associate pastor.

Alice, as she was known to everyone who worshipped at First Presbyterian in Suburbia, USA, was the ever capable, ever available, and, it seemed, everlasting mainstay of the church. Few could remember her arrival more than 30 years earlier. Few had been around longer, none of the professional staff and only a dozen old-timers among the congregation.

Serving an upper middle-class community, First Presbyterian experienced a sizable turnover among its membership. That membership was made up of upper-echelon officers of major corporations with home offices in the metropolitan area, many young professionals with growing families, a few academics, among them the president of Midtown U, and a number of singles and several retired couples.

Dr. MacKiver-O'Brien was indeed an honest-to-goodness Ph.D. in theology from one of the country's leading universities. Nonetheless, she remained known to all, including the teenagers, as Alice.

She arrived fresh out of seminary as an assistant to the minister of education and youth services, still short of her 25th birthday. It was easy for everyone to wrap her in the same identity for the rest of her career. Neither deacons nor elders made recognition of her steady and uncharacteristic advancement which seven years earlier had brought her to the associate pastor's chair.

And the church was not without a periodic crisis. A six-month interim when the pastor suffered a heart attack was followed by a scandal in which the minister of music was fired for molesting two young boys. But the event that got the most coverage was the indictment of the treasurer, a highly respected banker, for stealing cash from weekly collections. First Presbyterian seemed to have them all!

But there was Alice. Throughout 30 years, she taught the children, visited the sick, filled the pulpit, righted the finances, and, it seemed, filled every void with her endless energy, talent, and love. Few other communities—her service reached far beyond the church walls—were fortunate enough to have an Alice.

And she remained Alice. Not Doctor, not Reverend—and her ordination had taken place 20 years earlier—just Alice.

But it was not Alice, many in the congregation had to be reminded in the months that followed, who threw the bombshell. Two deacons suggested the Reverend MacKiver-O'Brien be invited to fill the pastorate upon the retirement of the incumbent, some ten months away.

By the time Bill Comstock became involved, the membership of First Presbyterian was bitterly divided with no easy solution in sight. The usual arguments were tossed back and forth.

"We have never had a woman as pastor." "Men are the leaders in holy matters; the Bible makes that clear in a thousand references." "Alice is not ready; she has never served as a pastor." "How could she?" someone asked; "our church would never give her a chance." "I'll leave the church before I agree to having a woman in the pulpit."

"Women have been put down long enough, and especially in the church." "Let's set history straight and do the right thing." "Women in other churches are treated equally. Must we stay forever in the dark ages?" "She has done the work of a pastor for years—and better than any we have seen!" "I'll leave the church before I'll be a party to such continuing blatant discrimination."

James Patrick O'Brien had seen it before. A distinguished lawyer, educated in Catholic schools from his earliest years, he had vicariously endured the crush of sex discrimination when his younger sister was denied her wish to serve at the alter of the family church, the very same request that had been quickly approved when he, a boy, had sought the privilege only two years earlier. And the different answers came from the same priest.

It was the same when he got to college. Young men were singled out, he among them, for special attention, personal advice, even financial help. Encouraged to go to an outstanding law school, one where he could not afford to pay the costs, the teaching brotherhood quickly found the necessary scholarship funds. Again, the younger sister—and she looked to her big brother for answers to so many concerns—was unable to find any encouragement among the faculty of that same university when she inquired about medical school two years later.

For a young woman, even a very talented one, those who wore the collar either on campus or among the practicing clergy seemed to feel that another role—marriage, children, church, and family—would be a more proper and fulfilling life.

And then Alice came into his life.

They met in a fourth-grade classroom of an inner-city elementary school where both were tutoring. As they listened to the regular teacher, a skillful and dedicated veteran, explain the special needs of her youngsters and answered questions from the half-dozen volunteers from the nearby campuses, Alice MacKiver and Patrick O'Brien soon found themselves as a twosome, responding on the same wavelength to the challenges they would meet. They worked together for the rest of the year. It wasn't long until they found it convenient to share a quick lunch, meet after each tutoring session to plan the next, and finally, to launch a serious courtship with regular dates for social events, campus activities, and an occasional concert. Visits to museums on weekends, something neither had taken the time to do previously, proved another shared pleasure.

No great threshold was crossed, no single moment stood out; but before either was fully aware, their relationship had become serious—so serious that each invited the other not just to meet but to get acquainted with the other's family. Neither had really thought about marriage. In fact, both Alice and Pat were proceeding under the tacit assumption that such matters would be dealt with in due time, well after each had settled into a professional career.

Religion had not been mentioned. There had been a few fleeting references but not a single serious discussion. Pat knew that Alice was studying at a local Protestant seminary and was in her last year of undergraduate work, and Alice knew that Pat had one more year of law school before facing bar exams and the job search. Their differing religious upbringing was apparent as the families got acquainted, but both seemed to accept the other without serious concern. No parent, aunt or uncle, or cousin even raised the question of "marrying out of the faith."

But Patrick O'Brien had forgotten about his local priest, the same priest who had so enthusiastically welcomed him to be an altar boy only a decade earlier.

"You will raise the children in the Mother Church (Catholic)," the priest told him, "and when they become of age, you will send them to our schools (Catholic), and, I hope, you will help us to welcome your wife into membership of our church (Catholic)."

Pat, as he later tried to recount the full admonition from Father O'Toole, could get no further. The rest was blurred—just ran together in his head, he said, as he tried to explain to Alice what had happened. "And, oh yes, Father O'Toole absolutely refused to participate in a joint ceremony," Pat added.

Quietly, stubbornly, unhappily, Patrick O'Brien walked away from his church, his family's church, the only church he had known. But he didn't walk into another, and 30 years later he was still on the outside as Alice made her way through the official ranks of her church and into the hearts of its members.

Supportive of Alice in all that she did, and occasionally worshipping in her church, Pat had not joined. And Alice had not pressed him; her respect for his judgment and love for her husband put proselytizing out of bounds. Some members of First Presbyterian, a few who knew him well, understood his feelings; most did not. Pat remained firmly by her side as the ordeal brought on by the two deacons unfolded.

Those two men had started a hail storm, or was it hellfire and brimstone! Would Alice have made the thrust had the deacons not first fired the cannon into the glass ceiling? Pat would never know—and maybe Alice would never know either.

But now the "fat was in the fire," and Alice clarified her position.

"I would like to become the next pastor of First Presbyterian." It was a matter-of-fact statement made in a low voice but loud enough to be heard clearly by all at the joint meeting of deacons and elders. With measured dignity and firmness, Dr. MacKiver-O'Brien left no doubts about her qualifications, her readiness, or her expectations.

While all of the elders knew Alice and her work firsthand, some of the deacons were young and quite new, not sure of their proper place in the church hierarchy. Perhaps the two who had first spoken out in nominating Alice would not have done so had they been aware that the ruling body of a Presbyterian church called the Session, and made up mostly of elders, holds all the power. Deacons are there to handle routine day-to-day pastoral affairs. But no matter, Alice was now a candidate, and her presence could not be ignored. She wasn't likely to spend her remaining ten to twenty years before retirement doing all of the chores which others couldn't or wouldn't do without being given the title of pastor. Associate, even though it carried both responsibility and recognition, was not enough.

Not a single deacon or elder around the table knew for certain what Alice would really do if she did not get called to the pastorate. Nor would she tell them.

Would she leave the staff? Take her personal membership to another church? And what about her husband Patrick? He had never joined the church. In fact, he was known to go to the golf course on some Sunday mornings while his wife pursued her duties at First Presbyterian. Some remembered that his family was Catholic, but couldn't recall Pat's participation in the church, if any.

"The only times I have seen Pat inside our church," confided one deacon, as the board hashed over the situation in closed session a few days later, "were the times Alice occupied the pulpit. Even then he seemed quite unconcerned."

It remained for the presiding elder, the one who had called the Session together in their special meeting, to add the clincher.

"I don't know," his words were cautions and measured, "that O'Brien is even a believer."

From there on the lengthy discussion went from basement to roof and back again.

"Can we elect a pastor whose husband is an atheist?"

"But I didn't say he is an atheist," corrected the elder. "I said I simply don't know."

"Listen," pleaded another, "Dr. MacKiver-O'Brien, giving her doctoral study due recognition, is the best thing that ever happened to this church." Continuing with growing courage, the speaker concluded, "Alice doesn't need anyone's help. She has done it on her own, and she deserves to be our next pastor. I, for one, will support her all the way."

As the meeting broke up, no one could claim victory and no one would admit defeat; but, in fact, they were all losing.

Those who supported Alice could not get the majority needed to put her in the pastorate. Comstock, busy with the always-present crises at Midtown U, sat on the sidelines for the entire episode, an inaction he would always regret.

Prejudice against a woman—or was it against all women—had prevailed. Many pastors, all men, came to First Presbyterian during the next quarter century, but suspicion, bitterness, and fear kept the congregation divided in a dozen little pockets of moral retreat. Visitors to the city, looking for an appropriate place of worship while away from home, found other sanctuaries more satisfying. As older members died or moved away, their places went unfilled.

Alice and Patrick looked elsewhere.

Would women ever gain equality with men—in the world, in America, in Midtown University? Comstock had given the matter much thought, and the older he got, the more it bothered him. As he looked back, he realized that it was not until the last decade of his professional life that he felt fully awakened to the unfair treatment accorded women in so many facets of society. Like many other busy, hard-working men, this academic had sought diligently the knowledge of his profession and the skills necessary for his own success, and the more he had struggled with such personal interests, the tighter the blinders had been drawn to the injustices all around him.

Bill Comstock, as he searched diligently for cause and cure, kept coming back to organized religion. And he centered his questions on his own Protestant upbringing.

Admittedly a non-scholar when it came to theology, his half-century of campus life brought him in regular contact with professors of religion, philosophy, biology, and all the other disciplines. Neither humanists nor scientists could provide, thought Comstock, much encouragement in resolving the dilemma.

Was religion too deeply rooted? Absolutely, concluded this exasperated campus leader.

For western civilization, the Old Testament prophets had set the stage for male supremacy. Prescribing the role of men in a God-fearing world, those who set forth the laws simply put women in their supporting, helping, serving place. As each law became further refined, rabbis, followed by priests, ministers, preachers—clergymen of all stripes—rewrote and restated the lower place of women.

"It was the holy men who assigned women to their fate," said Comstock as he discussed the problem with one of the deans. "Whether Protestant or Catholic, Jew or Gentile, orthodox or reform, our hands are collectively tied by our own religious heritage," the president continued.

But the university president was wasting his breath. To convince a religiously devout dean to appoint a woman to direct a major research program in his school was impossible. Had not the man broken his own daughter's marriage to a husband outside the family's faith? Was not his wife "going her own way" after 30 years of married life because the dean was so authoritarian in his behavior?

It was a man's world on campus, in the church, at corporate headquarters—indeed around the world. Put a kaleidoscope anywhere on earth, either now or at anytime in history, and the pictures are the same—men reign, women serve. And, unfortunately, the foundation of such dastardly behavior—the wall behind which it is all hidden—is religion! What irony, thought Comstock.

Vows of poverty, of chastity, of love, of service, and of a hundred other things, but no vow of equality for men and women!

All such questions raced through his mind as Comstock sought to unravel the problems of conscience and responsibility, opportunity and prohibition, which surrounded him and his work.

Yes, he had appointed women to greater responsibility at Midtown U. But the five highest-ranking women at the university were all gone within two years after Comstock retired.

Better to light a candle... Take one small step... Don't curse the darkness.... Comstock reminded himself of the same admonitions that he so frequently gave to others in moments of despair.

Progress was being made, and Comstock was a part of the remedy. When he made himself face up to the facts, women were gaining in the overall struggle for fairness, he recognized, but the journey was long. The overriding disappointment was his realization that one lifetime, his own, was not enough.

Recounting the decade of the eighties, Bill Comstock could see the culmination after all the years of blindness on the part of one major segment of society—the world of big business. In many boardrooms, those of the largest corporations in America, women were taking their seats, being welcomed alongside men. Suddenly there was a burst of "finding eligible women and minorities" for service as "directors, trustees, regents, overseers, and governors."

"Dr. Comstock, would you be able to suggest the name of a candidate or two for our board who is black, Hispanic, or female?" It was a common refrain, voiced by some who were only camouflaging their prejudice against both women and minorities, and by others who realized the period of denial to both groups was coming to an end.

While he would not live long enough to see discrimination completely eliminated, he recognized that his own professional life had concluded with a major step forward in bringing both women and minorities into the main stream of academic and corporate governance. He saw the first woman appointed to the presidency of an Ivy League university. He saw his own nominee, a well-qualified black woman, chosen to be a director of a prestigious non-profit organization and soon afterward elected to the board of directors of a major American corporation. Comstock would remember every detail for years to come.

Invited to suggest new members of the board to replace retiring trustees, Comstock went straight to the confidential file he kept for just such purposes. Except on this occasion, the names had all been collected for those times ahead when new trustees would be elected to the board of Midtown University. He looked only to the first name: Christine Kinsey MacIntire.

Still under 50, Dr. MacIntire had dug her way out of a small town in Florida, had worked her way through a segregated, all-black teachers' college, and had taken her first job as a teacher of mathematics in a newly integrated junior high school. Years later she could laugh and explain that she was really hired because math teachers, even those with minimum qualification, simply could not be found in her part of the country.

Three years in her first job, with each summer spent in more advanced mathematics courses, brought "Miss Mac," as she had become affectionately known to her students and their parents, an offer of a graduate fellowship at the state university. A master's degree was followed by the Ph.D. whereupon "Dr. Mac" was appointed supervisor of math teachers for the entire state, a post she shared with one other colleague.

After ten successful years, Washington beckoned, and so Dr. MacIntire joined the national office of education to work with a small team of educators on revising the teaching of mathematics for the entire country. She became impatient with the federal bureaucracy and entered a large city school system as assistant superintendent. Her next stop was the superintendency of the same city. It was in that spot that Bill Comstock got to know her and her work.

It was generally conceded to be one of the toughest jobs in the country—schools surrounded by crime, poverty, breakdown of family, child neglect, drugs, the whole range of human misery—but the determined, experienced black woman dedicated herself to the task. When people began saying within a year of her assuming the post, "Dr. MacIntire is the best thing that ever happened to our schools," the university president put her on his carefully selected list.

"How would you like to have a brilliant woman as your next trustee?" Comstock asked the CEO of National Researchers, Inc. "That's exactly the kind of person I'm looking for," was his quick reply. "Now, can you find me a minority also?" The request was genuine.

"The woman I'm suggesting is black," Bill Comstock quietly added.

"Then, I get two for the price of one!"

Openly criticized for being too slow to appoint either women or minorities to the board or to employment in National Researchers, Inc., George H. Gilchrist felt immediate relief from a major embarrassment.

Gilchrist was very thin-skinned (sensitive would be a more kindly way to put it). He had moved directly from a brilliant career in research and exploration to the presidency of NRI, not having given either thought or preparation to the responsibilities of managing such an enterprise. He really believed he had removed all impediments to good management by insisting that employees address him by his first name, including his driver. Unfortunately, the forced intimacy backfired. Through it all, George was looking for ways to stay out of the limelight and get back to his research.

"And what is the lady's name?" By the time the question was asked, the answer didn't really matter. Gilchrist saw Comstock's suggestion as a welcome way out of so many of his current headaches that the name seemed immaterial. As the two made their way through MacIntire's resumé, however, George seemed to come alive enough to realize that he was being offered a gem.

Election to the board was without challenge. Preliminaries, including a luncheon hosted by Comstock where MacIntire and Gilchrist got acquainted, followed by another at which George arranged for the senior officers at NRI to meet the candidate, went off without a hitch. Two trustees, well-known for their strong belief that only white males should be entrusted with responsibility for our major institutions, raised no questions as the CEO described the candidate.

Comstock did allow himself a personal smile as he listened to George who, by the time of the introduction, was taking major credit for finding Dr. MacIntire.

How true the adage, thought the academic: "One can get a lot done if he/she doesn't care who gets the credit."

But Gilchrist wasted no time in informing the world of his coup.

News releases were distributed nationwide, announcing the election of the new trustee, and it seemed that every publication of National Research for the next 12 months carried at least one picture of Dr. MacIntire or a reference to her.

One in particular caught Comstock's attention. It was a picture of George with his new trustee, appearing in a seventh-grade classroom of an inner-city school, handing out toy replicas of a radio-controlled robot used to explore the ocean floor. It was, as both participants explained, an introduction of the youngsters to science.

Soon after the burst of publicity, Comstock and other trustees learned that NRI had added a professional public relations person to the senior staff. He was, fortunately for the company, remaking the public image of this heretofore publicity-shy leading researcher.

Before another year had passed, Dr. MacIntire had been elected to the board of a major regional bank and a nationwide merchandising company. Bill Comstock had helped in each case by responding to confidential inquiries from the two chairmen of the organizations. He was indeed a participant in the old boys' network; he was just using it for new and different purposes.

But it was a slippery slope. Three steps forward seemed always to be followed with two steps back. North Potomac University was the campus; Jennifer Worthington was the casualty.

In her early fifties, successful in every step of a career up to that point, Dr. Worthington was the innocent victim of a changing tide which swept away the very foundation of her entire professional life. A newly appointed president of North Potomac called her to his office, a thousand miles away and three months before he officially took up his new duties, to tell her "there was, unfortunately, no place for her in his new administration."

Twenty-seven years earlier Comstock had first become acquainted with Jennifer Worthington when she went to work at North Potomac, fresh out of graduate school. Now, she was being informed by a president whom she had never previously met and who knew nothing about her ability or her experience that she had reached the end of the road. Apparently, the new president had not even bothered to learn what she had done in all those years at NPU.

Senior administrative officers, faculty members, student leaders, trustees—the entire campus community of NPU—knew well the outstanding contributions Dr. Worthington had made.

Her first job was assistant dean of students. That was followed by the deanship and then by university compliance officer (a law degree completed through night school back at Midtown U had prepared her for this tedious, often frustrating responsibility). Next came a two-year special assignment as assistant provost with responsibility for planning, along with a university-wide committee, the university's next decade of development, including finances. Through all her administrative chairs, Jennifer believed it to be important that she maintain direct contact with students and faculty. To accomplish this, she taught one course in the field of her doctoral research, clinical psychology. Departmental faculty members had encouraged her more than once to leave administration and become a full-time professor.

Her superiors in central administration over the years—she had seen three presidents come and go—and especially her immediate boss, the provost of North Potomac, had kept giving Jennifer more and more responsibility. Solving knotty administrative problems, something she did with great skill and with a quiet, confident demeanor, and seeing the results move the institution forward really prevented Worthington from considering other professional opportunities, including that of full-time professor. So settled was she in her work that when Comstock recommended her for positions at other campuses, all judged to be advancements, she politely declined to explore a single possibility.

Associate provost had been her title for five years before that fateful encounter. The provost, looking to retire one year later, had carefully groomed Dr. Worthington to succeed him. She would be the number two executive of NPU; the entire campus community recognized the forthcoming succession—and approved.

There were those who suggested that Dr. Worthington go even further and enter her name in the bidding for the president's office. She was pleased that so many of her colleagues viewed her with such respect, but she firmly declined. Assuming that she would be the next provost in only a year, she did not want to be viewed as a competitor to the person eventually selected. She felt that to do so could possibly make her relationship with the new leader a bit awkward, and she wanted to be of maximum help to whomever was chosen. Furthermore, Jennifer was not fully confident that she could be effective on the alumni fund-raising circuit. Confident though that she could be of continuing service to the university, this experienced administrator was not only selling herself short but also was putting too much faith in reason and decency.

She was totally unprepared for the message of the new president: "There will be no office of provost in my administration." And then, as though he was waiting for the pain to penetrate, "Thus, I simply have no job for you."

Harold J. Herter, the president-elect of North Potomac, had taken charge. It was already obvious that he knew how to spread fear and uncertainty throughout an institution of higher learning. Having signed a five-year contract, Herter was already making a mark. To some it proved to be more of a brand, like a hot iron wielded by a rancher on his herd of cattle. For Jennifer Worthington it proved to be a scarlet letter, permanently burned into her forehead.

Returning to North Potomac after her career-shattering message from Herter, she first reported to her boss, the provost. Next she went to Midtown U to see President Comstock, whom she knew to be both mentor and friend.

To both provost and president her story was the same; and as it turned out, each man gave her the same advice: Your treatment was so unprofessional, so shabby, so unfair, and your service has been so superior that you should sue North Potomac University and its new president for damages. One man was her immediate supervisor, and he could speak to the details of her outstanding work over 27 years; the second, from another campus, had known Dr. Worthington even longer, and he could speak to her high standing among senior administrators across the entire country.

"If you sue," each man added, "I'll be a witness for you."

Three more months until July 1 when Herter would arrive; three more paychecks before I shall be unemployed; how much longer can I pay my mortgage? These questions and a thousand others crossed her mind. Devastated by the ultimatum that had been dropped across her path, Jennifer, not surprisingly, had trouble picking her way through the rubble. She asked her two older advisers, both of whom she knew had only her best interests at heart, to allow her time to think.

Before the middle of the next week when they talked again, Comstock did some thinking, too.

Jennifer Worthington was not one to jump without considering all the consequences. Should she decide to bring suit, Bill Comstock could see a bright moon rising over the entire world of higher education, and as the full story unfolded, he envisioned the justice of public opinion pinning Herter to the mast. While Comstock would regret the negative publicity that would come to North Potomac, its new president would be getting his just desserts. The institution would recover. Fortunately universities were able to survive the damages of even the worst scoundrels.

But what if this woman, so severely hurt by the most damaging blow possible to her career, decided not to seek redress in the courts? Comstock could help her relocate, but that would leave Herter free to continue his mischief. Then, too, relocation in anything close to a position of comparable pay and responsibility would be almost impossible. But if that is her decision, where might she go? It was a question Bill Comstock did not wish to pursue, but recognizing Worthington's personal makeup and professional behavior, he recognized that there was simply no way for him to predict her answer.

Aware of how disciplined she was in her work habits and how tenacious she was in pursuing solutions to even minor problems, Comstock could not recall a single instance in the many years he had known Jennifer in which she had issued a serious challenge to one of her superiors. Always considerate of the opinions of others, here was a woman who, it seemed, supported the decision reached in whatever group she found herself. This did not at all mean that she remained silent; her disagreements were expressed clearly but always with dignity and courtesy. Having made her point, she felt there was no necessity of pushing, demanding, or scorning those with different views.

Dr. Worthington told Comstock of her decision in precisely the same manner that he had remembered.

"I have decided not to sue Mr. Herter."

The dissatisfied look on Comstock's face required Jennifer to proceed. She did, without raising her voice.

"If I sue, it is bound to become a high profile case, and I can see my name, as well as that of Herter and North Potomac University, spread all over the papers. Also, it will be the topic of conversation and gossip in every meeting of people in higher education for the whole year." She hesitated, but it was apparent she was not finished.

"To bring a suit of this kind would brand me for life, and I'm afraid I would be blackballed from every campus in America because I would be marked as a troublemaker." With a perplexed look, Comstock still withheld comment.

"Dr. Comstock," (others might address him by his first name, but to Jennifer he was still the president of Midtown where she had been a student) "your offer to go to court on my behalf is appreciated. To know that both you and my boss at North Potomac are willing to go to bat for me in such a public way is something I shall never forget.

"I would like to work another ten to fifteen years in higher education," Dr. Worthington continued in her calm, unhurried way. She knew her listener would appreciate knowing the full rationale for her decision. "From all I have seen of other cases, a woman who challenges presidents or governing boards in such decisions always loses.

"Not only does she lose the contested decision, but also rarely will she be given another chance on another campus." Jennifer was well informed on such maters.

From his thorough knowledge of higher education, the president of Midtown U could not dispute her observations. Sadly, Comstock realized, even with all the support he might muster on Jennifer's behalf–and he had friends in high places on many campuses–it would be well nigh impossible to find a comparable position for a woman who had resorted to the courts to settle a grievance.

"Uppity women," was one of the more polite terms used to describe such persons, and it was too easy to lump them all together!

But to go quietly as Jennifer had decided to do would still not guarantee a satisfactory relocation. A couple of years beyond 50, facing a tight job market, with essentially all her experience in one institution, Dr. Worthington faced a very uncertain future with her decision.

Comstock knew her well enough to know, however, that the decision was final. She had chosen the course with which she was most comfortable, and so he could only ask, "What now?"

"I'm getting acquainted with the want ads in the Chronicle," she replied with a good helping of humor. "Fortunately," she went on to explain, "I have six months, counting the summer, in which to find something and to relocate."

It was the voice of confidence of one who had succeeded in each position held over the past soon-to-be three decades. Dr. Worthington could not envision the frustration and disappointment that lay ahead; her professional life had been one of uninterrupted progress.

"You know I will do everything possible to help," said a worried Comstock as Jennifer left.

Within the week Dr. Worthington had applied for three positions advertised in the Chronicle, and she had listed Comstock as one of three requested references. In two cases he was personally acquainted with senior administrators on the other campuses, and he made telephone calls. Maybe, just maybe, Jennifer could pull it off. With her impeccable record, it should be possible.

For the next three months, however, Comstock found himself explaining that record. Questions all centered on the obvious. Why is Dr. Worthington leaving North Potomac if her service has been so valuable? In explaining that her position was being abolished by the new president, each questioner knew, as Comstock knew, that no matter what titles were given to people, the work was still there to be done.

What he couldn't say was what he thought—Harold J. Herter was an arrogant jerk. A well-traveled CEO, he had been the center of controversy wherever he had served. North Potomac U is in for a rough time, he thought. Knowing the man had caused Comstock to make his offer in the first place—to go to court to support Worthington in confronting the culprit. But it was too late to do that now.

With such strong credentials, Dr. Worthington found herself among the finalists, usually the three most promising candidates for some six positions, all of which were at the same or higher level of her role at North Potomac. Encouraged with each invitation for a personal interview, and confident that she could make as strong a case as any other applicant, Worthington refused to become either impatient or discouraged.

But somehow each job disappeared as Jennifer watched and waited. Two of them were filled by other candidates, two were withdrawn, and decisions were deferred in the others.

Three months had slipped by. Dr. Worthington had cleaned out her office at North Potomac, said good-bye to a dozen staff members and close friends, deposited her final salary check, and faced the first Monday morning of her adult life unemployed.

"I have taken a job," was her telephone message to Comstock as a new academic year approached in September. "It is a two-year assignment, and I'm eager to tell you all about it," a bit of enthusiasm could be detected in her voice.

"This calls for a celebration. Let my wife and me take you to dinner. Betty (Mrs. Comstock) will want to hear all about it, too." Jennifer's seven-days-a-week search had ended.

"South Central State College," a small, public institution in the Washington suburbs which they all knew, "has received a foundation grant for planning its growth and development. I have agreed to serve as the chief planning officer. It will be fun," Jennifer continued, "to work with deans, faculty members, students, and trustees. And I was favorably impressed with the president when he talked with me about the work."

It was a relaxed group—friends sharing a moment of triumph with a dear colleague. But Dr. Worthington's professional career had not returned to a solid track; she had gained a two-year reprieve.

Two years and she would again be in the job market. She was forced to take a sizable cut in salary. In her new job, she could pay her mortgage and live by cutting expenses here and there; and the title of vice president on her resumé would be a plus. Still, she would be two years older when making another move, a bit more of a handicap. All of her friends, and especially the Comstocks, who considered Jennifer practically a member of the family, remained uneasy.

It turned out to be a routine piece of work. Dr. Worthington, having done the same thing years before at North Potomac, went through the entire period without the slightest hitch. Everyone was delighted with the final report of the planning group, written entirely by Jennifer, but the credit was given to all the others. There was no permanent spot for her, though, at South Central.

Another all-out effort to find a job produced only further frustration. For the first time in her career, Dr. Worthington was told she was overqualified for some positions she sought. Was it another way of saying she was too old, thus avoiding the charge of age discrimination? While she had suspicions, she successfully warded off despair and depression. Remaining confident that she was the master of her own fate, Jennifer took her next work in stride.

She would be a consultant in higher education for the rest of her professional life. It wasn't what she had planned; it simply rolled over her like a gently rising tide.

Having served on special panels for the department of education through the years, and having been called as an expert witness in several discrimination cases, Dr. Worthington built a reputation as one able to untangle complex problems and to maneuver around ordinary roadblocks in higher education. Thus, she found herself responding to numerous calls for help as she continued to look for a permanent job. A month of such work ran into a semester, then into the academic year. Before she fully realized what was happening—hurrying the conclusion of one study or reviewing material before beginning another—two full years had elapsed since she left South Central. In fact, the search for a permanent slot had lost some of its urgency.

Problems that she tackled and invitations she accepted proved increasingly challenging. As her reputation grew, more and more clients turned to Dr. Worthington not only because she had proved to be so effective but also because she was a woman! Some needed to prove their freedom from bias, so a woman on the team was a safe—but temporary—course with no long-term commitment necessary. It would be her way of life for the rest of her professional career.

All the way into her seventies, Worthington found herself spending a few days here, a week there, making a return visit, reporting to governing boards, meeting with faculty groups, soothing student gripes, living in different hotels, working most weekends, and traversing the country several times each year. Carrying with her from one task to another the knowledge and skills that only a person of her ability and capacity could muster, this woman who had been so content with her role on a single campus was, by the time she finally retired, one of the country's foremost authorities in all of higher education.

She paid off the mortgage, bought a larger house, acquired her own sailboat, and appeared in public only to testify before congressional committees on educational legislation. Comfortable in retirement, she limited herself to a few close friends, including the Comstocks. Many in the world of higher education recognized Jennifer Worthington as one of its most constructive leaders. The prejudice of the times, however, and the arbitrary action of one person, Harold J. Herter, had prevented her from gaining the presidency of a single, major campus.

VII

BOARDS, COMMISSIONS, COMMITTEES, AND OTHER FILTERING DEVICES

One more board, thought Comstock, and the camel's back would break. At one point in his career his memberships included some 52 such commitments, a number that he considered a bit of trivia until he realized the whopping amount of time all the meetings took away from other things he must do.

It was true, as President Robert Sills of Bowdin College had pointed out many years before, academic leaders are supposed to be experts in all fields, and, furthermore, they are required to give of their time and talents to every cause under the sun. But 52 memberships! Ridiculous, to be sure. For the remaining decade of his active career, Bill Comstock steadily cut back on his board commitments.

But the world's business was run by groups, far more so in the United States than elsewhere around the globe. So as he took his regular seat around the bank's boardroom table in the chair clearly marked with a brass nameplate on the back, he waited for the CEO's gavel to signal the opening of business. All those hours spent around meeting tables suddenly came to mind.

Dentists worked in patients' mouths all day; accountants checked and re-checked numbers, having reams and reams of printouts, usually working alone; farmers rode tractors or tended cattle from dawn to dusk; but university presidents sat around tables. Only when he began to muse about the ways people spent their days was Comstock concerned about the way he spent *his* days—invariably long days.

The CEO was already into the first substantive item on the day's agenda, with approval of minutes and other routine preliminaries out of the way. Comstock glanced at his watch, knowing the exact time the meeting would end because the old chairman ran each session by the clock—it was one and a half hours, always within a minute or two. A call from his secretary beforehand might inform directors that some special problem would require another 15 or 30 or whatever number of minutes. That information was offered with a note of apology by the secretary and repeated again at the meeting by the CEO, who seemed to feel that taking more than the usual one and a half hours of directors' time was somehow a weakness of management.

Comstock headed back to campus and braced himself for yet another meeting that same afternoon, this one of Midtown U's faculty senate. Reflecting on the just-ended board meeting and mentally preparing for the one ahead, he recalled the adage that America's business was conducted in a businesslike way, whereas academic decisions were to be made only as a last resort. For all its verbosity, however, a university's faculty had become over the centuries, and for good reason, the most powerful group in the entire institution.

Bill Comstock from his earliest days as a young professor had come to look upon the faculty as a second governing board. The faculty controlled the curriculum of the university—what courses would be taught, what the content of those courses would be, and what configuration of courses would qualify a student for graduation. The cliché that only the professor controlled what took place in his classroom or laboratory after the door was closed held a world of truth—and power. Although this responsibility had been delegated to the faculty over many decades by the board of trustees, which officially held the charter of the institution and therefore all the legal power, it would be unthinkable—and in practice impossible—to roll back the academic clock.

Midtown University's faculty senate, while not on the president's list of 52 boards, was, nonetheless, one of his most important. He used the group as his eyes and ears to the entire university community. While students and alumni were also important constituencies, professors could be counted on to reflect the interests of all groups as well as their own, and usually with great accuracy.

Bill Comstock tried never to miss a meeting.

Taking the presiding officer's chair—no name plate on academic seats—he had arrived, as always, just one minute before the time of the call of the meeting. After a routine roll call, the first order of business was to establish the presence of a quorum, and then the formal meeting began.

Well-established rules guided Comstock's behavior. As presiding officer, he did not enter the debate; his position was well known to the group, and although all members might not agree, most respected his point of view. Comstock believed the senate was the faculty's policy-making body and that the administration—Comstock, other senior officers, and, indeed, the board of trustees—should not interfere as the faculty hammered out its various positions. He wanted, too, the opportunity to consider recommendations of the faculty apart from the on-going debates. Upon receiving a report or request from the faculty, Comstock and his staff tried always to respond promptly. The president had also learned that such behavior yielded other dividends. If, in the course of a debate, the administration were unfairly attacked, some other member of the senate would defend the administration. And it was a professor who was voicing the rebuttal!

Comstock came to each meeting with a special mental outlook. "Expect," as he explained to non-academic friends, "to be the last to leave, to conduct each meeting with even greater deliberation than the group would like, thus putting them in the position of having to push things—and to warn your wife that you will be late for dinner!"

Academic politics represented the height of intrigue for those who did not understand, and most of the general public felt completely baffled. It was seen as the depth of inefficiency for most business-oriented citizens. For Bill Comstock it was a game of utmost interest and importance, and he played it masterfully.

Henry Kissinger, among others, is credited with the observation that "academic politics is so serious because the stakes are so low," but such comments fail to explain either the role of the faculty in university affairs or the importance of professors in the educational experience. Comstock found that many academicians treated service in the faculty senate as a heavy professional responsibility; others steered clear of service at all because of the frustration in arriving at decisions; and still others wanted only the faculty's self-interest to be protected with administrative officers left to worry about all the rest.

Like Marshall McLuhan who wrote, "The medium is the message," Comstock came to regard the academic process as the reward in its own right. To him it was a poker game, and this university president enjoyed each turn of the cards! There were times when he felt that he was the dealer, able to control the flow of the game, if not the precise result. As he watched his counterparts in business and industry, Comstock concluded this to be a particularly satisfying part of the workplace which they were missing. Psychic reward! Call it what you will. Playing the game and winning at least a reasonable share of the time was gratifying. For one who loved competition, academic politics resembled mortal combat—without the bloodshed

Corporations did indeed have other centers of power. In some industries labor unions exerted substantial influence on company policy, and there were always stockholders to be heard. Comstock, a participant in the governing process of both the academy and private enterprise, and a serious student of both, doubly appreciated its defeats and successes. "What have I learned from our most recent difficulty?" was an ever present question, as he walked away from yet another board meeting, either university or corporation.

Over the years, Comstock had concluded that public universities, especially those so-called flagship institutions such as Texas, Ohio State, Wisconsin, and others where capital cities also serve as the geographic home to the academic center, were in the worst of all locations. Political interference, often led by the governor, was handy, frequent, and all too intrusive. It was so easy for the politician—governor, legislative leader, or staff assistant—to call the president of the university for information, favors, or support. It was also easy, as history had demonstrated, for a governor to move from that office to the university for personal ambition or for convenience. More unusual was a move from the university's presidency to that of governor, although that had occurred in a number of states over the decades.

For an academic leader to feel the presence of another governing group just a few blocks away was not far-fetched; too many examples existed across the country, even among the greatest of public universities.

Where the corporate board was all order and discipline, the faculty senate was marked by rambling discourse, planned diversion, and infinite delay. Motions to table, defer, return to committee were all devices used to avoid even a tentative decision, but the chief delaying tactic of all was just plain talk. Every side of every question had to be restated again and again with each speaker adding his own particular twist or flavor to the debate.

Bill Comstock was masterful as the presiding officer of such a body. He had learned from his years as a professor the many aberrations of behavior found in faculty groups. Above all else, patience had to be the ever present guide, the prerequisite to accomplishing anything. Discussion must run its full course; in academe there were no shortcuts. For a university president whose campus activities seemed bound to interminable discussion, service on corporate boards often served as welcome relief. Years later, he would look back and smile at what he described as his "how-to-survive-faculty-meetings behavior."

"Even if the President of the United States should call," Comstock instructed his staff, "I am not to be asked to leave a faculty meeting." Of course, he knew that should the man at 1600 Pennsylvania Avenue ever wish to speak to him, it would be some presidential assistant who would be searching for him, not the President himself. He knew, too, that some university CEOs became so tired and impatient with faculty meetings that they would arrange to have "urgent" messages delivered in order to escape.

But Comstock had an inherent faith in the fairness of faculty decisions, and leaving aside such a one sided item as professors' compensation, he had seen convincing evidence over the years that decisions, with few exceptions, were made with the university's long-range welfare in mind. So it was not difficult for him to remain attentive, no matter how long and boring meetings became, since a careful observer could detect potential problems—or even opportunities—as comments from the participants were laid out among the group.

Even as he welcomed the change to the corporate boardroom, Comstock had to concede that procedures of faculty groups had their advantages. Too many times he had witnessed the business CEO, under the guise of "keeping on schedule," cut off discussion, place a heavy heel on dissent, or simply fail to understand an important problem. Particularly disturbing to this academic was the pattern of corporate boards in stifling discussion on the part of inside directors. They invariably entered the discussion only as the CEO directed or requested their contributions. There were no dissenting views to those of the CEO from inside members; rarely was there even a question raised. This gave rise in

American business in recent years to the emergence of what some called two separate boards—one made up of insiders and the other of outsiders. By the nineties internecine warfare had broken out between the two in some of America's biggest corporations.

Somewhere, thought Comstock as he moved from the campus to the profit world and back again, there must be a middle ground more desirable than the two extremes. His resignation from one corporate board, where he felt the CEO was deliberately misleading him and other outside directors, further convinced him of the shortcomings of the generally accepted "order and discipline" of the private corporate world.

Service on boards, however, always carried its surprises. It was from the Midtown University faculty senate, the one Comstock considered the second of the university's governing boards, where he met one of his most troublesome problems. It occurred during the chaotic days of the late sixties when all the campuses around the world seemed to be in upheaval. For Midtown, located in the heart of Washington, the setting was ideal for constant crises.

The torch was carried by Fred Clark, the associate dean of the law school. His proposal was not totally unexpected. It came on the heels of similar developments at a dozen or more other campuses across the country. Why not establish, he argued before Midtown's faculty senate, an all-university assembly where every constituency of the institution could, through democratically chosen representatives, consider matters that the total assembly agreed were important to Midtown. The assembly would then make recommendations to appropriate student organizations, faculty groups, and alumni bodies, and ultimately would forward such advice and counsel to the board of trustees for final disposition. Think of all the pressure such a body would take off the backs of trustees, of the president, and on and on.

Since the proposal came from Clark, some in the faculty senate, including the presiding officer, Bill Comstock, were immediately suspicious. Clark was known to be among the most liberal—some called him radical—of the entire university faculty. To get from him a proposal that could at first glance be considered rational and reasonable was a little too much to expect. Yet, as developments over the next four months proved, he had done a lot of work on his proposal before the day he introduced it to the senate. Various student organizations quickly aligned themselves in support; Clark had promised them strong representation in such an assembly. The most powerful of alumni groups, the athletic council, had come aboard, and most surprising of all, the Midtown chapter of the American Association of University Professors held its first meeting in ten years to endorse the plan as "worthy of serious consideration."

The president was caught off guard, something that didn't often happen. All-campus assemblies had been established in several colleges and universities, but they were to be found in the country's most liberal institutions. Comstock had seen them all too closely–in Latin America. There, many major universities had been paralyzed by the manipulation of such assemblies by skillful politicians. Without effective governing boards, in many cases no boards at all, the campus assembly had taken shape to fill a vacuum. Invariably, during periods of unrest, they were taken over by a small, radical minority, usually a group interested in acquiring political clout within the country's power structure rather than for any concern about the quality of education that the campus might provide.

Having visited universities in four South American countries, Comstock was well acquainted with the institutional assembly as a way of running a university. Among his most vivid memories was that of a conversation with the chairman of the assembly at Colombia's National University in Bogota. They met in the student center over a cup of coffee.

"Who is to be served by the university?" was the chairman's first question to Comstock as soon as the latter identified himself as a Ford Foundation representative from "the States."

"Obviously," replied Comstock, "the university is here to serve the student. That pertains whether the student is a beginning freshman or the most advanced researcher. It is to serve the learner."

"Exactly," was the firm response.

"Then who would best know what learning the student most needs?" Quickly moving on and answering his own question, the chairman added, "That is why the students should shape the curriculum of the campus, and that is why we at this university have given the largest number of seats in the assembly to undergraduate learners."

"How does the faculty share in the assembly? How many seats for them?" Comstock wanted no misunderstanding of his belief that the most advanced and experienced learners, namely the faculty, should determine what knowledge would be of greatest worth to the least experienced learners. But the chairman would have none of it. The fact that National University had been closed for five months because of a student strike seemed not to faze the chairman. It was the student who was the central figure in the university, and the faculty was simply on hand, serving as a convenience as the student might request its help and guidance. Neither experience in learning nor experience in life made the professor any more able to choose the most important knowledge or skill for the student; instead it was the student's appetite and choice that should determine the content of his or her studies. So went the platform of this radical leader of one university assembly.

Although he had been warned of the posture which the chairman would likely take, Comstock had difficulty in accepting such absurdities. Leaving his adversary after two hours and four cups of coffee, he moved on to visit with the faculty of the chemistry department where the chairman, upon learning of the educational consultant's presence on campus, had sent a messenger to seek him out at his hotel.

Yes, it was true, the faculty of chemistry confirmed that the university had been closed for five months.

"Then, why are you here?" inquired Comstock, to which the group numbering more than a hundred responded with a hearty laugh.

"This is just the way we like it." "We don't care if the students ever come back." "They're only interested in politics; let them go to the devil." "With them on strike we can get our research done."

These were the voices of professors of chemistry; they were interested in a wide range of research topics, some of which affected their country's economic life. Most were dedicated to strengthening Colombia's industrial base, allowing its citizens to reach a higher standard of living, providing a better diet, or controlling health hazards. They saw the intrusion of national politics as a powerful force for unnecessary trouble for the university. The all-university assembly was the means by which such political shenanigans paralyzed an otherwise vital institution.

Two lengthy visits to South America, with appropriate stops on four university campuses, gave Comstock an indelible picture of the anarchy that the assembly inevitably brought to each university. Back at Midtown, the question was how to deal with the proposal organized and masterminded by Dean Clark—and gaining momentum—for the creation of an all-university assembly.

The president of Midtown U had worked out his answer in time for faculty senate consideration at its very next meeting one month later. Acting after a series of meetings with the university's major constituencies, Comstock proposed the appointment of a Presidential Commission, whose charge would be "to study the desirability of creating an all-university assembly for Midtown University, and to make such recommendations as to its membership, powers, and conditions as it may see fit; and to deliver its final report to the president and board of trustees, along with such further suggestions as alumni, students, and faculty may wish to attach."

As the tiring debate droned on and on—it turned into a six-hour session with a thirty-minute recess—only a single voice from the group branded the proposal for what it was: "a grand scheme for delaying action." It was the truth, and Comstock had hit upon the plan because he didn't know any other way to slow down the movement without causing a student strike, which he knew would be masterminded by Dean Clark and three other radical professors.

But it was Clark whose argument carried the day. So convinced was he that the all-university assembly was an idea whose time had come that he looked upon the charge to the commission as a directive on how to create such a body, not anything so Machievellian as Comstock had in mind. It probably never occurred to Clark that the president was capable of such an ingenious diversion.

Fifteen months later, sitting with Dean Clark in the privacy of his office, Bill Comstock lowered the boom. "No," he said, quietly but firmly. "I cannot recommend to the board of trustees the creation of an all-university assembly."

"But Mr. President, you said" Clark attempted to begin his appeal.

"Turn to the charge of the commission," Comstock interrupted. "There you will find what I said," he added as he picked up a copy from the table.

"You were directed 'to study the desirability of creating an all-university assembly,' and I am quoting, 'and to make such recommendations, as to its membership, etc.'

"Well, you have done that, and you are now reporting the results to me, and I, of course, shall send them on to the board. I am simply telling you now what my recommendation will be, as a courtesy, to be sure. I, too, know much more about the all-university assembly than I did 15 months ago, and I don't believe such a body is appropriate for Midtown U." Clark was stunned. He knew that without Comstock's support the commission's expectations were dashed.

It was the middle of June. No chance for a student protest; even Dean Clark's two strongest supporters among the faculty had departed for the summer. Then, too, he realized that the initial clamor for the assembly which began a year and a half earlier had faded. While he had been able to keep the commission focused on its task by sending delegations to various campuses around the country to see such groups in action, Clark was fearful that the fall term, a whole summer in the future, would not find enough student and faculty support to resurrect the idea. But his own leadership of the commission had made the dean an authority on university governance, and he was not about to give up easily.

Bill Comstock, for his part, had used the time since the appointment of the commission to box in whatever recommendations might come out in its report. In a keep-you-informed session with board chairman, Glen "Parky" Parkinson, soon after the appointment of the presidential commission, the president of the university laid it all out on the table.

"I'm simply playing for time," explained Comstock. "Knowing what I do about such assemblies, both here in the States and in South America, you can bet that I'll never allow one to be set up at Midtown."

Parkinson needed no convincing. He, too, had given some thought to the subject.

"The way I see it," responded Parky, "an all-university assembly of seventy-five to one hundred members representing alumni, faculty, students, and even the non-academic employees, could quickly become the power center of the institution. It would be difficult, if not impossible," he continued, "for the board of trustees to do anything except approve their recommendations."

"You are absolutely right," agreed Comstock. "Except, of course, the assembly would have absolutely no legal responsibilities. As I see it, the governing board would become a rubber stamp, liable for all the institution's actions, but in practice unable to overrule or depart from assembly recommendations."

"Parky, as always, I appreciate your understanding of this situation," Bill explained, always grateful for the support of this quiet, most astute leader of Midtown's trustees.

Parkinson answered questions from other trustees during the period of the commission's study, deflecting pressure that would have landed on Comstock, and without revealing his already firm conclusion, met with Dean Clark in two lengthy sessions at the dean's request. "As a board, we shall be interested in your findings," was Parky's measured response.

Glen Parkinson was certainly the right chairman for his time. Being the seasoned lawyer that he was, Parky had learned to listen, and in listening he heard—and understood—both immediate and long-range implications of the proposal for an all-university assembly.

But Clark wasn't finished yet. He still held a powerful set of cards, to be sure most of them dealt to himself, and he saw more than one way to beat Comstock, whom he could now brand as a double-crossing university president. Believing in his own powers of persuasion, he thought he might convince Chairman Parkinson to accept his proposal. After all, Parky had been, while non-committal, open-minded on the subject.

If approached in just the right fashion, perhaps Parkinson will give me, thought Clark, the privilege of presenting the complete report to a meeting of the full board of trustees. There he could count on seeing at least three friends. Weren't they, after all, former students of his from their law school days! With them, together with other trustees who didn't know much about the proposal, he could envision a solid block of support within the governing board.

He would beat the president at his own little game.

But the vice-chairman of the commission, whose ear Clark sought immediately following his disappointing session with Comstock, had a more immediate suggestion.

"Why not call the executive committee of the faculty senate into special session and get them to endorse the proposal? Sure, it's summer, but I know the chairman of the committee well, and I'll bet I can persuade him to call a meeting immediately." Dean Clark now had two forces at work, both of which would put pressure on Midtown's president.

It was late July when the faculty senate's executive committee convened in special session to hear Clark, and since Comstock had made no secret of what his recommendation to the board would be, he was on hand to defend his position.

"Mr. President, I never dreamed you would act on the commission's report before the board of trustees had a chance to consider it," was only one of the critical comments directed at Comstock as the meeting progressed. "Then, too, to use the summer period, when students and faculty are scattered all over the world, seems to be a bit sneaky." Not exactly complimentary, as Bill Comstock explained, smiling, when he reported the session to Parky a few days later.

But the university president wasn't greatly concerned. Professors, he knew, love to bark; they will do almost anything to keep from biting. So calmly responding, he explained.

"Dean Clark delivered the commission's final report, as it is so labeled, one week before I gave him my assessment of the proposal. True, I could have waited until September before indicating what my response would be. However, if I had done that, some would then have accused me of burying the report, keeping it away from the trustees, or worse yet, demanding that I implement the all-university assembly without waiting for the board to act."

Continuing his well thought out defense, the president nailed the lid on his case.

"We sometimes must be reminded that we all serve this university at the pleasure of the governing board. It is they who hold the charter of this institution, and that charter gives them complete authority over all of us and over everything we do. Furthermore, they hold the liability. In the parlance of the day, the trustees hold the bag. Now an all-university assembly has no authority except as a governing board may delegate responsibility, but can such an assembly be liable for its actions? Hardly.

"Finally," (it was a short speech, but most members of the group were already uncomfortable with the confrontation), "in several South American universities I found these assemblies to be true instruments of anarchy, and members of Dean Clark's commission found the same to be true at some of the campuses visited in this country." It was true, but Clark didn't know that Comstock knew of the disappointment of at least two members of the commission when they made their visits. He could only wonder who squealed.

"Now, unless you have further questions of me, I'll take my leave." It was Comstock's habit, although an ex-officio member of the group and therefore privileged to attend all meetings, to excuse himself on such occasions, giving the regular members an opportunity for private discussions and avoiding any embarrassment his presence might cause.

The executive committee decided to take no action. Various reasons were given, the campus grapevine reported! There had been a quorum, but not all members could make the meeting; the full senate should have a chance to study the report; let's wait until fall when everyone can digest the recommendations. But perhaps the most convincing argument of all was that Bill Comstock was going to fight it tooth and nail. Some had no appetite to take on the president when he felt strongly about an issue.

Dean Clark never got to the board of trustees; he didn't even ask to argue his case with Glen Parkinson. By the time the fall semester rolled around, the all-university assembly was an idea whose time had passed—almost. Officers of the student government, elected the previous spring on the wave of interest in the university assembly, worked hard to revive the idea upon their return to campus. Previous tactics in such situations usually focused on strikes, sit-ins, harassment, hostages, or destruction of property. Their strategy this time was different.

They would show their disgust with Midtown U, its president, the governing board, and the faculty—yes, even the faculty since that group had rolled over and played dead in view of Comstock's opposition to the assembly—by voting itself out of business! This would show the world just how unimportant and insignificant students had become at Midtown University. Students didn't have a role in institutional affairs; alumni should withhold contributions until President Comstock and the trustees came to their senses, and prospective students should be discouraged from coming to Midtown.

With a full year to publicize the many negative factors about the university—the one that had lured them with false propaganda—the duly elected officials of the student body (only 17 percent of the students had voted) would tell the world of the gross inadequacies of the institution and the astonishing stupidity of its faculty and president.

Battle lines were drawn. Student officers set to work in planning the year-long campaign; neither Comstock nor professors took seriously the students' threat. It looked good on paper, but the plan to discredit Midtown U proved ineffective at every step.

On behalf of the student government of the university, its officers demanded that each recruiter sent out from the admissions office be accompanied by one of them so that prospective students could hear the truth about Midtown! The director of admissions would have none of it, and besides, he had no money for such nonsense.

Next came the student newspaper. Its editor had strongly supported the idea of the university assembly all the previous year as the presidential commission had slowly pursued its task. Approached in the fall, having interviewed Comstock and having learned both his position and the rationale of the assembly plan, the editor had determined that he didn't welcome the prospect of bad-mouthing Midtown, his university. As he explained, the editorial staff was studying the matter; but neither support nor opposition ever came.

The same message was sent by the alumni council. The vote of their executive committee was unanimous: "to take no action regarding the request of the representatives of student government."

As academics know, controversy dies slowly on a campus. What had begun as a movement to install an institutional assembly at Midtown had now become an issue of survival or demise of student government. That item became the sole agenda for those who had been elected the previous spring to represent the students' interests in university affairs. They wanted their fellow students to vote themselves out of business when elections were held the following spring. They succeeded in reaching their goal. Student government was abolished.

By picking only candidates who agreed with their position, by campaigning vigorously, by appealing to friends who would vote as directed, and by downplaying positive roles for student government, the officers had achieved their goal. For the first time since World War II, when the campus had been completely mobilized for the war effort, Midtown University had no student government.

President Comstock, while disappointed to see it happen, clearly understood the cycle of student activism. Waited upon one week before the election by the three top officers of the student governing body, Comstock had expressed his wish that their government not be abandoned should their slate of candidates win. Go back to the students with a referendum; keep at least a skeleton of student government alive. It had been useful in the past, and it can be an important part of campus life in the future.

The advice fell on deaf ears. The morning after the election, all newly selected officers submitted their resignations.

"Now, Mr. President, what are you going to do?" asked the student body president who had just been elected as he handed Comstock his written resignation. He was accompanied by the out-going president, who had arrived at his moment of triumph: the end of student government.

It could have become an angry exchange; Bill Comstock chose not to make it so. Unless the occasion required otherwise, his voice to students was always that of friend and counselor, never that of the military officer nor the policeman.

"I am sorry, " he began, "that you have found it necessary to take this step. What has been done cannot be undone, however. And I shall not try. You see," his tone calm but serious, "student government was here when I came. It has been a part of this university for decades," pausing to let his message sink in.

"What do I expect to do? Nothing."

Answering his own question before either of them could respond, Comstock explained, "Student government will return when the students themselves want it, not until then. But I don't expect the wait to be too long. It is truly unfortunate that we face the year ahead without the usual participation of students in university affairs. You may not believe it, but what you have done is a disappointment to all of us—faculty, alumni, trustees, and, yes, to me personally."

Both young men (no women had yet reached the point of seeking the top student office) were beginning to feel a bit of guilt for their actions. Having arrived in the president's office wearing a brave front, they left with serious but quiet doubts.

In the few weeks remaining before another summer recess began, organized efforts were taking shape for the rebirth of student government. One year after being voted out, it was reborn.

Dean Clark had retreated to his teaching and research; few remembered the sequence of campus events—or cared. Midtown University was too centrally located to be long focused on its own affairs. National and international events were too fast moving, and many faculty members, students, and alumni were deeply interested or involved in them.

Whether it was another crisis in Russia or China or the Middle East, the emergence of yet one more threat to world health, a civil war in a not yet discovered third world center, or a natural disaster which was straining all humanitarian efforts, Midtown University felt its direct effects. No matter where the fever might rise, anywhere on the planet, Washington felt the chill, and the campus where Comstock worked (he never accepted the term "presided") always seemed to field first-team players. No wonder students arriving on campus for the first time could sense the flow of history through every building, book, and street corner.

It was the unique environment of Midtown University that permitted a pulling back from the precipice of a possible all-university assembly. Fortunate, thought Comstock that such a misstep could be sidetracked. In sharing responsibility, a manager could indeed bring about delay, denial or even achievement. It was good to know where any group might be headed.

Just when he had concluded that committees and commissions, star-studded or plain like vanilla, were a potential menace, Bill Comstock was awakened to an overwhelming story of success by the work of a group on his own campus—a group most of whom he had appointed. It was Midtown's Commission for the Year 2000.

Chaired by the provost of the university, nine members selected from various constituencies of the institution had labored diligently in searching out the most promising path for the next century. By reviewing current developments on other campuses (every member of the commission had visited at least one other institution of higher learning where some publicized innovation was being tried), by assessing Midtown's limitations and opportunities with hard-headed rarity, and by listening carefully to respected colleagues, members had put together a practical document for the future—a rare product in academe.

Upon first reading the report, the president could hardly believe his eyes. He had seen so many such documents before, most of which set out unrealistic goals, claiming usually that the college or university should be all things to all people. Often the report pointed out that new resources—money—would be required, but that was the president's job—not really a difficult task if he would only pursue it! Shelves were filled with such volumes, most of which accumulated the dust of the ages. But Midtown's commission had produced a refreshingly down-to-earth analysis of their institution's strengths and opportunities, wisely leaving unmentioned the weaknesses and the many areas of specialized scholarship in which nothing was offered.

But Midtown's president was not the only reader the report satisfied.

Reviewed by selected groups from the faculty, alumni, students, and trustees, the study brought forth much praise and only minor suggestions for change. From those reviews the president took the document to Midtown's governing board where it received both a thorough review and a unanimous vote of approval. The Commission for the Year 2000 had done its work well. University spokesmen could now clearly relate to the areas of scholarship, the courses of study, and the kinds of service that Midtown would pursue in the foreseeable future. Personally, Comstock felt especially indebted to the commission for giving him the substance for all of his own fund-raising efforts for the remainder of his active career.

There was a place for collective thinking after all. The filtering which the commission had done—taking promising ideas and programs from other campuses, weaving them into the already existing offerings of Midtown, and assessing their potential for the future—would be critical to the decisions that had to be made immediately as well as later.

With his confidence thus restored in committees and commissions, Comstock would never again write them off as useless. Instead, he would look for the circumstances that would best promise a worthwhile result—a clearly prescribed purpose for such a group, an able and dedicated leader, and sufficient support in both staff and money to get the job done.

Could private business and industry benefit from group work, or was such a device as the commission useful only in the not-for-profit world? Appointed to just such a group at General Power and Light, the open-minded academic would learn more about profit-making enterprises.

Much had happened in the ten years since Bill Comstock accepted the invitation of the CEO of General Power to become one of fifteen directors. GP&L, as it was known throughout the Washington region, had recruited its chairman from the upper Midwest, and Comstock had not gotten to know Christopher A. Burke before being asked to join the board. Since the company was a regulated public utility with a reputation of respectable community service, the president of Midtown felt complimented to be invited. Since he had voluntarily left another board a few months earlier, one that was requiring increasing travel away from Washington, Comstock also believed he could find time without neglecting his campus duties.

Another factor, one always present in decisions made by Midtown's president, was the prospect of making new friends—and supporters—for the university. Most immediate, however, his close friend Ray Radcliff was a senior director of General Power. It was Radcliff who had suggested Comstock to Burke even before the new CEO arrived in Washington, and it was he, in turn, who went after Comstock to join. Such are the ways of corporate America.

Comstock felt especially fortunate to number Raymond Radcliff among his closest and best friends. Here was a Washington attorney, another respected criminal lawyer who was also a trustee and generous supporter of another university. Yet he was big enough to embrace the president of Midtown as a friend and confidant. It was easy for them to share their deepest concerns because of the high level of respect between them. Having discussed even the most confidential matters, each returned to his separate world.

It was an unusual friendship which began in a casual meeting.

They introduced themselves to each other on the handball court at the old YMCA. The game that both men loved would bring them together again and again. Although the playing field is a meeting place for many—whether tennis, golf, squash, or other—few such encounters lead to lifelong friendships. This one did.

So when Bill Comstock sat down to lunch with Chris Burke, each knew the agenda and each knew the outcome. One would invite the other to his board and the invitee would accept. It was that simple. The luncheon provided only the opportunity for these two leaders, one a newcomer to the community and the other a well-anchored part of the establishment, to get acquainted.

Ten years later it was a different world in which GP&L was doing business. Some public utilities in the country, General Power among them, had entered the world of competition. Regulatory agencies no longer allowed them a minimum level of earnings, and General Power was having to examine all its activities in order to survive. Bill Comstock had witnessed the entire transformation. Even Midtown U, a major customer of General Power, had looked at other possible sources of power to see whether money could be saved by shifting to another supplier. So important was the matter to the university that Comstock had considered resigning from General Power because he was afraid of being caught in a real conflict of interest. His chairman insisted that he remain.

Having decided to stay on the board, Comstock was asked by Chris Burke to serve on the committee to downsize the company. "Downsizing" was in its ascendancy. Few corporations in the country were exempt from the worldwide competition requiring every enterprise to examine its way of doing business. Both finished goods and raw materials entering the United States or leaving the country were being subjected to intense competition from around the globe.

When Ray Radcliff agreed to serve as chairman of the committee, Comstock knew that he must join the group as well. He didn't think he would have the time that would be required, but like other busy people, he made the time. Months later, he would candidly explain, "It was one of the most valuable experiences I ever had. On that committee I learned more about production, what the costs are, and how they can be controlled than I ever imagined."

What he didn't say was how do we in academe apply some of these same innovations to learning. That part would bother Bill Comstock for the rest of his life.

Downsizing at GP&L became the mission for Jean Bosco, the vice president for personnel. One of the first women to hold such a position in a major American industry, Mrs. Bosco had quickly proved that appointing her had been no mistake. After only a few years in the job, she knew every position in the company, the knowledge and skills necessary to perform well, and the level at which the incumbent was either succeeding or falling short. Equally vital to the task of downsizing–doing more with fewer people as the process was often explained–Jean Bosco knew where jobs interlocked, overlapped, or separated.

To guide "The Radcliff Committee," as it became known, and to lay out an overall strategy for achieving the goal, Burke engaged the top consultant of the day, Michelle Burnside, a management consultant who had established her own company, Burnside Associates, as a result of her early successes in helping corporate giants like IBM, General Motors, and AT&T reduce their work forces.

Within weeks, every employee of General Power was analyzing his own job, that of the person who brought him his raw material, if any, observing the task of the worker beside him, reporting it all to the supervisor above, and offering alternatives that promised savings in time or energy. When it was all over, examples could be found at all levels in which employees recommended elimination of their own jobs.

With a goal of 25 percent reduction in the work force, what started out as inconceivable and impossible to most employees turned out to be a payroll one-third smaller. It was shocking, a head-shaking, unbelievable result. Those whose jobs were eliminated saw the waste and duplication which had gone unnoticed for years. Perhaps most surprising of all was the almost total absence of ill will, undoubtedly due in part to the generous separation packages offered by General Power to all whose jobs were eliminated. But the knowledge of duplication and overlapping was so widely known since every employee participated in the complete process that no one had to depend on the grapevine to learn the facts. They had seen first-hand that GP&L was badly bloated.

Chris Burke offered retraining at company expense for all who could be assigned to new positions. The opportunity for early retirement with unusually attractive financial inducements was chosen by many, leaving relatively few to look for new employment. Even they left feeling good about GP&L because of an innovation in the financial settlement provided to each employee–shares of stock in the company.

With one-third of the payroll disappearing within two years–it would take that long to achieve the full reduction–GP&L was certainly headed for the best period in its history. Every employee, even those who lost their jobs, would benefit from the anticipated increase in earnings. The usual job referral services were provided as well, but ownership of stock was the most talked about feature of the entire process.

The Radcliff Committee had done its work well. Comstock would look back at what appeared in the beginning to be a most unwelcome, difficult task and marvel at the results. He would also learn something that he would worry over—how could the same kind of review be applied to Midtown U or any other campus?

Would he ever be in a position strong enough to lead such a review? Would any university president? He could hear the debates. What kind of committee, commission, or other filtering device could possibly accomplish such a feat?

It was a possibility worth remembering.

VIII

Philanthropy: A Way of Life Only in America

It was the one part of university life that made William Comstock most uncomfortable. How could he ever bring himself to ask anyone for money? When he was faced with the invitation to become president of New England University, raising money was the only responsibility of a university CEO that truly scared the otherwise knowledgeable and confident academician. Having come up through the professional ranks step by step, he well understood the special relationship of the faculty to the institution. The same could be said of his confidence in dealing with the student body and alumni groups. The general public gave him no particular concern, and although he had never worked directly with a governing board, the soon-to-be university president was confident of his ability to learn on the job.

But asking for money? His mentor (Comstock was in his fourth year as chief assistant to Ivy Wall's president) simply answered each inquiry on the topic with a shrug and a short assurance, "Don't worry. It will be easy for you in due time."

When such comments failed to soften Comstock's worried look, his relaxed, confident, and highly successful mentor would add, "You just ask, like reading a menu in your favorite restaurant."

And that's just the way it turned out. Years later, Comstock would tell other aspiring presidents, "Raising money should be among the most pleasant tasks of your presidency." He was also able to cite the most flagrant mistakes he had made as he moved from novice to expert in this delicate arena.

As he accepted his new responsibilities for raising funds for New England U, Bill Comstock, always the student, learned much of philanthropy and its unique role in the culture of our country. He came to see the many ways in which the generosity of people, many of modest means, added the vital "civilizing" factor to our daily lives. He rediscovered the definition of a rich man: "One who wants less than he has," one of the oldest of proverbs. And he recalled Mahatma Ghandi, of whom it was said, "He wants to give more than he takes." He would also learn that many who have little give much, and the opposite: Some who have much give nothing. Each person, like each snowflake, is different.

But Comstock would come to realize that our own America was the birthplace and is still the home of the world's most generous philanthropic activities. Indeed, he came to see that giving–giving by both individuals and corporations–is part of every community across the country. Among the insights he gained was that many great universities had been made possible only through philanthropy. He came face to face with the wealthy, the greedy, the generous, and the callous. People in businesses became known for the responses they gave to others' needs. NEU's new president focused for the first time on the vital relationship between private giving and the world of learning.

Facing a recently met alumnus across the luncheon table in Cleveland, Bill Comstock would make his first mistake in fund-raising. He would try to avoid such a misstep again. For years to come, he would look back and point to the encounter as a prime example of a blunder, the kind made when preparation is sloppy and incomplete.

Steve, as Roger S. Blaine insisted president Comstock address him, although the two had met only two hours earlier, was among NEU's most successful alumni. An outstanding undergraduate in chemical engineering, Blaine went directly to Cleveland where he found work in a small company producing an additive for motor oil. Imaginative, industrious, and thoroughly honest, Steve had no difficulty persuading the company's owner and founder to follow a new idea–one that Detroit's car makers and the country's drivers quickly accepted. It was an additive to prevent motor oil from congealing and gumming up the engine in cold weather.

Touring the plant with Blaine as his guide, Comstock quickly sensed just how successful this fast-growing company had become. Now employing some 1,500 people (the total work force numbered 32 when Steve came to Cleveland only 20 years earlier), occupying a new plant with unbelievably clean, bright, and well-ventilated work stations, the scene was not the kind Comstock experienced all too often in American factories. Instead, it was a sparkling example of the new kind of smoke-free industry that communities all across the country would seek to attract for the remainder of the century.

The businesslike but unhurried tour had followed a brief chat in Steve's office. Now the two were sitting in the company lunchroom—no executive suite, no exclusive dining room, but with enough privacy to engage in conversation without being overheard.

"Bill," began the host, "I know you didn't come here just to see our plant. I've read the material you sent about the plans you have for strengthening my alma mater, and I want to help."

Here, thought Comstock, is an unusual man. Friendly, sincere, businesslike, no pretense, Blaine had come right to the point—no dodging, no evasion, no hesitation. This new-found friend was, in his own way, offering to give before the messenger even voiced the request.

"As you might guess, I'm particularly interested in advancing the engineering programs, and it is that part of the university I want to support financially." As Comstock listened, he actually became embarrassed at his own hesitancy. Blaine, perhaps sensing the growing discomfort in his guest, continued.

"Tell me quite candidly, Bill, how much do you think I ought to give?"

He must answer. But, if he asked for too much, he might lose the respect of this obviously brilliant graduate of NEU, and if he asked for too little, the institution would fall short of the next step upward. Mulling it over—as long as he dared—Bill Comstock replied, "Steve, I hope you can give $100,000 to the university."

There it was—out on the table. Not until later did the academic, inexperienced at that time in an art in which he would become expert, learn that Steve Blaine expected to be solicited for one million dollars, a sum that would have stretched him a bit but an amount he was prepared to give, provided he could contribute it over a period of perhaps five years. Comstock erred on the wrong side. He failed to live up to expectations that the donor already had in mind, an unforgivable mistake in the world of fund-raising.

Blaine was such an unusual alumnus and corporate executive, however, that Comstock's inexperience proved not to be at all damaging to New

England University. As the friendship grew between the two men—it would last a lifetime—Blaine gave much more than a million dollars in financial support to his alma mater, and even more in terms of work, promotion, and help. His company became a regular employer of NEU graduates, offering them, as Blaine said, a similar opportunity to that which he had been fortunate enough to find upon graduation. Unlike many, Steve Blaine continued for the rest of his career to give credit for his successes in business to the exceptional quality of the education he received at NEU. Comstock would meet all too many alumni of universities who were quick to blame their failures on the institutions they had attended rather than take any responsibility themselves.

Blaine, as the CEO of what became a major American corporation, had lots of company among other business leaders as he increased his activities with his alma mater. Elected first to its governing board, he served through a series of assignments, culminating in the chairmanship of the finance committee. Bill Comstock, at the time of his departure for Midtown University some years later, tried to persuade the governor to name Steve to the chairmanship of the board, but state politics dictated otherwise. Most would never know the full value of Steve Blaine's help in furthering the fortunes of New England U; the governor's political debts prevented them from ever learning.

But as Comstock observed in the years to come, senior officers of America's corporations, and especially the CEOs, seldom hesitated to serve as trustees, advisers, and fund-raisers for colleges and universities. They also gave of their personal resources. Too bad, thought the academic, that uninformed professors level criticism at business without appreciating the interdependence of education and industrial advancement. Likewise, Comstock would many times observe the lack of appreciation the entrepreneur had for learning.

Like other academic leaders before him, Comstock came to realize that wealth—all types and levels, present and historical—was a subject that would occupy more and more of his time and thought.

Great wealth! What does one do with it? Early American tycoons—Andrew Carnegie, John D. Rockefeller, and Henry Ford—set early precedents. Another economy, new in some ways, would bring new names to the philanthropic roundtable. Gates, man and wife, was but one new name, but the foundation bearing that name would count sums unheard of in earlier years. More high-tech companies would join.

But monarchs and merchants in other parts of the world, some of whose wealth was unmatched, seldom exhibited such benevolence. Knowing that private (often personal) philanthropy is a uniquely American phenomenon, Comstock sometimes wondered what factors came together to produce this unusual characteristic of our society. He could name the income tax laws—or the absence of them in the early years—your brother's keeper syndrome, ego satisfaction, personal fame, public recognition, humanitarian interests, buying immortality, or a hundred other factors. Whatever the motivation, this keen observer of fellow human beings came gradually to realize that philanthropy had proved to be a basic component of our civilization.

The drama of philanthropy was intriguing as Comstock saw it played out in the boardrooms where he participated. Personal friends in the legal profession, officers and directors of financial institutions, physicians and family members—those who managed trust funds, foundations, or other philanthropic endeavors—were all a part of this great American endeavor.

There were elements of this special altruism which Comstock quickly found distasteful: lawyers maneuvering clients into positions so that their estates would be left to the lawyer's disposition; bankers who gained control of trusts and then used the resources to meet the bank's charitable obligations; family members who squandered resources meant for broader community causes; and physicians who allowed themselves to be appointed guardians or executors of their terminally ill patients.

And the greatest foundations were not immune from political bias, personal influence, or arbitrary decisions. With billions at stake—charitable giving had long since passed the hundred billion threshold—it was perhaps naïve to think that all philanthropic decisions would be made on merit. Fortunately, the get-all-you-can group, no matter what the source, remained a small minority among those who handled charitable funds. Comstock just didn't want to see a single dime misused. He kept that thought foremost in his mind as he continued to raise money for Midtown University. The steps and missteps would be many before his academic career, spanning more than four decades, ended.

Perhaps, as he reflected in later years, the most important move he made when he arrived at Midtown University was to assemble a small team of development people and to serve personally as their leader until the task could be turned over to a full-time vice president. Mrs. Comstock had done her share as well. Together the two rallied alumni groups in every major city in the country, finding high levels of pride and personal warmth where inactivity had been the pattern before.

It was ironic, thought Comstock as he remembered those early years, that he, in company with a fund-raising consultant already employed by the university before his arrival, actually received only one pledge–the magnificent sum of five thousand dollars–in their first 12-city trip across the United States. The new president learned much more, however.

The consultant, a veteran of 25 years in university development work, was at the president's elbow every minute with advice for the moment and guidance for the future. The only problem was the president had to do everything; the consultant actually did nothing except advise. Addressing Comstock as Bill from the moment they met didn't bother Comstock at first; he wanted in no way to be regarded as too formal or stuffy. But as the exaggerated familiarity continued, especially in the presence of elderly alumni and the youngest undergraduate when meeting for the first time, Comstock began to look for substance in his highly paid consultant.

What he saw was form, procedure, and ritual; there was no substance. It was "Bill, you must meet this one, call on that one, cultivate the assistant who will in turn lead you to the rich alum or philanthropist." Every wealthy American, whether the person had any relationship to Midtown University or not, whether he or she was miserly or generous, whether any interest in the broad field of education had ever been exhibited–nothing seemed to matter. If the person, the foundation, the company, or whatever had money, Comstock should go after it, according to the consultant.

Never one to telegraph his shots, Comstock surprised his associates and even the development committee of the university's board of trustees by dismissing the consultant. It was no big issue. The trustees were quite willing to turn over to the new president responsibility for fund-raising, development, alumni relations, and all the rest. Now that Comstock was in the chair, they could go back to their own affairs and await signals from the new leader, hoping not to be bothered too often.

And Comstock was ready to take charge.

Goodwill and generosity overflowed among alumni and friends brought together in the president's meetings. People came out to see and greet their new leader. How touched he was to receive a telephone call at his hotel in Denver from a man who identified himself as a graduate of some 60 years earlier, now housebound and confined to a wheelchair. Nonetheless, he would be represented at the evening's activities by his wife, "not a graduate of Midtown U," he explained, "but a loyal supporter."

Some ten days later a check for $1,000 arrived in Comstock's mail from the couple with a short note, written by a shaky hand: "I only wish it were more."

Generosity and greed, thought the president. What is the factor that prompts one person to share money or food or kindness and another to hold his purse tightly, seemingly content only when his wealth is stacked higher and higher?

History records so much greed. That misers are alive and well is probably a condition of scarcity better known to college presidents than to those in most other walks of life. To Comstock, the university was first in overall service to mankind. It was worthy of everyone's support through work and wealth and even sacrifice. After all, shouldn't we be willing to sacrifice for our children and our grandchildren and for the world in which they will live? The university is society's most promising instrument for bringing that better life to more people. So convinced was Comstock of this that no other work could pull him away.

Yet this president, believing ever more strongly as the years went by, knew that others had different priorities. And he respected them. What he couldn't abide was the miser, the Scrooge, and it seemed to be his luck to meet one every day.

That first year at Midtown U brought enough for a whole career. The conflict—Comstock called it a collision in later years—began in an innocent enough way. It involved a respected alumnus and trustee of Midtown U, a career diplomat who had risen to one of the key ambassadorial posts in the world. By all measures the Honorable Reginald Lawson was a person of considerable wealth and one who had made some modest gifts already to other educational institutions. His seemed the perfect name to put on the university's new library. For at least five years faculty members, students, alumni, and even the trustees themselves had acknowledged the inadequacies of the present building. There was simply no space for one additional volume. They recognized the dangers to academic programs if a new library were not built promptly.

Preliminary plans were in place, but not enough money to begin. A naming gift of one million dollars was required. President Comstock invited Ambassador Lawson to lunch.

The ambassador declined but suggested instead that he come to the president's office for the discussion. Lawson knew the topic to be addressed, and he came prepared, better prepared than Comstock could have guessed.

"You know, Reg, how critical the new library is to the university," began Comstock. "As an alumnus and trustee, you have read the reports of consultants and accrediting teams and the petitions of students. We all know our present library is totally inadequate to support the academic programs now offered. Student recruitment is suffering, faculty research is far more difficult, and both new faculty and the very best students are turning away from us after they see our library."

The president then led the ambassador through a concise but complete review of the plans, handily displayed on the center of the rather modest boardroom table.

"Reg," Comstock continued, "will you make the naming gift so the new library can be built? While it is a large sum, one million dollars, it's only one-fifth of the total cost."

The ambassador appeared in no hurry to respond to the request. He must be mulling over the way he will phrase his acceptance, thought Comstock as he proceeded.

"Such a gift, coupled with funds already at hand, will give us enough to start construction immediately. When everyone sees the library is being built, raising the remaining funds will be a certainty. And, oh yes," Comstock added the clincher, "the board would insist upon putting your name or your family name–whatever identification you would choose–on the library."

Lawson still appeared to be deep in thought and still in no hurry to reply. The president moved ahead with more salesmanship. "Andrew Carnegie is probably remembered today because of the libraries that bear his name more than for any other reason. Princeton has its Firestone. One after another of our great libraries bears the name of someone who had a vision for the future. If you do this, Reg," Comstock concluded, "I'm sure you will always be proud of your actions." It didn't seem necessary to him to point out that Lawson would be buying a permanent monument for a fraction of the construction cost.

While it had taken Comstock 30 minutes to lead the trustee through the full presentation, Lawson used a full hour to respond.

The ambassador took a circuitous route in giving his rationale. Perhaps diplomacy had taught him that to say no a person (or government) must cloak decisiveness in a soft wrapping. But there was no doubt about the message.

"Under no circumstance could I do such a thing," said Lawson.

The explanation was new to Comstock; indeed, it was unique. The president of Midtown would never hear it again— never in his long years of searching for money!

"You see," said Lawson, "the estate which I have (estimates ranged between 25 and 40 million dollars) is not really mine. I am only the trustee of these assets. My father passed along to me a very generous inheritance—it would have been much bigger except for the damnable tax policies of our government. It is for my use during my lifetime but must be held in trust for my children and their children after them."

"So you see, Mr. President, I don't really own anything. I am only a trustee of the estate, a trustee for the family. I must do my best to see that it grows while it is in my care, and then I must find every way possible within the law, of course, to transfer it to my children and grandchildren."

Comstock felt numb. Running through his mind as this fellow talked—it was hard to think of him now as an ambassador—was the image of a man filled with self-serving greed, carrying messages to other peoples round the world for America and Americans. In this case the ugly American came in the guise of a mannerly, protocol-minded, immaculately dressed, even debonair diplomat.

Having explained that the million-dollar naming gift could be paid over as long as a five-year period, Comstock couldn't avoid thinking about the annual income from Lawson's estate. It would certainly grow, as it indeed had already, under this miser's management.

Government tax policies, redistribution of wealth, socialism, revolution—Lawson gave new life to those topics.

Comstock went home that evening with a heavy heart. Were he not so convinced that better education was the only true avenue to a better life for all Americans, he could have succumbed to real depression. But although people in high places frequently disappointed him, there were others whose actions surprised and delighted the president and all those who worked tirelessly to move the university forward. Two pleasant social activities concluded another full day for Comstock, and the disappointment had at least dulled by bedtime.

As the president shaved and showered the next morning, new ways of solving the problem were already bubbling up in his mind. A good night's sleep had helped him see things more clearly. He did his most creative thinking with the rising sun and seemed to enter each new day with an extra push of enthusiasm.

But the ambassador was still there. It was midmorning when the subject of the "lost two hours," as the president later described his "high diplomatic encounter" with Lawson, came up again, this time from E. K. Lindstrom, the board chairman.

"Say, Bill," Lindstrom began, "I had a call this morning from Reg Lawson." The chairman had known Lawson for many years and was a contemporary of the ambassador's father. He still viewed this veteran of protocol as not yet quite dry behind the ears. It wasn't difficult for Comstock to respond when EK recounted the ambassador's call.

"He told me," began EK, "that you and he had discussed the new library and that you had a difference of opinion on the matter. Reg said he thinks he should resign from the board." Comstock, waiting for the chairman to indicate how he felt about the matter, allowed EK to proceed. "What do you think, Bill?" the chairman asked.

Comstock didn't hesitate; his answer was quick and clear.

"Let him resign."

EK let out a little chuckle. But it didn't signal complete agreement with Comstock's reply. "You really think so?" the chairman drawled. "Yes, I do," the president shot back. Then he launched into a review of his session with Lawson. He explained that he didn't think the ambassador would ever do anything for the university and that he was only wearing his trusteeship as window dressing for his resumé that went to foreign governments. Lawson had done nothing during his first six-year term on the board, Comstock added. He made it clear that his own relationship with Lawson in the future would be cold and distant. "Anyone with Lawson's wealth," Comstock concluded, "who doesn't have some conscience for the well-being of others is in a very sad state of mind."

"Well then," EK said, "I'll tell him that we regret his departure but since he feels as he does, perhaps he might not stand for re-election." His six-year term was just coming to a close, and the ambassador's letter of resignation pointed to his "great pleasure in serving as a trustee." "New responsibilities," he said, "would require my absence from Washington to such an extent that I would be unable to carry my share of the load." The resignation was reluctantly accepted, and the ambassador was never seen again at a Midtown University function. A year later, however, the president was surprised and amused to receive a check for $25,000 with a short note from Lawson.

"Bill," it read. "I'm enclosing a small contribution to my alma mater. Use it for whatever purpose you and the other trustees may decide. I continue to admire your leadership of our university."

Well, thought Comstock, the man does have a conscience—but not a very sensitive one. The annual income on 25 to 40 million was running at 10 to 15 percent annually, at least 2½-million dollars.

Human nature and human behavior, thought Comstock, as he marked the note for his personal reply and sent the check to the treasurer for deposit, is forever unpredictable. In his first course in psychology he had been warned about errant behavior. Aberration, deviant, perhaps different and unexpected would be better descriptions, but then what could really be foretold?

This note with the check was the last word from the ambassador. Invitations went unanswered, or excuses came from secretaries and housekeepers. Rumors began to circulate that Lawson was ill, that he was in the hospital, that he had gone to New York, to the Mayo Clinic, to the sunshine belt for treatment of an undefined health condition. Some seven to eight years after his resignation from the board of trustees of Midtown U, Ambassador Reginald Lawson died. Only in his early sixties, Lawson was a victim of cancer, but neither he nor his family had felt comfortable in publicly acknowledging the cause of his illness. As with the disposition of his estate, only close friends and family knew the details. The widow, children, and grandchildren, through carefully crafted trusts that minimized inheritance taxes, got it all. Not a single charity benefited. Ambassador Lawson had lived up to his trusteeship.

Comstock had learned that a president's personal behavior carried a strong message to those from whom he might seek financial support for the institution. Alumni of New England U, true to their Yankee tradition, let it be known to all concerned—especially senior officers of their university—that stretching the dollar was not only their personal lifelong practice, but that they also would watch closely to see that every dollar given to their alma mater was carefully used. Some of his colleagues, those serving NEU and presidents of sister universities as well, writhed under such scrutiny, but Comstock could not have been happier. Being completely dedicated to the work of the institution, he found it easy to tell professors or others on campus to seek employment elsewhere if their chief objective was to get the highest possible income.

Philanthropy became a personal matter to Bill Comstock. Early in his professional life, he adopted the tradition followed by many religious groups—tithing. But he didn't do it for religious causes! Many people learned in private conversations with Comstock that his religion was not of the usual kind—church, synagogue, or faith group. It was education. He would state over and over, "Since I believe that education is man's best hope for improving life on this earth, it is to education that I will direct my own giving."

"And since education is my religion," he would explain, "I must do as much for my beliefs as others do for theirs."

In spite of the costs of buying a home, providing for his young family, and beginning a professional career—Comstock had finished his formal education after World War II without a dollar in his bank account—this academic was soon supporting the charities of his choice with more than 10 percent of his income.

In later years when his giving went far beyond the 10 percent guideline, Comstock never hesitated to explain, "It's a small price to pay for our blessings and only a modest investment in our civilization."

With such convictions, beliefs so strong that no one who knew

Comstock could really doubt them, it became no problem whatsoever for him to solicit financial support for the educational institutions he served.

Some among his closest associates felt otherwise.

Woodward D. Grayson was a distinguished professor of sociology when Comstock met him after becoming president of Midtown U. Grayson had come directly from the University of Chicago after completing his Ph.D., and had quickly climbed the professional ladder, making friends, gaining respect for his scholarship and teaching, and at the same time attracting increasingly favorable attention to the institution itself. A frequent lecturer to both private and governmental groups that paid him sizable fees, Grayson was the kind of professor most university presidents are happy to find.

It was only natural that president and professor would soon get well acquainted. Having been informed of Grayson's reputation and having met him at a number of campus receptions, Comstock's first opportunity for an informal, friendly conversation came at the community table in the faculty club. Spotting a vacant chair directly across the table from the veteran professor, Comstock joined the group. In addition to Grayson there were a half-dozen faculty and staff members from various parts of the university, some of whom the new president now met for the first time. It was a friendly group, and they seemed genuinely pleased to welcome Comstock. Not until later did he learn that his predecessor never sat at the community table, although Grayson's words should have warned him.

"This is an unusual pleasure, Mr. President," Professor Grayson began after the necessary introductions. It was soon obvious, too, that others at the table deferred to Grayson.

What began as a friendly luncheon conversation between a new president and a veteran professor soon became a monologue. Grayson gave others at the table, including Comstock, no opening. Referring often to his old teachers at Chicago as though everyone in the group knew them as well as he did, quoting his own scholarly writing with the assurance that all were as conversant with the field as he, and paying no heed to the silence with which his exposition was being received, the seasoned lecturer simply treated the group as another audience, waiting for his self-created gems of wisdom and knowledge to fall.

Comstock had witnessed the biggest bore in the entire faculty for the first time. Other encounters brought forth more monologues, and the new president, like his campus colleagues, found other places to sit when his routine permitted visits to the faculty club.

After a decade in retirement, years in which he continued to publish well-received books with generous royalties and to deliver lectures for large fees, Woodward Grayson died, just six months after his wife had succumbed to a lingering illness. There were no children, and only a grandnephew came to the funeral, a ceremony that had been carefully detailed in the professor's will.

Having listened to many of Grayson's monologues, Midtown University's vice president for development was quick to point out that since the well-known professor spent his entire career at Midtown and since there were no children or other close relatives, surely the estate, or most of it, would be left to MU.

Comstock offered another possibility to the vice president. "I heard so much about the University of Chicago that I won't be surprised if Chicago gets it all."

When the details of the will were finally disclosed, neither MU nor Chicago got anything. And nothing was left to promote further scholarship in sociology. Neither graduate nor undergraduate students would benefit. Nothing educational was mentioned. The entire estate, some two million dollars after all debts were paid, went to a private club in Washington, a place where the Graysons spent their leisure time, far from the academic scene.

Again, Comstock quickly admitted his ignorance of human motivation. What moves people to action? And what kind? He conceded he would never really know.

And there was Ed MacKiever. At 50, following a successful quarter-century of law practice, Ed took on the job of professional fund-raiser for Midtown U. Perhaps bored, but certainly with more money than he and his wife would ever need, MacKiever quickly accepted Comstock's offer to become MU's "Vice President for Institutional Development," a euphemism for fund-raiser.

To be sure, MacKiever's appointment was unorthodox. He had no professional training for the work, no experience with alumni or public relations programs—facts which Ed quickly recounted when Bill Comstock made the offer. Both men would enjoy that moment in later years as each recalled the conversation.

"I want you to be vice president," said Comstock deliberately drawing out each word of the full title, "for Institutional Development at Midtown University," as they began their luncheon. The lawyer had been invited without really knowing what Comstock had in mind.

Working together on a number of community charities and serving together on a corporate board, Comstock and MacKiever had gotten to know each other well. But Ed MacKiever was both surprised and flattered by his friend's offer. He quickly reiterated his shortcomings.

"It doesn't matter, Ed, that you know little of alumni or development programs or that you didn't graduate from Midtown (another assumed weakness that Ed had pointed out several times). Your real job will be to raise money, and you can do that. I've seen you do it! All the rest you can learn in 20 minutes," an expression Comstock often used to minimize exaggerated hazards.

Bill Comstock hadn't tried to anticipate his friend's reaction. It was simply a hunch that Ed MacKiever might be ready to conquer new worlds. A graduate of Ivy Wall University and its universally respected law school, MacKiever had advanced rapidly in his profession. Everything he did pleased everyone concerned. Whether it was a settlement out of court or lengthy litigation, neither loser nor winner spoke ill of the brilliant, warm and friendly, and always fair young lawyer. Did he need a new challenge? Comstock was only playing a bit of unbridled intuition.

"Ed, I must tell you up front that it won't be a bed of roses," Comstock hastened to explain. "You know the academic world well enough to realize that your income will drop precipitously, your workweek will be longer, and vacations will be shorter and less frequent. But I strongly suspect you may find some real satisfaction in helping the rest of us make Midtown U a greater university."

The academic had read his friend correctly. Ed wanted the personal satisfaction of doing something with more meaning than making money and gaining respect in his profession. He had done that. The idea of helping to build something greater than himself—a university that would be around long after his departure from this earth—seemed to be the answer to MacKiever's search. Two days later, Ed called to accept.

Putting his lawyer life to bed, carefully completing each outstanding obligation, and leaving no client dissatisfied, the new vice president took up his duties with enthusiasm.

For the president it was a marriage made in heaven. Fifteen years later, after he had become known as the most effective fund-raiser on any university staff in the country, Ed retired with the praise and thanks of the entire Midtown U family and with personal friendships that lasted through the remaining 20 years of his life.

But Ed MacKiever had forgotten his own mortality and perhaps his legal practice. He died without a will.

Life income agreements, charitable trusts of all kinds, disposition of estates—these had been daily fare as MacKiever advised alumni and friends in providing financial benefits to Midtown U. Like a former Chief Justice of the United States (and many others to be sure), this brilliant lawyer, turned fund-raiser, failed to do for himself what he had so carefully planned for others.

When Mrs. MacKiever died within a few weeks of Ed's departure, the estate was in such a mess that distant relatives—the couple had no children of their own—new claimants, and the ever present tax collectors, each with armies of lawyers, succeeded in dissipating what had been a sizable estate. As the final court orders were recorded some four years later, the university that had been so much a part of the MacKievers' life for more than a third of a century, got nothing. And neither did Ivy Wall, Ed's alma mater.

Strengthening the financial base of Midtown U had proved again to be an uncertain science. A slipup in planning or a "t" left uncrossed could cancel a lifetime of good intentions or long held expectations. However, Comstock's efforts on behalf of the university fortunately resulted in more good luck than bad.

Often unannounced and unexpected, Midtown U received gifts, bequests, and other benefits well beyond those planned or pursued. The case of professor Thomas L. Harris was an example.

Harris had retired in the January of Comstock's first year at Midtown. The two men had met only a couple of times, so the new president had no way of knowing how Harris felt about his 20 years as a professor of biology in the institution. When a check for $5,000 arrived the following August with a short note asking that it be used by the biology department to help some graduate student with his or her research, Bill Comstock was quick to find out more about the heretofore unnoticed scientist.

Professor Harris had retired a little early, colleagues advised the president, in order to move to a warmer and drier climate because of chronic respiratory ailments. Other faculty members in biology were somewhat surprised to learn of the contribution (it was a bit large for Midtown in those days), but they did recall that Harris had bought research equipment for graduate students who were particularly hard up. On at least one occasion he and Mrs. Harris had taken a student to live in their home for a year, and it was doubtful that the student had been asked to pay for room or meals. Tom Harris, as colleagues knew him, was just a very fine human being, genuinely interested in students, an excellent classroom teacher, and a reputable researcher. It was too bad, they all agreed, that he felt it necessary to leave so early.

Comstock called Harris and engaged him in conversation beyond the usual thanks for the gift. The call evoked a warm response from the quiet professor. A check in the same amount arrived in each of the next four years. Graduate students who benefited from the contributions were asked to write directly to the retired professor to express their appreciation. After five years there was more to come.

"Mrs. Harris and I," the professor wrote, "would like to make permanent our modest support for the biology department of Midtown University. Please use the enclosed to establish an endowment fund, taking $5,000 for current needs." The check was for $55,000.

"We expect to send a like amount next year so that you may have another $5,000 for immediate use and enough to raise the endowment to $100,000. A 5 percent payout (the practice was well known at MU) will make available the usual amount annually."

By this time Bill Comstock had learned much more about the Harris family. Having benefited from modest inheritances, both Tom and his wife, Judy, had enjoyed the comforts of middle income Americans while carefully preserving their financial nest egg. They raised three children who were surrounded by good books and enriching music; each in turn entered the world of work fully prepared as a professional. While Comstock did not get to know the children personally, he learned that they were enjoying adult life on the model of their parents. It would be difficult, concluded Comstock, to find a more stable or, in the vernacular, a more successful family.

Since education–learning and teaching–was such a way of life for Tom and Judy Harris, the establishment of an endowment of $100,000 should have come as no surprise. Midtown's president was not ready, however, for the next development. It came by way of an unexpected telephone call from Professor Harris.

"Mr. President," Harris began with a salutation that he always used in addressing Comstock by phone, "Judy and I would like very much to do something more for Midtown, and we want to do it while we are still around to see it happen."

While pointing out that the retired professor and his wife had already done so much, Comstock knew enough about philanthropy to wonder what "it" would be.

"We would like to establish a professorship at MU in biology. If I understand the conditions correctly," Tom continued, "that can be done for one million dollars."

"What a magnificent thing to do," was the only response Comstock could utter. He was absolutely stunned. Here was a million dollars from a couple whom he had concluded had already done as much as could be expected of them. In fact, the best information from university colleagues who had known both Tom and Judy Harris for the entire 20 years of his stay on Midtown's faculty suggested strongly that the $100,000 endowment had already stretched the family resources, leaving little room for any more contributions. Comstock recalled how surprised he was to receive even the initial gift of $5,000.

Tom Harris continued. "We would like to deliver the million to you over a five-year period, income tax laws being what they are, if that schedule is satisfactory?"

Satisfactory? How could it possibly be otherwise? Midtown's president tried to offer his thanks, searching for words to express his overwhelming joy and gratitude.

Tom Harris proceeded to put in place each specific piece of the well-planned gift. "Our commitment is outlined in a letter being mailed to you this afternoon. And, oh yes, I have asked my broker to get in touch with the treasurer of the university directly since we wish to transfer stock to cover the first installment." Harris even spared the president of any uncertainty by adding, "Our attorney will give you a copy of the codicil to our wills covering this liability in case we should both be hit by a truck!"

And some people say professors are fuzzy-headed and not businesslike, thought Comstock.

In the entire history of Midtown University, only a handful of gifts had been so large. And it had come from a retired faculty member, one whose name had never made the *New York Times* or weekly news magazines. Known favorably by undergraduates, and highly respected by his graduate students, Harris' scholarly peers could be found represented in some half-dozen professional journals. Retired, already several years away from all professional contacts, living as comfortably as continuing health problems would permit, Tom Harris was providing for generations to follow what had been for him and Judy, and their three children, the most satisfying experience of life. They were making education a bit more accessible to others.

As for fund-raising, the president could never separate two professors from his thoughts: Woodward D. Grayson and Thomas L. Harris. How many people—students, colleagues, and acquaintances well beyond the campus—would ever see the likes and differences of these two men? They served the same institution for many years, even taught some of the same undergraduates in the liberal arts college, but did they ever get to know each other? Did they ever discuss how college students should be educated? Did the absence of children in the Grayson household make a difference in the way students are nurtured? Comstock would never learn the answers.

There were many ways to raise money for a university, and Comstock, by this time, was determined to master them all. Every member of the development team at Midtown was expected to pursue every lead, to put together a sound plan for proceeding, using each tool as effectively as possible, yet making sure that no corners were cut or any commitment broken. As a result, the annual giving program grew each year and reached further and further into the pool of alumni and friends. Potential for those capable of making special gifts was continually researched and sharpened, and cultivation of lifelong benefactors became the underlying responsibility of all hands. The overall strategy for strengthening the financial foundation of Midtown U included every member of the institutional faculty—every clerk, faculty member, and administrator within the campus, and every friend or alumnus beyond.

For a person to give more than token financial support, Comstock had learned that the purpose had to be something that a prospective donor believed worthy—worthy of real sacrifice. He spent much time and energy preaching, as his wife, Betty, described his efforts, the worth of education and the special niche the university played in the whole arena of teaching and learning. When he returned from any one of hundreds of speaking engagements where he carried the message of education, she would greet him with, "Well, did you use your usual text?" His reply was always the same, "It is the only text I have!"

What a change, thought Comstock. "When I first became a university president, raising money, which I knew very clearly to be a key part of my responsibility, was the activity that I dreaded most." Within a few years, however, looking for money became his most satisfying endeavor. Confident that he could articulate the purpose for which funds were sought, confident himself that the university was one of our most useful institutions, Comstock made no apologies for asking others to give of their resources in its support.

And then he had learned another way of placing financial building blocks in the foundation of a university—invest in real estate. He had watched as Columbia University collected the annual rent from a 50-year lease on the land under Rockefeller Center. He followed events as the lease negotiated in the mid-twenties moved toward expiration in the mid-seventies. Would there be another lease? A sale? A long, drawn out court battle with lawyers, real estate magnates, and bankers expounding both expert knowledge and partisan positions?

No, the problem was solved in a civilized way.

Each side chose a representative, and those two chose a mutually acceptable third member. He was William McChesney Martin, former chairman and highly respected head of the Federal Reserve. Within a short time, both sides reached a settlement, apparently without rancor or disappointment. To Comstock, the results were not unexpected. The press reported that Columbia sold the land and placed the proceeds, 400 million dollars, in the general endowment fund of the university. Only a few years earlier, Bill Comstock had chosen a similar path for Midtown U. But a war had to be won before the policy could be launched.

Pleased that Comstock had been chosen as the new president of Midtown, the longtime treasurer was eager to guide the institution toward property investments just because he believed the time was right. Henry W. "Bucky" Hardart, as Comstock was soon to learn, was both long serving and long suffering. But shortsightedness was centered in the governing board; the chairman firmly said the university should not be in the real estate business. He carried along two other powerful trustees, and Hardart's proposal never received a fair hearing. It had been the same way for 15 years.

The university had acquired a mishmash of town houses, storefronts, and small shops over the years, properties that it would not have the resources to develop for decades. Further, there had been no pressing need for additional academic space. The treasurer had simply wanted to put the land to more productive use. Why not build income=producing properties and thus keep student costs at Midtown as low as possible?

When Comstock took office as president, however, the trustees elected a new chairman—but one handpicked by the outgoing chairman! Not too encouraging, but a change at least.

Sensing that one small project might serve as a breakthrough without setting off too many alarms, Comstock and Hardart planned their strategy carefully. They would find a desirable tenant, explore the prospects of a long-term lease, put the necessary financial information alongside, and then take their case to the vice chairman of the board. Their rationale for bypassing the chairman—in the parlance of management it was an end run—would be that the vice chairman's advice was needed before they bothered the chairman.

Hardart's instincts were perfect. Charles Vann knew a good business deal when he saw one, and for the first time Bucky Hardart had found a friend, a knowledgeable one, among the trustees. Midtown U's financial base was about to receive its first infusion of real estate income.

No great mystery surrounded either the first or later investments. Land which Midtown U acquired in small pieces and built into consolidations was used as collateral for loans which in turn were used to finance the construction of office buildings. Long-term leases to good creditors supplied the cash flow for untroubled amortization. Since maintenance and operating costs, insurance and security, and all taxes were born by tenants, new income began flowing immediately to Midtown. What had been an expense to the university, as bankers might say, was now turned into an earning asset.

But Charles Vann supplied the power behind the scene that launched Midtown into the local real estate business. In retrospect, Comstock's analysis suggested several ingredients for the successful chemistry that brought a reversal of previous policy. Most importantly, perhaps, Hardart and Vann fully respected each other, although each had had few opportunities in earlier years to work together. Both were quietly stubborn, conservative in fiscal matters, and completely dedicated to the welfare of Midtown University. Perhaps, too, Vann wanted the new president to succeed since bickering and ill will had marked the previous CEO's brief tenure. But as Comstock would see over the next several years, Charles Vann was a real asset to the university. He would later advance to the chairmanship and leave Midtown a stronger institution by his wise leadership and personal generosity.

As the initial venture into real estate took shape, Vann took charge. He persuaded the chairman in a session of private lobbying–an aberration to his usual straightforward way of doing business–to call a special meeting of the board's executive committee so the matter could be acted upon without bringing the entire group together. As these plans were put in place, Hardart voiced his worries to Comstock.

"We are bypassing the finance committee, and I'm afraid of the members' reaction when they learn what's going on," he said.

"But the chairman of finance is a member of the executive committee," the president reminded Hardart. "Can't he bring along his committee?"

"Well," the treasurer replied, "he has always insisted that any financial matter be first considered by his committee." Jurisdiction, thought the new president. It rears its ugly head in every governing body. No wonder the U.S. Congress is tied in knots, he thought.

More personal lobbying helped to ease the difficulty. Hardart was dispatched to inform, and hopefully persuade, the head of finance. Citing all the reasons, adding a bit of urgency, and getting only a stoic response, Hardart played his last card.

"Mister Vann is willing to arrange a loan of five million at 5 percent just to push the project along if we move promptly," explained Hardart

"He can't do that! Nobody can get a loan today for less than eight. Is the man crazy?" It wasn't an encouraging exchange.

Hardart clammed up. It was a behavior which over the years had earned for him the designation "sphinx." Faculty members who sought information from him usually came away reaffirming the title. Seeing the treasurer's disappointment—a reflection of the anger and frustration from years of beating his head against the wall of stupidity—the finance chairman broke the silence.

"All right, I'll come to the meeting and hear the story," he said, ending the meeting.

Members of the executive committee who weren't already alerted to the business to be considered were not happy to be dragged in from the beach, golf course, or other leisurely pursuits for a special meeting on a hot August day. Has the new president created a crisis already? Some wondered. A sense of duty, curiosity, not wanting to be left out—the combination was enough to get all members to attend.

It turned out to be a four-hour marathon, beginning at ten in the morning and adjourning at two in the afternoon, with lunch delayed. Some thought a conclusion would not have been reached if everyone had not become more interested in food than in continuing the battle. But the session was worth it, Comstock and Hardart agreed as they walked back to their offices. Even the finance chairman said he would call his committee together before the next full board meeting to "try to persuade any doubters to approve" the proposal.

Neither Comstock nor anyone else could foresee either the agonies or the benefits which lay ahead. As trustees argued with trustees in the final board meeting, Comstock learned much about those with whom he would be working for the next several years. He noted, for example, that Mr. Vann said only a few words, content to sit back and watch the chairman (the very one whom he had found it necessary to convert) carry the case for the new policy. Skillfully neutralizing the substantive challenges to the proposal, he brought around the uninformed and doubters with careful explanations and well-founded financial data. This chairman, thought Comstock, may have been handpicked by his predecessor, but he has a mind of his own, and he wants to push Midtown into the ranks of the best universities in the country. How fortunate to have the leadership of such a chairman backed up by a Charles Vann. In spite of the short war over real estate, Comstock felt better about Midtown U than at any time since he was first interviewed for the job.

The new way of raising money by investing in land and buildings was good for the institution, but it would always bring controversy. Before long, students branded the university "Real Estate U," the press accused Midtown of being just another developer instead of an institution of higher learning, and some local officials bemoaned the loss of tax income.

For Comstock and Hardart, it took session after session, meeting after meeting, and answer after answer in the months and years to come. Patiently, courteously, and factually the general public and Midtown's many constituencies were addressed. After years, questions still arose, but thanks to the tireless efforts of more and more people who understood and approved of investments, the tide began to ebb. Even the mayor and city council stopped criticizing when they saw that each project brought new tax income to the city. One enterprising reporter, however, intent on writing a great exposé, wouldn't give up. Under the ruse of wishing to discuss a university's appropriate role in conducting classified research (secret investigations for military or CIA dollars), Howard Kerod, a well-known investigative reporter, was granted an interview by Comstock.

"I understand you have some very valuable real estate," Kerod observed early in the conversation. The question neither embarrassed the president nor caught him off guard. What the reporter was not prepared for was the president's answer.

"Would you like to see some of our real estate?"

"What an invitation," thought Kerod. "This academic suspects nothing. I'll get the lowdown before he realizes why I'm here."

"Come with me." Comstock's invitation was all innocence. Grabbing his coat, the president led his guest to a busy street corner within full view of a new library.

"Tell me," he challenged the reporter, "what is that corner worth?"

Sure of his ground, Kerod replied, "Judging from property values in the area, I would guess it to be very valuable."

"Yes," agreed the president, "if we were to build a plush office building or a modern hotel on the spot. But we spent ten million dollars to build the library, and we spend five million each year to run it. Now, you tell me what it's worth."

Irritated because the reporter had made the appointment under an umbrella of deceit, Comstock twisted the knife a bit further as they parted. "Why don't you find out the square-foot price of land under the White House while you're looking around town. You might find the federal government sitting on a gold mine." The otherwise questioning reporter had no response.

A very smart investigative reporter wrote no story. He came face to face with the obvious: Location is indeed important in establishing the value of land, but so is the use to which the land is put.

When the new president became the old president and retired some two decades later, income-producing properties (the now accepted terminology for such investments) had increased well beyond the first hundred million. Although far short of Columbia's four hundred million, it was not impossible to think that Midtown could come close to that mark given another thirty years. Furthermore, other non-profit enterprises were pursuing similar investments. Officials of several universities had come to Midtown to see how similar projects might be developed on their respective campuses, and Comstock was being singled out for his farsightedness. The persistence of an old treasurer and the shrewdness of a vice chairman had made it all possible.

Having explained a thousand times, or at least it seemed that many, having answered the same questions over and over, Comstock was in for still one more surprise as a veteran of the business school faculty paid him a visit in his last year as president.

"I want to write down the full story of the Midtown University saga of investment properties as a case study in management, and I want to do it before you retire, Mr. President, because you are probably the only person still around who has seen the full story." Quite a change, thought Comstock, from the dozens of faculty senate meetings where questions always seemed to carry an accusation that investing university funds in real estate was stupid, illegal, or immoral. Too often, faculty members seemed to be saying those dollars should come to us as salary increases, and if not that, at least to buy more books for the library.

Although he was complimented by the professor's understanding, the president declined to furnish the substance of a case study. Comstock had no appetite for revealing the subtleties of negotiation among trustees and senior administrative officers that made each project a kind of unseen puzzle to be pieced together. Then, too, there remained other properties to be acquired. Every real estate agent in town was waiting for the university to begin putting together yet another consolidation of land so they could jack up prices ten to twenty fold.

"Maybe in 50 years someone writing the history of the institution can plow up the story," said Comstock as he bid the professor good-bye.

Fund-raising, as Comstock looked back on some 50 years of university life, was a vital part of academe. Intriguing, challenging, frustrating, rewarding, but never boring, searching out money for educational purposes was a labor of love for the veteran administrator. He had seen so many individuals, guarded and suspicious in early discussions of even small contributions, change into proud and deeply satisfied donors after doing something worthwhile with their money. Not only did they loosen their own purse strings, but these converts also often became emissaries in their own right. It was alumni and friends of the university who were the most effective fund-raisers but only after they had made gifts of their own!

Again, in retrospect, Comstock had been instrumental in raising a lot of money for Midtown U, but as he liked to put it, "I was only one of many who wanted this university to play an increasingly important role in the nation's affairs." Before he was through, a complete development organization had been built—annual fund, parent's program, special gifts, deferred giving, and capital campaigns. His own attention was often focused on the special gift or on the person who might bring such a gift to the university. It became for Comstock a personal challenge, a poker game, to go after some "Scrooge" and to see him part with money, a possession often viewed as more valuable than his right arm.

And, of course, some got away. Many wealthy prospects were written off by the president and his senior colleagues as "having found a way to take it with them"—to the next world.

Comstock lived through the era in which universities and other nonprofit entities were making philanthropy a common denominator and the business world was adopting hundreds of worthwhile causes as an everyday activity. Many such efforts, while self-serving—scholarships or summer camp for children of employees, health services for the family, or special programs for the handicapped—were broadened to include support for the performing arts and other community-wide benefits.

It was the period of broadening private benevolence that Comstock viewed as the time when volunteer giving assumed responsibility for many of society's needs and services that tax dollars could not and should not meet. In the corporate boardroom, on the campus, and in the community he saw the period of "social responsibility" arrive. To some of his colleagues in the three camps, the change was unwelcome, but their resistance couldn't hold back another tide of history.

Knowingly or unknowingly, a few pioneers, individuals, and families—those who had acquired colossal fortunes—had set the wheels of private philanthropy in motion.

Within Comstock's experience, three names kept coming back as representative of those who had used their great wealth to fuel the machine—Andrew Carneigie, John D. Rockefeller, and Henry Ford. All three names became permanently engraved in the charitable causes of our country and the world. Did the circumstances that led to the creation of these great fortunes give way to the charitable work that followed? Was it a kind of single-minded greed that drove these men initially to build, acquire, grab, push, control, defeat, or destroy? Did the compassion that led to their philanthropy come later, or was it always present? Comstock had long since given up any serious attempt to analyze the complexities of human motivation. Clinical psychologists and psychiatrists and other professionals could have the field as far as he was concerned. Knowing that a little knowledge is a dangerous thing, he decided to keep his diagnoses to himself.

And, of course, many more names were added to those of the three giants as philanthropy grew through the years.

What does one do with great wealth? Perhaps, he thought, each person has to be placed in that uncertain position before a decision is possible. In his widely diversified activities, Bill Comstock had worked closely with individuals who were second and third generation members of wealthy families, and he had also gotten to know some whose fortunes, equally large, were still held by the original builder. Among both he saw greed and generosity, concern and sympathy, ruthlessness and cruelty.

In the boardrooms of both business and academe, Comstock witnessed year after year the struggles for fortune and power side by side with compassion and generosity. Sometimes the contrasting personalities sat shoulder to shoulder. No two human beings could be further apart than two trustees who served Midtown U for many years. Comstock, in order to avoid their names, would refer to them for the rest of his life as Pat and Mike. The fact that neither was Irish made his disguise more complete.

At 60 years of age Pat was recognized as one of the most successful lawyers in America, a reputation he already had earned when Comstock first met him some 20 years earlier. Always busy, but never overburdening himself, this able lawyer, whose fees were notoriously low, was in great demand. He accepted clients who had nowhere else to turn, it seemed—a young writer who claimed that a motion picture producer had stolen the plot for a new movie from an obscure short story he wrote just a few months before the film was shown; a shopkeeper whose business was being destroyed by the construction of a new major highway; and a waitress whose wages were withheld after she was fired by her notoriously amorous boss. All the stories and humorous jibes about lawyers did not stand up when one got to know Pat.

On the other hand, Mike possessed an ever unsatisfied appetite for money. And with money, as he accumulated more and more of it, came increasing conceit, arrogance, and lust. There were those who said they simply couldn't believe what had happened to Mike in the 15 years it took him to go from nothing to a vast fortune. His avenue was greenmail.

Not particularly complex, the game as played in the final quarter of the 20th century called for a raider to acquire, as clandestinely as possible, enough stock in a company to demand representation on the board of directors or a direct role in management. The company was then forced to pay an exorbitant price for the stock in return for an agreement from the raider to go away.

Long before Mike arrived at the point at which he had enough capital to enter the greenmail game, he had shown his aversion to bullying, cheating, and exploiting. His selection as a trustee of MU was achieved in the same way.

Knowing that he was the biggest borrower from the bank whose CEO served as chairman of Midtown's finance committee, Mike strong-armed the banker to nominate him and lobby for his selection. Bullying had won him a seat on the bank board, and the same behavior modified only by increasing arrogance brought him to the trusteeship of the city's most prestigious university.

Comstock found both these men deeply involved in university affairs when he arrived at Midtown. He quickly realized that Pat never allowed Mike's intimidating behavior to go unchallenged. Observing them as they faced each other across the boardroom table, the new president marveled at the calm, effective way Pat put down embarrassing or downright stupid positions suggested by Mike. Yet Pat seemed never to put himself in the crossed-hair gun sights of the obstreperous fellow trustee. When Mike spoke up loudly, volunteering to raise funds for the football team—not the highest priority in MU's development program—Pat was the first to commend him for his leadership and hard work, in spite of having little interest in athletics himself.

But greed wouldn't quite let loose.

After browbeating a number of his associates to cough up money for football, Mike added only a token contribution of his own. Comstock took no part in that fund-raising effort himself, but Mike insisted on explaining to him nonetheless just why he was not able to do more personally. "You see," he said "everything I have is completely leveraged. I can't pry loose a single ten-dollar bill. But you'll hear from me when my next acquisition takes place."

Midtown's president knew not to hold his breath. Mike's last greenmail adventure reported in the financial news only three months earlier had netted this corporate raider almost 200 million. If a fool and his money soon part, Comstock thought, then it was equally true that a miser and his ill-gotten gains remain glued together—forever.

Would this single-minded, merciless billionaire—it had taken him only 15 years to reach that point according to Forbes annual listing of the super rich—ever soften? Would he discover any activity in the world for which he would part with some of his easy gains? Provide for others in his will? Continue piling wealth upon wealth until his last breath? Would he take note, ever, of Carnegie, Rockefeller, or Ford?

In a sense Mike seemed personally driven like some of the earlier tycoons. But in spite of what biographers and others had written of the three historical philanthropists, it was hard for Comstock to believe any one of them could have been as ruthless as Mike. He had put together a company, bought three small businesses through government loan programs, and launched his pseudo-friendly buyouts that were nothing more than one greenmail attack parlayed into another. Unlike Carnegie, Rockefeller, or Ford, Mike didn't produce, make, or manufacture anything. He added nothing to the world's goods or services. Rather, he extracted from those who had worked to build, forcing some of them into bankruptcy. So despicable were his actions that Congress and federal regulatory agencies tightened restrictions that made greenmail raids much more difficult in the years ahead.

But it was too late to help Mike's past victims. He had already done his damage.

As the university president would later tell his grandsons, "I never found a more greedy or repulsive person." To those who knew something of Comstock's many acquaintances, his statement covered a lot of territory.

But it seemed that each time Comstock encountered a Scrooge in his search for financial help for Midtown, he turned up many more cases of generosity and deeply felt benevolence. Such was the case of Stanley D'Orazio, a classmate from their little high school in a small mining town only a few ridges and valleys from the Ohio River.

Few students even knew Stanley's first name, and teachers saw it only on printed reports. Like many other first-generation Italian boys, he was branded as "Tony" at an early age, a moniker he would carry throughout his life. Fortunately, it bore no particular stigma, and since he was a well-liked youngster, Stanley D'Orazio earned respect for his family and for other Italians throughout the community. He did well in his studies all through school, and he was always polite and well-behaved. No one was surprised when his name appeared near the top of yearly honor rolls and other academic rosters. The whole community felt an added measure of pride when Tony won the mathematics award in the 11th grade, an annual competition held among the best students from more than 20 high schools in the region.

Tony was the first in his family to finish high school. That he went on to complete college was even more precedent setting. If Southeast Appalachian College had not been located 20 miles from his home, that would not have been possible. Even so, it was not an easy thing to do. The country was in the midst of the Great Depression of the thirties, yet Tony was able to work his way through four years of college by a succession of part-time jobs, and as he would say many years later to his family and friends, "a lot of good luck."

His first break—maybe the most important one of all—came only two months into his freshman year. An upper classman, who was getting his board and room in exchange for tending the furnace at the president's house, came down with mononucleosis and had to leave school. Tony, having already made the rounds of all the campus offices looking for work and having made a good impression everywhere he stopped, was tapped to fill in temporarily. His work was so satisfactory that he stayed on through his full four years.

The job paid for his board and room, but even more important for Tony was that the president and his wife got to know him. Their interest in this young, modest, and hard-working student would continue for many years. Some 50 years later, their help and interest would bring important benefits to the college. For Comstock, who was able to witness the whole saga, it was a prime example of the best of all ways to raise money for an educational institution.

With limited course offerings, Southeast Appalachian College could give its graduates only the minimum of courses in most disciplines. Thus, Tony's degree in mathematics, accompanied by his second field of chemistry, did not reflect the same level of achievement as degrees of graduates from leading universities of the time. When he applied for a job after graduation, personnel officers quickly pointed out his shortcomings. Because his record was especially strong, however, and since Tony was so sincerely dedicated, one employment counselor among the six companies to which he applied advised him to return to college, get additional courses, and then come back.

D'Orazio returned to Southeast Appalachian and shared the conversation with the professor of chemistry. As a one-man department, Dr. Cyrus J. Wagoner was known for the extra mile he always seemed willing to travel to help his students. Tony was hardly prepared, however, for the full measure of help he was about to receive.

"Since you have all the mathematics you need for that job, I can arrange for you to get the additional courses in chemistry," said Dr. Wagoner quite matter-of-factly.

"But I need two year-long courses that will run for four semesters," observed Tony, knowing he couldn't put together the money for two more years of college. He also knew the job wouldn't wait for two years.

"But I can tutor you through both courses during the summer," explained the professor.

At the end of that grueling summer, D'Orazio had earned 12 semester hours of credit through "Special Studies," and he reported for work with his new employer. Dr. Wagoner had gone to his office each morning where he met Tony for their daily sessions. His own laboratory next door to the office had become Tony's home for the whole summer, and the president had waived all student fees. But Professor Wagoner was the one who gave the most; the college had no funds for such instruction. It didn't matter. And when Mrs. Wagoner insisted that Tony join them each week for Sunday dinner, he vowed never to forget either the people or the college.

Ten years later D'Orazio handed a check to Dr. Wagoner for $10,000, "to be used for the benefit of the chemistry department in such ways as you see fit." Dr. Wagoner retired after another five years, and he and Mrs. Wagoner were honored at a surprise dinner; Tony had arranged the affair and had invited all former chemistry majors to attend.

In thanking the Wagoners and the former president (now retired) and his wife, Tony voiced his feelings with deep emotion.

"There isn't another college in this country where a student could be as well treated as I was here at Southeast Appalachian." He then recounted in detail his four years of work and study, capped off with the tutoring from Dr. Wagoner. It was a touching story, reaffirmed by each of the more than 30 other alumni present.

"Only in America," D'Orazio observed "could the son of Italian immigrants find such opportunity and encouragement. There is no way I can ever repay my professors, my alma mater, or my new country—but I shall try." No one present doubted Tony's sincerity; no one present, including Tony, knew what form his remembrance would take.

Fifty years after his graduation, Stanley D'Orazio returned to campus for that milestone reunion. With his wife and two grown children present, he gave the college a million-dollar gift, to be used "toward the establishment of the Cyrus James Wagoner Professorship in Chemistry and such other purposes as the president and faculty may decide."

For little, still isolated Southeast Appalachian College, the gift doubled its endowment. Bill Comstock, who had raised more than 500 times that much with the team he had put together at Midtown, saw in Tony D'Orazio's action the best example of all fund-raising. Without the opportunity to attend Southeast Appalachian College, without the superb preparation in mathematics and chemistry, and without the personal guidance of both president and professor, Tony could not have taken a job at the bottom rung of the professional ladder in a major American corporation and risen through the ranks to head his own research team by mid-career. It was the American dream, and Comstock saw it played out by one of his own boyhood friends.

Although he was not a chemistry major, Comstock had been a special guest at the affair honoring Dr. Wagoner.

Undoubtedly, Comstock held a close personal affinity for Tony and all that had transpired. Instead of a personal debt to a single institution as was the case with D'Orazio, Comstock could attribute his own success to a respect for learning and the place of education in the whole scheme of things. With both parents as teachers (his mother gave up teaching after only three years to raise the family and look after the home), education was assumed to be the most important activity in one's life. Learning was the way to personal satisfaction, to the solutions of an individual's as well as society's problems, to economic independence, and to intellectual peace. To his father, learning was a continuous process—to be pursued at home, in school, in the field, anyplace a person happened to be.

Books were special treasures to be acquired, used carefully, and never damaged or destroyed. But learning was not limited to books. Knowledge was all around to be observed, to be understood, and to be used. Walking in the woods, working in the fields, Comstock's father was always the teacher. Flora and fauna carried knowledge for all, and Bill could recall from his earliest days that poison ivy was to be found in every nook and cranny of those hills and valleys, except valleys were "hollers" to the hill folks. Longfellow's spreading chestnut tree was real to Bill and his friends. As they grew up, they harvested the tasty nuts season after season and then watched sadly as every single chestnut tree died from a blight no one could stop. More than fruit of a tree was lost; chestnut lumber was used in dozens of ways by the Comstock family on their hillside farm, and by all their neighbors.

Education, learning, knowledge—there could never be enough—each step opened another river of exploration and study. Bill Comstock learned early that its pursuit was worth all his energy, and to raise money for its furtherance was the closest he could get to serving fully his fellow human beings. Many times he would find others who felt differently; it was particularly hard to swallow when one of them was a fellow university president. That person was none other than one of his own predecessors.

Prescott C. Vogel was on every alumni list that had been put together over the past 25 years. With a fortune estimated at several hundred million, he was solicited for every cause anyone at Midtown U had promoted during the entire quarter century after his name was carried on the Forbes list of wealthy Americans. No one had ever gotten a cent from him. Furthermore, he refused to see anyone from Midtown U, never returned a phone call, and even refused to see the two or three former classmates who remembered him as a friend. No Vogel children had ever applied to Midtown; a curtain of no contact had been drawn.

President Comstock was both pleased and surprised, therefore, when Mr. Vogel agreed to see him and invited him to lunch. Beforehand, he supplied this very special alumnus with the details of Midtown's major fund drive. They met in a private club in New York. Vogel was a most gracious host throughout the lunch even as the two-hour conversation at one point brought tears to his eyes. Some years senior to Comstock, Prescott Vogel poured out his painful story.

"Unfortunately, I can't feel kindly toward Midtown University," Vogel began solemnly. "It's a long story, and while it happened many years ago, the details are still vivid. I don't think I can ever forget." Comstock listened intently.

"It happened in my junior year. I was running for president of the student body and felt that I could win. My grades were good (Comstock had learned from the registrar that Vogel graduated fifth in his class); I had been active in student government, debating, and a few other activities. So far as I could see, there was nothing in my way to winning the election. In fact, the campaign was really free from any big, overriding issues. Then I got a message that the president of the university wanted to see me. I had met him before on several occasions; the campus was much smaller then, so I thought nothing of it.

"'Mr. Vogel,' the president began, although I'm sure he knew my first name, 'I'm going to ask you to do something which you may not like, but I hope you will help me, and in so doing I'll say you will also be helping the university.'"

"Frankly, Dr. Comstock I had no idea what was coming, but I wasn't expecting anything serious," said Vogel.

"'I would like you to withdraw from the race for president of the student government,' the president said bluntly.

"I was so stunned I couldn't speak. In my silence the first thing to cross my mind was that I had done something wrong, that the president of the university (he never referred to him by name) had heard something terrible about my behavior or something that had gone wrong in my campaign. Finally, I asked, 'Why?'" Comstock sat quietly as Vogel painfully recounted the event.

"You see,' the president explained to me, 'it isn't anything you have done. As a matter of fact, you have been quite a model student. The problem is that you are running against the son of a very prominent family, a family which for three generations has made important contributions to Midtown U and who are now grooming this young man for a political career—aimed at the highest office in the country. To win the campus election and serve as student body president here would, to the family, be an important first step to future political success.'

"After what seemed an interminable silence, the president simply added, rather nonchalantly, 'Think it over. If you choose to withdraw, it could be your greatest contribution ever to Midtown University.'"

Comstock had listened attentively, perhaps as shocked as Vogel had been as he sat years earlier in the president's office. No wonder, thought Comstock, Prescott Vogel has been hard to pin down for appointments or responses to Midtown requests; no wonder he had not been supportive of solicitations for funds; no wonder he has looked elsewhere for the education of his children.

"In retrospect I may have made the wrong decision in withdrawing. But I still don't know. It is something that has weighed heavily ever since.

I did stay at Midtown for my senior year," Vogel continued. "I really had no other choice. None of my family had ever gone to college. I didn't feel I could go to my parents for advice. So I bit my lip, withdrew from all campus activities, spent every waking moment on my studies and my part-time job at the hospital, and left Washington as soon as I got my diploma."

What does an educator do in the face of an account of downright injustice done by another highly placed educator? Apologize on behalf of the institution, in this case Midtown University? Comstock didn't have an answer; all he could do was lend a sympathetic ear as his host completed his sad story.

"Embittered, confused, and very angry, I came to New York. After one week, I had a job and visited the dean of the law school at NYU to see if I could be admitted. He advised a couple of summer courses, which I could take at night, leaving me free to work during the day. After the dean received my transcripts, admission was routine. He didn't even ask me to supply letters of recommendation.

"Looking back, the worst part of all," Vogel said, beginning for the first time to show his emotional trauma, "was the distrust that I carried away from Midtown University. Would I face similar treatment in other universities? Could I ever trust deans, presidents, or professors to be fair in their assessments of me? Even after graduation, what could I count on in the way of recommendations? Would they be based on my family, on other factors which I couldn't even imagine, or would they show only me and my record?

"Not knowing what to expect and not knowing where to turn, I simply buttoned up. I refused to share my deep-seated anger, my bitterness with anyone. I simply gritted my teeth and plowed ahead. I was alone and afraid. I realize now that the only thing that saved me was a stubborn, bulldoggish determination to get ahead—to get a good job, to get money, to become self-sufficient—and never to be dependent on anyone."

Having told his story, Vogel settled back in his chair, dropped his shoulders, and let his whole body relax.

Then he picked up the account again with a bit of anti-climax.

"It was years before I learned to trust other people. I didn't even tell my own parents about Midtown until much later; I was afraid that they would not understand."

As Vogel spoke, Comstock, appalled, tried hard to find a response. Finally, he spoke. His words came from the heart.

"I have never heard a more damning indictment of one's own action, and to think it had to occur at Midtown University. Mr. Vogel," addressing him now eye to eye, "I now truly understand why you have stayed away from our campus."

Leaning forward, eager to explain, Vogel added, "I just concluded that you, Dr. Comstock, should hear my story. I can't expect that either you or anyone else can correct the mistake of half a century ago, but you are certainly due an explanation."

As the two men ended their luncheon, Comstock, expressed both thanks and understanding, "No one from Midtown will bother you again. I'm sorry that anyone at our institution could behave in such a dastardly fashion, much less the president. For what it's worth, and I realize it can't be much, I apologize for all the grief and agony your years there have brought you."

"It wasn't your fault." Sadness had replaced anger in Vogel's voice; and the sadness was especially burdensome for Bill Comstock whose faith in the goodness of all colleges and universities was being sorely tested.

As they prepared to go their separate ways for the afternoon, Midtown's president–always ready with just the right comment–was still groping for words. Vogel, on the other hand, was ready to return to his office, donning the fixed, businesslike but friendly smile that had helped carry him to the heights of the corporate world.

"Say, Dr. Comstock," Vogel whispered as they neared the street, "I know it costs money to visit New York. At least I should contribute enough to cover your trip." With a sickly smile Comstock could only reiterate his inadequate apology.

It was a relief for Comstock to step into a waiting cab. After a short ride back to his hotel, Bill Comstock began to turn his attention to the evening's activities: a visit with the president of Midtown's New York alumni club followed by a reception for parents and prospective students. Then he and two colleagues who had accompanied him from Washington would spend the evening with some two hundred alumni. Comstock was forced to put the Vogel matter out of his mind, but unfortunately it would only go away temporarily.

Ed MacKiever was the first to call when he arrived back on campus. "How did it go with Vogel?" he asked. Confident that Comstock could deliver a convincing plea to this thus far unapproachable alumnus, MacKiever was only doing his job as chief development officer. Prescott Vogel could make a real difference in Midtown's fund-raising campaign.

"It's a long story, and not easy," Comstock began. "Let's just say for now that I came back empty-handed."

How much should he tell his close associate and longtime friend? They had been through so much together, and yet Vogel's treatment as a student at Midtown had been so demeaning and such a terrible reflection on its former president that Bill just didn't know how much to tell MacKiever. Quickly concluding that he would not reveal the full story yet, the president of Midtown smoothed over the matter.

"Vogel had a very unhappy four years at Midtown." Comstock responded. It was the truth, of course, but not the whole truth. And in order to get away from the subject, he added, "I'll fill you in when we have more time."

A routine letter of thanks went from Comstock to Vogel, "for a sumptuous lunch," with no reference to the substance of the conversation. No response ever came from the host. They would never meet again.

Do a person's student days affect his relationship with his alma mater in the years to come? How critical is it, thought Comstock, that the student emerge from those undergraduate years—those first years of adult life—with a strong reaffirmation of fairness, honesty, high ethical conduct, and all the other human virtues so carefully molded in the ideal home, rather than leave childhood's cocoon and move into a world of deception and chicanery. Vogel's shadow would extend over Comstock's relationships with students forever; the image would never disappear.

As students crossed his path in the years ahead, some simply asking questions for information, others requesting recommendations for further education or employment, and still others appearing before him in student groups, Comstock always asked himself: Am I being completely fair and honest in my reply? Is there something else this student should know? Will my answer convey what is best for all concerned? Comstock was aware that he would never know what influence a chance remark, a bit of advice, or a genuine attempt at counseling would have on the student he addressed.

Prescott Vogel had made one thing forever clear: A devastating experience in the student years was poor preparation for financial support to an alma mater in future years!

A trip to Connecticut the following week proved to be a timely cathartic for Comstock.

Bob and Cynthia Woodruff were among Midtown's most supportive alumni. They had met while undergrads and had married the day after Bob finished law school. Cynthia had spent three years following graduation working as a laboratory technician in Midtown University's medical center, making good use of her chemistry major and building a little financial nest egg for the couple's new life in New York City.

Bill Comstock needed no briefing on the Woodruffs. His trip to see them was the result of a personal call from Bob.

"We have sold our home here in Connecticut," explained Bob who, like many others, had spent his entire professional life commuting from the comfortable suburbs into the city, "and we would like you to spend a night with us and see the place before we leave at the end of the month for Florida. Can you work us into that hectic schedule you keep?"

"I'll call you back, Bob, and let you know the date," was Bill's reply to this longtime personal friend and loyal alumnus of Midtown U.

Anytime Bob or Cynthia called, and she shared equally in the friendship with Bill and Betty Comstock, a way would be found for them to get together. An invitation from the Woodruffs was never a command performance. Both were always gracious and considerate, but the Comstocks knew that such an overture carried something of importance; it was not a whimsical message. It would be interesting to see Bob and Cynthia again, thought Comstock, as he waited for his plane to land, but he rightly suspected that more than a social visit was on their minds. It must have something to do with their estate, perhaps a change in bequests, but Bob had given him no clues.

Comstock arrived a couple of hours before dark on a pleasant fall evening. Bob and Cynthia promptly took him on a tour of their beautifully landscaped two acres. Like many of their neighbors, the Woodruffs had spared no expense, it seemed, in putting together a showplace of trees, shrubs, and flowering plants. Adding "40 years of tender loving care," as Cynthia described their efforts, "resulted in what you see today."

"It won't be easy to leave," commented Comstock as they approached the end of their long walk. It was really the only remark which seemed appropriate, but his hosts only smiled.

"Oh, we've crossed that bridge," Cynthia said. "You see, Bill, we made the decision five years ago that we would sell this place and move to Florida when we both got to be 75. Well, that time has come, and instead of dwelling on our departure here, we're really looking forward to a new and different style of living."

"Bill," Bob interrupted, "we wanted you to see this place before we leave, but we also want something else–we want you to have a piece of it to take to your own 'Shangri La' out in Virgina that you have talked about from time to time."

"See this seedling," Bob explained as they all stood under a colorful Japanese maple. "Seeds from the tree drop to the ground and, rather frequently take root. This one," and he pointed to a particularly strong and healthy looking plant, "is about five years old. As you know, this tree is very slow growing, and if it does well, you will have one just like ours in another 35 years! Seriously," he concluded with a chuckle, "we just wanted you and Betty to have an offspring of this tree, which we have enjoyed for 40 years."

As Bob led them back to the house, he added, "We'll leave it in the ground tonight and have it ready for you when you leave tomorrow."

As Comstock enjoyed a leisurely dinner with the Woodruffs, he felt the satisfaction of complete, unguarded relaxation with genuine friends–no need to be on guard, no danger of saying the wrong thing, no worry that a comment might be taken out of context–a rare evening in the life of a university president!

As dessert and coffee arrived, Bob turned the conversation, almost casually, to their wills.

"Bill," he began, "Cynthia and I want to add to the trust funds for the two children. Both were created five years ago with $500,000 in each. The income is to be paid to our two daughters during their lives, with the corpus to come to Midtown U upon their deaths. Then we wish to leave the rest of our estate to that wonderful campus where we met." With a wry smile, he added, "Assuming there is something left after we kick up our heels in Florida!"

Watching the little seedling through the coming years—it had been set in a choice location where Bill and Betty could see it from their breakfast table—was a constant reminder of their friends. It remained so even after Cynthia Woodruff died at 93 in a nursing home. She had survived Bob by two years. In the intervening 18 years, the Comstocks had remained in touch by telephone, personal letters, and one or two visits each winter.

As most college presidents learned, at least those in the eastern half of the country, a trip to Florida was necessary every winter just to remain in touch with alumni and friends of the institution. For the Midtown president the trip meant a full round of calls, meetings, and various activities, but he always made a point of scheduling his final evening with the Woodruffs before heading back to Washington. It was with Bob and Cynthia that the Comstocks felt most relaxed, able to let down their hair and leave with a renewed sense of dedication to their tasks.

It had not seemed that long since he brought the maple seedling to Virginia, but 18 years had seen substantial increases in the two trust funds for the Woodruff daughters. Annual additions by the parents now insured a sizable income for life for each.

The estate was settled promptly because the Woodruffs had planned their departures carefully. Midtown U received a bit over eight million dollars, the largest gift or bequest in its history. Ultimately, somewhere through the years—Comstock was sure he would not live to see it—the corpus of the two daughters' trust funds would also come to Midtown.

As he and Betty discussed their treasured memories of the Woodruffs, Bill Comstock could not help wondering at the lack of understanding on the part of some faculty members of the truly humanistic concerns of people like Bob and Cynthia. Cynicism, they both knew, could be found in any group. Around the community luncheon table on campus, Bill seemed invariably to sit next to or across from a professor who seemed unable to see high-minded humanitarian concerns in anybody—and certainly not in a businessman, public official, or corporate lawyer. Futile, thought Comstock when he heard some disbelieving professors hold forth, and he seemed unsuccessful in attempts to convey to them the reasons behind actions of people like the Woodruffs. Their fundamental feelings and values appeared even less understood.

Unless we get to know members of other groups—business, professional, religious, racial, ethnic, or whatever–as individuals, our opinions of them are likely to reflect the least flattering stereotypes. A lifetime in academe had shown Comstock that the so-called objective scholarship of the campus did not render its practitioners immune from such propensities. He also realized that misunderstandings were of such magnitude across the country and across the world that they resulted in the worst possible violence. Taking time to learn the other person's perspective seemed to be something not enough people were willing to do, he thought.

How many Woodruffs, he wondered, were to be found in our society? Many to be sure. Some in every group, undoubtedly, but never enough.

IX

Parting With Power: Fired or Retired?

"Will you be attending any more meetings?" Jim Kranz was calling with a question Comstock had answered repeatedly for others, one that he had foreseen over the years as he saw fellow directors, trustees, and other CEOs leave their positions.

It had been ten months since the academic had retired from the board of Sanders Kauffman Publishing Company, and he had not been back. Since retirement, he had been traveling–a leisurely trip to the Orient, which included a month-long cruise in the South China seas, and a nostalgic visit to Scotland and Denmark to find long-lost descendants of two of his grandparents. After such a long absence, the question from his good friend Kranz came as a bit of a surprise.

"No, no, no, Jim! I won't be back," was the reply.

"Bill, we miss you." The sincerity in Krantz' voice made Comstock realize that his friend was not just uttering a flattering cliché; he was making a genuine appeal.

"It's nice to be missed, Jim. I'm flattered, but long before I retired, I decided that honorary directors are a bit of extra baggage in conducting the ongoing business of an enterprise."

"But I'm not the only director who feels this way," Kranz responded. "Two others have made the same observation at recent meetings."

"Jim, I deeply appreciate knowing that some of the directors feel that I might play a useful role. But it just won't work. I have seen too many board members over the years who wore out their welcome all too quickly after retirement."

As he talked, Comstock recalled a former vice chairman of Sanders Kauffman who, after 45 years with the company, came back for one board meeting each year only to make a fool of himself by demanding answers to questions which long ago had been resolved. To make matters worse, he felt compelled to offer advice to the directors and senior officers at the luncheon that followed each meeting, an affair meant for relaxation and where speeches were taboo.

"Let me ask you about a couple of matters that are before us now," Kranz broke in. While he knew clearly that no one could persuade him to resume attendance at board meetings, Comstock thought so highly of Kranz that he could not cut him short or dismiss his question. A lengthy exchange followed between the two, one an active director and the other retired, one with two years' experience and the other with twenty-seven. Both took their responsibilities seriously. Unfortunately, Comstock allowed himself to make reference, at least once during the discussion, to a troubling situation that had occurred when he first came on the board. It provided an opening.

"You see," Kranz said, "you have all this institutional memory and the rest of us do not."

"No, Jim. Among the senior officers and the board itself are very knowledgeable people who go back further than I do. How much each of us may choose to remember of the old days is another matter. In retrospect it's clear that some of the decisions were good and others not so good. But Sanders Kauffman is a well-respected, major publishing company with an effective CEO and able directors." As a final comment, putting the matter to rest but in a friendly tone, he added, "You certainly don't need me."

"But we don't want to lose track of each other," Jim came back at his older friend. The reference was not to their personal relationship because the two men and their families were close friends, vacationing together at least once each year. The concern was that the retired director would lose track of Sanders Kauffman.

"Don't worry, Jim. I'll keep a beady eye on you and our favorite publishing company. And if I find something in an annual report or even a quarterly one which I don't like, I'll be after all of you."

Giving up power, leaving the position, either that of CEO or board member, was a routine action for some, a crisis for others. Whether fired or retired, the behavior of the person affected was often surprising. Midtown's now retired president had seen every extreme, none more distressing than the post retirement actions of his friend Jerry McCoy.

Adams Park University had benefited over the years from a generous legislature, a large and supportive alumni group, and an intellectually superior student body. Following the lead of the most selective private colleges and universities in the northeast, Adams Park, having taken half of its name from an early colonial family, was among the leading universities in the country. Gerald McCoy became its 17th president. It was here that Comstock came to know, to work with, and to become personal friends with a new colleague.

McCoy's leadership, lasting almost ten years, proved to be a period of further enhancement of the prestige and respect for the already well-known university. Building institutional partnerships with research centers and universities in Europe, South America, Russia, China, and Japan, Adams Park became a leader in international education. Much of its newly acquired reputation was the result of McCoy's directions. When an important ambassadorship became vacant, the President of the United States turned to the leader of Adams Park U to fill the post. It proved to be a wise appointment.

Jerry McCoy served brilliantly. He understood diplomacy, needed no tutoring in economics, had read history since a teenager, mastered three foreign languages, and found himself at home with world leaders. So well did he do his job that when a new president of the opposite political party came to Washington, McCoy was asked to continue. He remained for four more years, bringing to seven his total service as an ambassador and pushing him well beyond the normal retirement age for academics.

But the transition from the corridors of power and the challenges brought by the complex relationships of the world's leading nations—tasks that had occupied his every thought and action for seven years—were too much for him to lay aside.

He was now separated from the ambassador's office with its many amenities. Another change in administration had created a state department that had no use for his advice. Having lost touch with the country's universities through years of complete immersion in foreign affairs, Jerry McCoy was left without anchor. Here was a very talented person, still in good health and with lots of energy, still years away from the rocking chair. Where would he go? What would he do?

It took several months of his hanging around Washington for him to decide, time in which his wife and friends could only watch and wait. The children were all married, making lives of their own. Grudgingly, McCoy had to recognize that he could no longer influence world affairs. Those who had sought his counsel while he was president of Adams Park University and especially when he held one of the most important ambassadorships in the world had suddenly disappeared. It was as though the mast of a great ship had been swallowed up by the earth's curvature.

When the decision was finally reached, it was one of desperation. Clinging to the only straw remaining, Jerry McCoy went back to the small New England town where Adams Park was the major activity. As if to invite continuous aggravation, he bought a house within the immediate environs of the campus, just across the main street and directly opposite the home provided by the university for its president–the place where McCoy had spent ten busy, successful years.

For some, the choice might have been most satisfying; for McCoy it was a disaster.

A new president had arrived just six months before McCoy took up residence across the street. Tom Peterson had been selected after a nationwide search, and the trustees were convinced they had made a wise choice. Jerry McCoy had never met him, however.

Harold Mann had moved into the presidency when McCoy departed seven years earlier. A former professor of English, dean of the college of arts and sciences, and finally chosen by McCoy as academic vice president, Mann was a popular, non-controversial choice. His years as president were calm, serene, and uneventful. There were no serious problems, but neither was there much excitement. Many liked it that way. Those who wanted to see a bit more activity got their wish.

Thomas Peterson walked innocently into a fire storm. Jerry McCoy supplied the gasoline.

Eager to establish a friendly as well as a professional relationship, Tom and Nancy Peterson arranged a small dinner party as a kind of welcome back for the McCoys, including just three other couples from the campus, all longtime friends and close associates of the McCoys. The evening began like old-home week; the mood changed well before dessert.

Taking over the conversation before the soup was finished, McCoy, buttressed with an extra martini, let the group know of his many achievements reaching more than once around the world since his departure as president of Adams Park. Presidents, dictators, kings, and prime ministers had all crossed his path, most of them coming out second best in what was recited as his own brand of conquering diplomacy. Mrs. McCoy, a quiet little lady, sat through it all, nibbling on her food, eyes focused mostly on her dinner napkin.

The Petersons patiently and bravely endured, striving mightily to be good hosts; the other guests were in shock. They had never seen their former president with too much to drink. The world of diplomacy had indeed changed this ambassador.

When Nancy Peterson announced after dinner coffee in the living room where an inviting fire was burning (it was already early winter), everyone left the table with relief. The reprieve lasted only until they were settled in comfortable chairs, carefully balancing cups amid tenuous smiles indicating some degree of recovery from the dinner table disaster.

Coffee didn't help Jerry McCoy; it only changed the subject. Almost immediately, he began questioning Tom Peterson on the university. What changes had been made since he left seven and a half years earlier? Why were they made? Whose half-baked ideas were they? And wasn't it about time for all universities to wake up and live in the real world?

Tom Peterson didn't answer the questions; neither did anyone else. McCoy answered his own questions—completing the ruinous evening.

Jerry McCoy's comments on higher education had started out as a monologue. When he finished, it was a diatribe.

By the time Bill Comstock caught up with McCoy, he was not even sure he wanted to renew what had once been a genuine friendship coupled with professional respect and admiration. Perhaps a previous meeting with Peterson had colored his opinion of McCoy. Jerry's telephone call left no doubt about his strong desire to see his old acquaintance.

"I'll be in Washington next week for a couple of days, and I must see you," McCoy said. "I'm working on a couple of things, Bill, and I need your advice."

Comstock briefly recalled his past relationship with McCoy as he searched for a response. The two had been together for several years while both were located in New England, and during that time McCoy seldom sought advice from anyone. Yet the two were friends even though each was a bit leery of the other. Although he had always found McCoy to be straightforward, Comstock also remembered some surprises in their past. More than once, Jerry had caught the various constituencies of Adams Park U off guard. It would be most interesting to see what the old warrior had brewing now.

Peterson's irritation with McCoy's behavior was not only already known to Comstock, but other presidents also knew about it—the academic grapevine had been at work. McCoy let the community know clearly that mistakes were being made in the way Adams Park was being run under Peterson, and, furthermore, the governing board, the state legislature, and the general public should wake up to the problems. When Comstock had a chance to talk with Peterson, he could detect genuine compassion in the young president's comments, making clear that he was worried about McCoy's mental and emotional well-being.

Jerry was writing letters to newspapers, the governor, the chairman of the board of trustees, and the student newspaper, citing mistakes, blunders, and faults of deans, admissions officers, coaches, and even the director of the marching band.

Comstock braced himself for an uncertain meeting with McCoy.

"Bill, I want you to be on my board of directors," McCoy said abruptly after being seated for lunch at the International Club where both men held memberships. "I'm forming my own consulting firm, and I've picked out a half-dozen people across the country to serve on the board. I'm seeing my lawyer this afternoon. I want him to incorporate the company right here in D.C. I figure that a lot of the business can originate in Washington, and..."

"Hold it, Jerry. Wait a minute. What kind of consulting will you do?" Comstock interrupted. He thought he knew the answer, but he wanted McCoy to state it and not to assume that a prospective member of the board was already informed and eager.

"Why, I want to show governing boards and young presidents how to run their colleges and universities both at home and abroad." It was the answer Comstock expected. "There are five or six hundred new presidents appointed every year right here in the U.S., and most of them don't know beans about the business. Also, I've seen a lot of the world in my day, and foreign universities need help even more."

As McCoy continued, Comstock interrupted him once again to ask a critical question.

"Jerry, as you know, beginning a consulting practice requires some start-up cash. Where do you propose to get it?"

"First of all, I'm going to work for nothing for the first six months. And then I figure that each board member will put up ten thousand initially with a commitment to add another ten for the second six months if needed. With sixty thousand up front and another sixty for a cushion, we will be firing on all cylinders." McCoy had the blueprint drawn, but only in his mind. He hadn't put a single word on paper. Comstock took advantage of the opening.

"After you are incorporated, let me see the document. I'll let you know then whether or not I can serve on your board." It was Comstock's way of avoiding an immediate commitment. Finding three incorporators (two besides himself, something the lawyer undoubtedly would tell him), leasing office space, hiring even a minimum staff, selecting office furniture and equipment—those and many more necessary chores didn't quite fit the job description of a former ambassador and university CEO.

"I have another reason for wanting you on the board," McCoy added. "You'll be retiring from Midtown before long, and then you can run the consulting firm." That prospect didn't excite MU's president.

Months went by with no further word from McCoy. Then Comstock answered his phone late one night to hear an inquiry from another retired university president and longtime friend now living on the West Coast. "Say, Bill, can you tell me what Jerry McCoy is up to?"

"I'm sorry, I can't, and I'd be afraid to guess," Comstock replied, just the hint of a chuckle in his voice.

"Well, he called me several weeks ago to tell me about a business he was starting and said that you were helping him. He wanted to sign me up for something, but he wasn't very clear."

It was the last gasp of a once highly respected ambassador, university president, corporate director, and community leader. He struggled mightily to hold on to some of the influence, prestige, and power he had possessed in earlier positions. Unfortunately, Jerry McCoy, with his misdirected actions following retirement, lost the respect and dignity he had rightfully achieved in a highly successful career.

A statesman-like leader had become a cantankerous, unhappy, and bitter old man. Newspapers no longer carried his letters to the editor; long-time friends from the campus had other pressing matters when he called to invite them to his home; and the Petersons, because of his uncertain behavior, no longer included him in their social affairs. Jerry McCoy lived out his years in increasing seclusion, the last five made even more lonely by his wife's death. Giving up leadership was more than he could accept.

Jerry McCoy had "borrowed power," as First Lady Barbara Bush defined it, from each of the positions he held over a period of decades. Upon retirement he simply could not relinquish that power to a successor.

How should one give up power, the power of the position? Of the person? The answers are as many and varied as there are people who go through the experience, thought Comstock: some with protest—kicking and screaming—others with dignity and grace, many with pleasure and relief. The academic watched as another President, Ronald Reagan, departed the high office with more elegance than most, at least symbolically. He and Nancy, after taking their leave of his successor, boarded Air Force One, made available by the newly installed president (Reagan could no longer authorize such a trip), and flew west into the sunset. The next day, the media carried pictures of him cutting wood on his ranch.

Bill Comstock, however, often saw the return of borrowed power become a struggle, one that exacted high costs. He watched as three generations of the Harris family suffered through the transfer of leadership of their highly successful business.

William Harris, between his second and third years at New England U, started a small shop, selling men's sweaters to summer tourists, just off the wharf where most yachts and sailing vessels tied up when they stopped in Bar Harbor, Maine. He shrewdly observed that young men, especially those on their first sailing trip down east from Boston or other New England harbors, arrived in Maine sometimes wet but always cold. They looked for warm clothing before putting out again into the mist and fog. With money to spare, they usually grabbed the heavy woolen sweaters Harris had brought over the border from Canada.

By the time the young entrepreneur opened for the second season, the shop had more than doubled in size. The sign over the door forthrightly but modestly invited the public, "See Henry for the Best in Woolens."

Harris had been busy in other ways during the off season. Not satisfied with the limited supply of stock his suppliers across the border in New Brunswick could furnish, he talked himself into a sizable line of credit with the First National Bank of Portland, no mean feat considering the tight-fisted Yankee bankers. The money made it possible for him to buy directly from mills in Scotland.

Special Imports, Inc., was born with William Henry Harris as its president. Other incorporators joining him in the new company were his banker in Portland and his landlord in Bar Harbor.

It was another of America's business success stories. "Henry" became the name for imports. First it was woolens for all the family; then came perfumes from France, with watches next from Switzerland. Branching into other lines of clothing, Harris added woolen suits from London for both men and women. Within a decade the name of Harris, and of Henry too, had been taken out of all advertising; Special Imports, Inc., had been installed over the entrance of ten major retail outlets in New England. Harris had long since given up all interest in further education, but his business didn't prevent him from pursuing and marrying a young woman who stopped on the wharf in Bar Harbor to buy one of his sweaters. A socialite from back bay Boston, she knew a New England treasure when she found it, and while Sally Compton set in motion the proper pursuit, she happily allowed herself, after a reasonable interval, to be caught.

Fresh out of Radcliffe, with a family name that led back to the Boston Tea Party, Sally Compton brought immediate entry into Boston society for her new husband. Henry Harris hardly needed the help. His reputation for honesty, hard work, and business acumen, coupled with the proper level of modesty, had preceded him. So when the founder of Special Imports decided to build his flagship merchandising center in Boston, the place that would service all his stores, bankers and real estate people stepped up, eager to help—and hoping to get a bit of the action.

Comstock arrived at New England U just in time to see the sun setting on the phenomenal career of William Harris. At 93 he was still running the company. Henry II, well into his sixties, had succeeded to the presidency of the company and the CEO's title more than a decade earlier. Those who knew the family well agreed that "Henry, the Founder," couldn't bring himself to part with the power of managing and controlling

Special Imports. As a result, his son, seemingly the pride and joy of the old man from the day he was born, had never been allowed to make a single, significant decision. Subdued, never one to show his frustration or disappointment, the son continued the role of dutiful underling in the business and obedient child in family affairs.

Comstock only heard the earlier history. Although he came late to the Harris family story, he came in time to see the problems created when the family empire shifted again to another generation.

Henry Harris III was a trustee of New England U when Bill Comstock arrived as president. "Henry three," as he was called, turned out to be one of the university's strongest supporters and one of its most generous benefactors. His relationship to Special Imports was direct—he inherited the company!

At age 40, Henry II was CEO of the still-growing business. His father was determined to handle succession more satisfactorily than his own father had done. Following the founder's death, he stepped aside at the end of only one year of bona fide responsibility in the CEO's chair so that the third generation could exercise complete control.

The youngest Harris was the embodiment of his grandfather insofar as ability, personality, honesty, and hard work were concerned. Within ten years Special Imports had doubled in size, tripled its earnings, and made the third Henry, along with his two sisters, who had inherited an equal share of the company, very wealthy. But the youngest Henry was troubled. Bill Comstock was among the first to hear about it.

"I've asked you to lend an ear, Bill, because I have great respect for your judgment and I know our conversation will remain confidential," Harris began as the two settled down to lunch in one of New York's exclusive clubs—a place where New England U's president only found himself when he was a guest of a member.

Henry Harris was not sitting down to a relaxed, cheerful luncheon. He was worried, obviously heavily burdened. A family crisis, personal illness, or business calamity? Poker-faced but genuinely concerned for his friend, Comstock waited.

"I have decided to sell our company," Henry, speaking softly, broke the news to his friend.

Comstock was shocked, astounded, amazed, speechless! Before

he could think of a repsonse, Henry asked, "Bill, am I crazy?" For the first time a thin smile creased the otherwise solemn, almost sad face of Henry Harris.

With the tension lifted, Comstock allowed himself a smile as well before replying.

"Henry, no one has ever accused you of being crazy, so I certainly won't become the first."

"The last thing under the sun I expected today," Comstock continued, "was what you've just announced. Some university matter, perhaps the education of one of your children–since you have sought my advice on such matters before–but never did it enter my mind that you might be thinking of selling Special Imports." After a brief pause, Comstock added, "There must be some reason that I can't see."

Henry proceeded to answer.

"Bill, you know the history of our company. My grandfather put it all in place; my own father, whom you got to know, handed the company to me on a silver platter; and here I am now, sitting in the CEO's chair, with Special Imports doing beautifully. Most CEOs in the country would give their eyeteeth to have a business running as smoothly as ours. Yet, I'm fidgety, impatient, and, yes, I guess bored."

Harris looked across the table at his guest in resigned anticipation. He knew that neither Comstock nor anyone else could tell him the best course to follow, but he was baring his deepest worry to a trusted friend, bouncing his tentative decision off a willing sounding board.

Taking the cue from his host, Comstock set out to find the rationale for his friend's decision.

"It's apparent, Henry, that you have been thinking about this for some time," Comstock began. "One doesn't wake up in the middle of the night and suddenly say, 'I'm changing my life.' Beyond being bored at the moment, are there problems down the road somewhere that you see?"

"Yes, Bill, I see something ahead that looks like a problem to me. Going back as far as I can remember, I knew that I would succeed my father as head of Special Imports. There was never any question as to how I would spend my life. In high school other kids took for granted that Henry III would inherit the top job in our company, and when I went to college, I knew and all my friends knew what my business career would be.

Dad waited long enough for me to complete the MBA at Ivy Wall University before he took me into his office as a young assistant. Just imagine, being the assistant to the president the week after graduation. I thought nothing of it at the time; it was simply taken for granted since the family owned the company."

Comstock made no effort to interrupt. Henry Harris was pouring out a story that in all probability no one had heard before.

"As you know, I have two sisters; I was the only son. It was assumed that each sister would attend the best college in the country—women's college, that is—marry an eligible young man and live her own life. But for me, my life was fully decided." Sensing that he might be giving Comstock a wrong impression of his parents and grandparents, Henry quickly clarified his statement.

"Don't get me wrong. I was completely satisfied with the direction given to my life. While my classmates, particularly those in graduate school, began their search for employment, often not knowing in what business or industry they might find that first job, I felt smug and complacent. My own future was guaranteed unless I made a complete fool of myself. You might say my success was signed and sealed."

Henry Harris saw clearly both the advantages and limitations that came with his inheritance, and he did not want his academic friend to see any ingratitude whatsoever in his feelings toward his father or grandfather. Such a career path may have been the subject of an executive case study in a business school—or in fiction—but Comstock had never heard one of this kind discussed across the luncheon table. Harris continued. More of his dilemma unfolded.

Neither of Henry's children, he confided, had any interest in Special Imports. There were two sons, as New England U's president knew, and no daughters. Both were able academically, and friends assumed that one, or probably both, would spend a lifetime with the family-owned business. The ground, however, had shifted.

"Neither boy," Henry explained, "wants anything to do with Special Imports. I couldn't get either to take a summer internship any place in the company. I even offered them a summer in Europe with our chief buyer, but there was no interest.

"Henry IV is determined to finish that Ph.D. at Chicago. You may remember he has been there a couple of years now." Comstock did indeed remember. The youngest Henry had talked with New England U's president about possible places where he could pursue an advanced degree in archeology. "Now with two extended field trips under his belt, Henry seems happiest when he is searching the dusty terrain of East Africa for further traces of early man."

"If he can't find a teaching job when he finishes, then he wants museum work. No matter which, it looks like archeology has won the day. And of course," Henry said candidly, "if that interest satisfies him, he should stick with it."

Harris trailed off, not ready to elaborate further. Comstock brought him back to the subject, perhaps inadvertently, with a question.

"What about Paul? Didn't he head for business school a couple of years ago?" Comstock remembered that the younger son had made a good record in one of New England's best prep schools before going to college. He had had no specific information since then, but surely the younger brother could not be written off so soon.

Henry's answer was devastating. It poured forth from a broken-hearted father. Yes, Paul had gone off to college only to be diagnosed near the close of his freshman year as HIV-positive. What began as a runny nose and a little fever turned into a burning 24 hours in the hospital before doctors confirmed the dreaded suspicion. It seemed that Paul had spent a few wild weekends visiting Boston, Hartford, and New York during his senior year in prep school.

"Right now," Harris concluded, "Paul is in Paris, undergoing an experimental treatment."

Neither man knew how to continue the conversation. Comstock tried. "Henry, all of our discussion today will remain between us for as long as you wish. Why not, however, wait a while to see how things turn out for Paul before you sell the company?"

Puzzled, Comstock asked himself: Did Harry invite me to lunch to tell me about Paul? Is selling Special Imports Henry's way of retreating from the corporate world where he is an accepted, respected leader? Will he disappear into his cave, hurrying away from a family tragedy he can't handle?

How inadequate I am, he thought, in helping a dear friend so deep in mental anguish. He could not remember another occasion when he was at so great a loss for words, and words were supposed to be the special equipment of academicians. No tool seemed sufficient for his friend's condition. Fortunately, Harris wasn't looking for words of comfort; he too knew their limits.

Their good-byes were brief, a quick handshake followed by a knowing, understanding look into each other's eyes. Sympathy and genuine friendship—it was all the academic leader could offer.

How long would it be before he would know the answers to the many questions facing the Harris family? Only time would tell. And it soon did when Harris called Comstock from New York.

"Bill, I'm sure you remember the conversation we had some months ago. I want to thank you for lending a sympathetic ear."

"Well, I'm afraid I didn't offer much help," Bill broke in.

"Oh yes you did. You were a great listener, and I took full advantage of your patience.

"I've made my decision, Bill. I have sold the company, and the story will break tomorrow," Henry continued. "I wanted to alert you before the papers come out. The Journal (his reference was to the *Wall Street Journal*) will carry an article, and we have sent out releases to all the media."

"Congratulations," Bill told his friend, aware and pleased that he was obviously relieved.

Special Imports, Inc., the story revealed, was being merged into the second largest merchandising giant in the country. Henry Harris would become vice chairman of the board, not a full-time executive position, the account pointed out, and the Harris family through exchange of stock would become the single largest shareholder in the new company. In addition, Henry and his two sisters would take away tons of cash.

Midtown's president, happy that his friend had succeeded in getting a heavy burden off his back was still concerned. Henry had always worked hard, filled every day with heavier-than-necessary commitments, found it difficult to take vacations—even short ones—and had been known to rush back to his office when matters may not have required his personal attention. Would he adjust to his new leisure? Would Henry Harris be content to see others in the new company making decisions he could otherwise be handling? Could a CEO who had had complete authority refrain from pulling back some of the power he had just given away?

Long after Comstock's own retirement from academic work, he and Elizabeth remained friends with Henry Harris. His wife, Cynthia, sadly, had died of breast cancer some five years after the sale of the company. While Cynthia was battling her disease and young Paul was living from crisis to crisis with his precarious health problem, Henry IV appeared to be the least worry of any family member. He was spending each summer working in some archeological project, having landed a professorship in one of the few first-rate departments in the country. Most important of all, his father had continued to recognize and support the youngest Henry in his professional career.

As for Henry III, he took a leave of absence from his new position after just one year. Cynthia's cancer had just been diagnosed, and the effects on the couple were devastating. The perfect world of a few years earlier had now collapsed. The Comstocks stood by and helped as they could; unfortunately, all help fell short of the need.

Paul's death followed his mother's by just six months. A grieving Henry Harris was now left without family, without his business, and without power.

"It was a good thing I sold the company when I did," he told Comstock only a few days after Paul's funeral. "Bill, you and Betty are great friends. I have leaned on you in many ways, and to tell you the truth, the happiest days of my life, and of Cynthia's, too, were the years we worked together for old New England U."

"Those were good years, Henry," Bill affirmed. "We can both be pleased with the results of our work then."

The two friends reminisced, both avoiding the pressing personal question: What does Henry Harris do now? It was not asked because neither man knew the answer. It came, however, within a few months.

Henry set up an office in the old Pan Am building in New York, hired an able young woman as his secretary, and began to devote his full attention to his investments and soon to those of his sisters. Prudent and cautious, Harris brought the financial affairs of all the family into commonsense, conservative, order. His secretary too had grown with the opportunity provided her and soon became expert under Henry's tutelage. In a sense she filled the void of the daughter Harris never had. When she married a few years later, Henry gave her away.

What happened to the power which had been concentrated in Special Imports in three generations of the Harris family? Comstock saw it transferred to another, even larger center of power—a bigger company. But there was no single owner of power in the new and enlarged corporate entity. It was more widely distributed, held by several senior officers in addition to the CEO. It was also shared by stockholders in spite of the presence of the one "largest" owner, and, of course, a board of directors held the final authority over everyone in the company.

Comstock's favorite analogy of the corner grocery store came back. He seemed always to be drawn to his pet illustration of power. If a person owns the family shop, he liked to say, whether it be grocery, dry cleaning, or what have you, his power over the business is then far greater than that of the CEO of General Motors or IBM. In the latter cases the CEO must share the power of his every action with many others associated with the enterprise. In the personally owned business, all authority is the owner's.

Comstock had learned that one need not be the CEO of a great corporation, the owner of a business, or the president of a university to resist giving up power. One of the most flagrant abuses of office was the chairman of the psychology department at Ivy Wall University—an abuse so extreme that it was ridiculous. Yet no one in the institution's hierarchy was willing to take action. It was Comstock's first lesson in academic politics, and he realized even then that the problem of transferring power was unpredictable and often surprising.

Arriving at Ivy Wall as a new assistant professor of history, Comstock moved into his modest but adequate office in Richards Hall, a century-old structure his department shared with psychology. The hallways were wide and the ceilings high; heating and ventilation cost ten times as much as they would in a modern building, but its location at the heart of the campus made Richards a choice spot. With no lecture halls remaining—they had long since been divided for more faculty offices—the large under-graduate courses in history and psychology were held in nearby buildings. Only graduate seminar rooms remained, along with libraries serving each of the two departments—an amenity that only a great university like Ivy Wall could continue.

It was an academic paradise for young Comstock, who had fought his way through two large public universities and shared choice reference materials with all too many others. Ivy Wall's main library, which held several of the greatest collections in the world, was just next door. Since he arrived two weeks before registration for the fall semester began, opening-term activities gave him another ten days before he had to meet his first class. "Professor Comstock," as he was already being addressed by graduate students and administrative staff, settled in with unmatched satisfaction and humble gratitude.

Having survived the great war when a number of his closest friends did not, having returned to graduate school to complete what the war had interrupted, having done his time as a research assistant and part-time instructor, young Comstock could now look forward to resuming his career—a career which he had known from his earliest days would be the world of learning.

Looking up from his large desk, so heavy he would soon learn that custodians seldom cleaned behind it, Comstock could see the wide expanse of grass and the aging elm trees that marked the original quad of Ivy Wall. Within a few days he added to his office the only missing component to an academic paradise—books. The university's budget for books must be inexhaustible, Comstock thought. He learned there was money for books that he wanted for personal use—in his own office; there was money for any materials he might like for the department library—for his needs and for those of his graduate students. The main library asked every faculty member each month to list any new publications in his discipline that might not have come to the librarian's attention.

William Howard Comstock—it was some time before the new associates began to address him as Bill—knew this was a rare opportunity. He happily set about to fulfill his responsibilities.

Before the fall semester ended, the new "professor" in history (all ranks were accorded the title) was already known as a good lecturer, one whom students, even freshmen, could approach for advice and guidance. Comstock had also outlined, tentatively, the first two books he would write. He found ten-hour days in the office, with a full Saturday morning added for good measure, to be no burden.

But the echoes from the psychology department, at first trickling across professorial lines and then thundering like Niagara, were beyond his imagination. Professor Risen, longtime chairman of the department and now professor emeritus, was raising havoc. It took five years for the drama to end, but for Comstock, who fortunately could stand on the sidelines and watch the parade go by, it was a full immersion in academic politics. To this intellectual Garden of Eden, Paul Risen had contributed a full measure of forbidden fruit.

Joining his new colleagues for a cup of coffee, for lunch at the faculty club, or for an occasional late afternoon chat, the new man in history soon learned the details of Risen's amazing career.

Not unlike many others who had been attracted to Ivy Wall, Risen came straight from a post-doctoral fellowship at a sister institution, having caught the attention of leaders in his field with two brilliant articles in the most respected journals of psychology. At only 30 he was soon promoted from assistant to full professor; he had hurtled the associate rank completely. Such ascent of the academic ladder was practically unheard of among the first tier of universities. Two years later Paul Risen was unanimously chosen by his colleagues, a large and diverse group, to be their chairman. The dean of the college and the vice president for academic affairs of Ivy Wall shared their enthusiasm. After all, this 35-year-old psychologist had already brought additional recognition to an aleady internationally recognized department.

For another 30 years the same positive record was played over and over. Ivy Wall's department of psychology was soon regarded as the best of the best, a position it held until Paul Risen reached 65, and because of institutional policy, was forced to retire. Legislation was not yet on the books that prevented age discrimination.

But Ivy Wall and a few others of the best universities didn't say goodbye to their retiring faculty members. Many—and all of the distinguished ones—were given emeritus titles, provided with comfortable offices, supplied with secretarial help, allowed privileges of the campus, and encouraged to remain at work on their research and writing for as long as they wished. It proved not to be a good policy in Paul Risen's case—for him or for the institution.

Instead of retiring, the chairman simply moved from the chairman's suite, located on the first floor just inside the main entrance of Richards Hall, to a recently enlarged office located at the end of the corridor and to the left, which was the west side of the building. In the original structure it had been a sizable lecture hall. When the building was converted to offices, there was ample room for secretarial staff, waiting room, a graduate assistant, and the chairman's office, plus his personal library. Aside from three common rooms, the west side of the building from the basement to the attic, including three floors of offices, all belonged to the psychology department. The east side was home for history, where young Comstock began his new life. His office, only half the size, was directly across the hall from that of Professor, now Emeritus, Risen.

Risen was such a gracious, friendly man that the still-in-awe Comstock could hardly believe the story as it unfolded.

A new chairman had been named long before Risen's official retirement. He was Fred Manson, a highly respected professor at a sister university, one of Risen's former graduate assistants. Everyone knew that Manson had been hand-picked for the post. The fact that no other candidate was seriously considered was, again, a reflection of the respect members of the department had for their retiring chairman. It was assumed that any new leader would be one cut in the same mold. After all, the man who had made Ivy Wall U's psychology department the best in the country could be expected to do his best to keep it that way. But the best laid plans... So it was with Manson.

Within three months of his arrival, Fred Manson found his friend and former mentor looking over his shoulder. As he prepared material for the new catalogue, an annual chore of listing courses offered and faculty assigned, along with instructions for students and general information for those from other disciplines who would be taking supplemental programs in psychology, Risen insisted on reading the final copy. He made changes and forced his judgment on the secretarial staff behind Manson's back. After another three months, Risen used the informal staff meeting, a sandwich lunch each Friday noon for those faculty members who were available, to question Manson on all sorts of departmental matters. While he leaned over backward to accommodate Risen, one to whom he owed so much, Manson seemed always to fall short.

Fred Manson began his second year disappointed, disillusioned, and already looking for a graceful way out. He was not alone; the entire faculty, a group of men (there were still no women in tenured positions, although they were now receiving one-half of all Ph.D.s granted by the department), proud of the pinnacle they had reached, of the acclaim that their scholarship was being accorded, were saddened by the dogged obstinacy of their former leader.

Across the corridor, Bill Comstock listened in shock. A great scholar found only disappointment in his successor. Refusing to stop his meddling, he drove Manson away at the end of two years. Marvin Nettles fared little better; he made it through only three years.

Such was the tragedy of Paul Risen, and he brought it all on himself. Comstock watched the transformation. It would take another five years for the department to find its way back to stability.

In describing his first five years at Ivy Wall to family friends in the business world (his two brothers spent their lives in private enterprise), he would often say, "I can look out my window and see the best of academe; I can look across the hall and see the worst."

Leon Wyclif was the third to tackle the complex task of restoring the psychology department and its still highly regarded faculty to reasonable quiet and stability. He took the chairmanship, he said, "not to make peace but to reduce chaos to disorder." That sense of humor, plus the capacity to use wisely the power of the position when necessary, gave Wyclif the advantage necessary to keep Risen at bay.

The struggle of these two chairmen, the 70-year-old, who had toppled his two immediate successors, and the 45-year-old, who was taking on his first responsibility as the head of a department, was one from which Bill Comstock would learn much. In later years he credited Wyclif with exercising his authority the most skillfully and successfully of any academic officer he ever knew. He said to Betty Wyclif, in the privacy of their home, "I learned more about dealing with a faculty from Leon than from any other source."

Not only was the youngest member of the history faculty able to see Paul Risen across the hall at his office and Leon Wyclif in the chairman's suite at the other end of the corridor, but he and Betty also regularly saw the Wyclifs, Leon and his wife, Ina, and their two teenage daughters, as neighbors. The Comstocks would look back years later and recall their good fortune.

Wyclif, too, was a "Risen scholar," a term used to designate all those whose Ph.D. dissertations had been directed by Risen. But he had strayed from the career path which others took. Instead of joining the psychology department of another university or taking on full-time research in the discipline, Wyclif took a temporary teaching job in Ivy Wall's law school. There he worked with a small group of criminal lawyers, researching the behavior of some of the worst offenders behind bars. Fifteen years later he was still there, having made a highly respected reputation for himself in a field which many mainstream psychologists refused to recognize. That fact didn't bother Wyclif; he was content with what he was doing.

Although it was somewhat in desperation that the faculty and the college dean turned to him to fill the chairmanship, nothing in the situation was a surprise to Leon Wyclif. He knew exactly how to handle the problem—and he handled it well.

Risen made it a point to welcome Wyclif with a full measure of enthusiasm. Most observers, including the bystander across the hall in the history department, saw a replay of the old chairman's seeming pleasure that an outstanding leader was moving into his old suite—and another of his boys. The display of goodwill lasted only a few days.

Little dust was raised, at least outside the chairman's office, but the confrontation was direct. More than a year passed before Comstock, still happily working away in the little corner office across the hall from Risen, could put together all the details. Small bits and pieces were supplied by Wyclif, more by his wife. Before Leon Wyclif took his new position, the two families were not only close neighbors, but they also had become close friends.

Risen went to Wyclif's office, as the story came together, under the guise of a trivial incident which had occurred earlier in the week. His real reason, however, was to ask the new chairman what he was going to do about a scheduled sabbatical for which a very senior colleague would be eligible the following term. Both items were routine and clearly the province of the chairman to determine. Neither required faculty consideration of any kind.

"Now, Leon, I don't want to meddle in your business," Risen reportedly began, "but you don't have to approve that sabbatical. After all, Smythe (the senior colleague and a longtime member of the faculty) is only two years short of retirement and why..." That was as far as he got.

"Look, Paul, I'll decide whether or not Jim Smythe gets his sabbatical." Fastening his sharp blue eyes on Risen, keeping his voice low but firm, he continued, "My friend, you had your turn at bat. It was a long and distinguished run. Now its my turn."

"But I only want to be helpful," Risen cut in.

"Oh, you can be. And I'm going to see to it that you are. You know how you can help me?" Wyclif continued. "You can let me alone so I can be chairman."

"But Leon..." the old man insisted. Again he was cut short.

"You ran two chairmen—two outstanding men—out of this chair after you retired. You won't run this one out. Do you understand what I am saying, Paul?" For once, perhaps for the first time, Professor Emeritus Risen had no response.

Wyclif continued, "Our working relationship will be quite simple. When I want your advice, I'll ask for it. Until then, keep it to yourself." Leon Wyclif looked out to see the serenity of Ivy Wall campus in late summer; he looked back to see a red-faced, angry ex-chairman.

Almost jumping to his feet, Risen rushed headlong past the office staff, through the waiting room, and down the hall to his office. After 30 minutes behind the closed door, he quietly emerged, carrying his always-bulging briefcase.

It was Friday afternoon. Would Risen come to the office on Saturday morning as was his habit? Leon posed the question to this wife, Ina, as he reported the dash which the old chairman made from his office.

Paul Risen did not come to the office, something Bill Comstock noticed. Not yet knowing of the previous day's clash, he was a bit anxious about the older man's well-being.

Piece by piece, the entire faculty of psychology learned of the Friday afternoon affair. It was variously described: an argument, a fight, a comeuppance, a victory, a defeat, a dispute. A whole list of nouns was exhausted before the story completed its rounds. Leon Wyclif offered little in the way of clarification. He waited. Risen didn't mention the matter to anyone, but it was a bitter, elderly scholar who lived among his lifelong colleagues for the next several months.

Then one day, unannounced and unexpected, Paul Risen came to the brown-bag, Friday luncheon, settled into a vacant chair just three seats from Wyclif and proceeded to eat his sandwich. He said little during the informal discussion, but as the group, some 25 altogether, picked up soiled paper napkins and coffee cups, several faculty members made it a point to let Risen know they were glad to see him.

Leon Wyclif made no special gesture toward Risen at the lunch; instead, he followed him to his office. Closing the door, Wyclif extended his hand, and with the simple comment, "Welcome back, Paul," took a giant step toward reconciliation.

Five years later, when Paul Risen left Ivy Wall to make his home with a son on the West Coast, some said he still remained angry and resentful of Wyclif. Others said he realized that he had been wrong, and that he regretted the trouble he had caused both Fred Manson and Marvin Nettles. Whatever the truth, a young member of a great university staff watched an academic drama of high intensity played out, one never to be forgotten. He had seen a distinguished scholar over time become an acrimonious curmudgeon. He hoped that he would never witness anything like it again.

There was agreement, however, on Leon Wyclif. He did what he had to do. He accepted the power, knowing ahead of time that he would have to use it. His explanation to his neighbor, Bill Comstock, was quite matter-of-fact.

"Bill, I couldn't stand by and see the biggest achievement of Paul's life destroyed. He had built the best department in the country, and it was being ruined. The fact that the same person who had built it was destroying it didn't matter. I wanted that department saved for all concerned—for psychology, for Ivy Wall U, and for the country. I can only hope that somewhere, sometime, before Paul meets his maker, he recognizes what happened with all of us."

"What's the use of holding power unless one is willing to use it for the good of the institution?" Comstock observed.

There comes a time, the two men agreed, when the transfer of power is necessary for the good of the enterprise. Would that all concerned might know when those moments arrive.

One power center Comstock learned to view with particular suspicion was the office of treasurer. The power of the purse—was it real? Perhaps his first personal confrontation made him forever cautious.

It involved Fred Younts, the treasurer of New England U when the erstwhile academic administrator arrived to take up his first presidential responsibilities. Attacking the institution's problems with youthful energy and enthusiasm, picking his way carefully to avoid hidden minefields, he simply never thought that a central officer of a university could be so deceptive. In January, six months after taking up his new duties, Comstock stumbled onto the mischief.

Pouring over budgets and financial reports from earlier years while home one evening, preparing himself for what he had been warned would be a long, grueling legislative fight over NEU's increasing needs, Comstock found an unusual entry. One hundred thousand dollars was included as a special reserve; a footnote straddled the fence between clarification and direct falsehood.

When asked to explain the entry the next morning in the president's office, Younts confessed that he had just squirreled away the amount from the previous year's "current operations." It was a kind of nest egg, he explained, which he expected to bring to the president's attention at the appropriate time. From the treasurer's red face and apparent embarrassment, it was obviously a case of deception. Comstock wondered how many other camouflaged items had been entered in the reports he had been reviewing the night before. He would never know. One thing was clear, however. He didn't need Younts' services any longer.

It was a sad ending to an otherwise uneventful career. Actually, the old treasurer had been asked to remain beyond retirement "to help the new president get a grip on NEU's finances."

Seeing the chairman of the board later in the week, Comstock used the incident to ask that Younts be retired immediately and that his assistant be named to fill out the remainder of the year in an acting capacity. When Younts' letter requesting retirement arrived a few days later, the new president responded with thanks for his long service to the university and with best wishes for good health in the years ahead. Other trustees learned details by word of mouth from the chairman, and before long, deans and other administrators had the full story. Coming back to the president for months ahead were tales of the treasurer's gathering power, most of it surreptitiously.

As the full story was put together, Younts would pick up the balance from numerous accounts throughout the university, hold the funds in earmarked reserves, then dole out dollars here and there to friends and activities in which he had a particular interest. An acting president who served for more than a year before Comstock arrived gave the old treasurer an open field to build his mini-empire.

In many ways it was like the old shell game; Younts built his ego by moving small sums from one hiding place to another, reaching in whenever he wished to show others his mysterious powers. While no audit ever showed downright misuse of funds or personal gain, those who worked most closely with NEU's treasurer during his last decade on the job, some 20 or more administrators altogether, were left to wonder. What a blemish to place on a career that lasted more than 40 years!

As Comstock learned later, Younts was not the only treasurer who reached for power. As president of Midtown U, he had a full view of another who played the game for far bigger stakes. His name was Roscoe M. Wolfe, and he was president and CEO of North South Trust Company, a very large regional bank. For reasons which no one really understood and few cared, he chose as chairman of the board a kind of easygoing, slow-moving ex-diplomat who appeared on the social circuits of Washington and Baltimore but did little else.

Wolfe not only ran NST with an iron fist, but as chairman of the board of one university and treasurer of a very large charity, he also yielded unbelievable control over them. With non-profit institutions and banks now under more scrutiny from the IRS and other government agencies, it would be far more difficult for such an abuse to take place, but Wolfe pulled it off and lived to enjoy a problem-free retirement.

For some 15 years this banker used his positions to put his own hand-picked selections into the offices of both president and treasurer of each. By doing so, he was able to bring the endowments of both to the trust department of NST for management, with the accompanying fat fees. Then by providing all other banking services which the two required, he benefited his own institution still further.

Scandals that broke when such practices were spotlighted by the media some years later came too late to catch Roscoe Wolfe, perhaps the worst offender of all. As Midtown's president assessed his view of such power-building to friends, Wolfe's retirement came before justice; the horse had been stolen before the lock was put on the barn door.

Was the mortal who handled the money, the treasurer of the enterprise, just too close to power to resist using what he could get of it for abuse? Comstock couldn't forget his longtime fellow president, Seeley J. Boothby, the dearly beloved and greatly respected leader of North East College. Leaving a professorship of philosophy at Harvard, Boothby spent his final quarter century in the top office of this first-rate liberal arts college, remaking its already strong curriculum, and raising record-setting funds for a completely new campus. At the same time he personally reached every student through his own classroom teaching. His work at NEC remains a stellar landmark in all of American higher education.

Arriving at New England U as the freshmen president in the region, Comstock wasted no time in making contact with Boothby whose reputation was already well known. He found in the old philosopher an immediate friend and mentor. One man nearing retirement, the other just beginning a similar journey, the two were immediately attracted to each other. It wasn't long before the simplest chores of the academic president or the most complex mysteries of campus intrigue became regular fare when the two men would meet and talk.

Budgets, money, finances–they made up a whole world which academic presidents could not ignore, or so Comstock thought.

"I never worry about money," Seeley responsed at the first mention of the topic. "Call me Seeley," the tall, distinguished scholar said. "It makes me feel younger." Each comment came with the same emphasis.

Seeing Comstock's perplexed look, Boothby explained.

"You see, I have a treasurer who is expert in things financial. To give him the complete responsibility for the entire college allows me to worry about other, more important matters." The new president couldn't quite believe what he was hearing. Is it true the most successful campus leader in all New England, perhaps in the whole country, really doesn't concern himself with finances?

"If I want to build a new dormitory, initiate a new lecture series, or acquire a new piece of art for our museum, I simply ask Don Seibert, our treasurer who has been with me all these years, if we can afford it. Of course, most of the time he has to figure out how much my new spending spree will cost, how best to finance it, and then tell me yes or no." What a wonderful way to delegate one of the most worrisome parts of the president's responsibility, thought Comstock, if it really worked that way.

As the neophyte got better acquainted with the veteran, he learned that it was indeed true—as was everything else that Seeley said. Seibert had the power to approve or to veto; it was also the power to pick and to choose among the various proposals that the president might make. Comstock had come to another conclusion. As the leader of a campus, he must always know enough about the finances of the institution to make such decisions himself. No treasurer, or other officer for that matter, should ever be in the position of overruling the president's priorities in the use of campus funds.

Carrying his power into the presidency of Boothby's successor, Seibert ran into trouble. His priorities for North East College ran counter to the new leader's wishes. Seeing his authority disappear, the treasurer, who had wielded so much control over the years, took the quiet way out; he retired a full year before the normal date.

Comstock, after learning of Seibert's early departure, probed no further. He would always question, however, whether Boothby had such loyalty from his treasurer as to assure support for his own priorities or whether the treasurer used his unusual position to substitute his wishes for those of the president. It was one more relationship that added a measure of suspicion to the ways in which an organization's chief financial officer might behave.

Again, non-profit endeavors seemed especially vulnerable for deceit or downright dishonesty. One of the most flagrant cases on record was that of Main Line Charities, a century-old institution, not quite as large as the Salvation Army or the American Red Cross, but equally respected. Richard Morton arrived to take over the treasurer's office soon after an anonymous donor dumped a hundred million dollars into Main Line's endowment. Presumably, the newly selected officer was an expert in money management. Years later, the general public and, all too late, the trustees as well would indeed learn of Morton's wizardly financial talents.

Coming to Main Line only a few months after Morton, surrounded by all the publicity the major gift had created, was a new CEO, James R. Cronin. He carried both titles, president and chairman, for no reason other than that his predecessor had done the same.

For Main Line a more dyed-in-the-wool blue blood could not have been found. Born into a Beacon Hill family of Boston's upper crust, "Doctor Cronin," as he was addressed immediately following the award of the degree from Harvard's Medical School, soon discovered that the practice of medicine was not really his cup of tea. Instead, he turned to things less demanding–memberships on boards of community groups, charitable endeavors, and other non-partisan efforts. He brought to each activity generous contributions from the family fortune–something which made his presence all the more welcome.

But James Cronin had other attributes. At six feet four, prematurely gray with a well-fashioned mustache, the doctor commanded attention wherever he appeared. After reaching Washington in his new role with Main Line Charities, every hostess in the city scrambled to get this unusual arrival to grace her dining table and drawing room. Yes, there was a Mrs. Cronin; unfortunately she lacked her husband's distinguished appearance. But that didn't slow down the couple's social life; it only made the doctor more conspicuous.

In contrast no one could remember ever seeing Richard Morton on the Washington social circuit. He was always at work, or so it seemed. Off to New York, returning from Detroit or the West Coast, the very busy treasurer was forever looking after the charity's affairs. Trustees saw him only at meetings or burning the midnight oil in his office; he was all work and no play. At least that was the image clearly imprinted on the president and the board. Facts were quite different. While the president and trustees were living the good life of Washington society, and paying their own way, their money man was living in another world of riches with Main Line picking up the check or, as was later discovered–much later–many checks.

It wasn't difficult for Dick Morton's expense accounts, airline tickets, hotel bills, and other documented outlays to go unnoticed. He was careful to build a cozy little group within the charity, each of whom benefited from almost non-existent supervision. In fact, the young woman, much younger than her boss, who approved all such expenditures and personally carried each through the accounting process, was not left without reward. She accompanied the traveling treasurer on many of his trips. That he was reimbursed more than once for some claims also went unnoticed.

It was only proper that Morton be paid well, and he was. Each board meeting found the organization growing in all aspects. Contributions doubled within a couple of years of the eye-opening hundred-million infusion, outreach efforts were touching new recipients, and Main Line was attracting even public grants which targeted special problems. It was an organization being asked to do specific things—feed the homeless in Richmond, direct a rescue mission through Project Hope, and carry medical supplies to a flood-ravaged population in India.

And who was responsible? Cronin claimed no credit for himself, something the other trustees clearly saw. Who, then? No great mystery. The hard-charging, well-organized treasurer. Yes, he certainly deserved a raise—something which also took place often and without much attention to details. Since most members of the board were themselves wealthy, either by inheritance or by current position, they believed Morton should be well rewarded. Because they failed to differentiate between profit and non-profit activities, the compensation package soon grew beyond reasonable boundaries.

Two leading newspapers broke the story; the IRS provided the ammunition. All charities were required to file annual reports of income, expenditures, and other facts, including in recent years the salary of the organization's top officers. In the case of Main Line Charities, the story didn't just break, it exploded.

Salary, perks, expense accounts, and pictures of the culprits made the front pages from coast to coast. As more and more underlings with Main Line talked, Morton landed in jail. Red-faced and apologetic, James Cronin bore the brunt. As he groped and floundered for answers to reporters' questions, he only reaffirmed his own ignorance of the institution for which he and his fellow board members were responsible.

A complete housecleaning brought a new board and new senior officers to Main Line Charities, but it took years for it to regain the level of support enjoyed when the disaster struck. For Cronin, the experience was personal. He withdrew from the Washington social circuit, yet he had no interest in returning to familiar haunts in Boston. He chose, instead, to spend his remaining years in the horse country of Virginia. Friends said, however, that he had no real interest in horses or other livestock; it was simply a place where he could hide.

Comstock added to "Fired or retired" another category: "Jailed." And, oh yes, watch the treasurer.

Some who held power did realize they couldn't hang on to it forever and prepared accordingly. One who did was Dan Allbright. The ten years Allbright served as CEO of the All American Insurance Company was, in Bill Comstock's opinion, the quietest, most serene decade he had ever spent as a corporate director. Unfortunately, the agony and worry following Allbright's retirement more than made up for the years of calm.

Daniel J. Allbright had come up through the company. Beginning in the legal office just one week after graduation from law school, he worked through all the steps before reaching the top office. His first assignments included work with agents and field managers, a kind of teaching responsibility where he explained, day after day, the lines of responsible salesmanship, the ethical standards of the company, and questionable practices which invited litigation. From those first years, Allbright established himself as a straight shooter, one who didn't cut corners and one whose word was his bond. That reputation followed him throughout his long career with ASIC, with senior officers, directors, every employee, and most importantly, with the general public. When practices of some insurance companies were questioned on ethical or legal grounds, Allbright could always be counted on to tell it straight.

His immediate post before reaching the top position was executive vice president, but in spite of the title everyone knew he was the chief operating officer of the company. His boss had preferred to carry both titles of president and chairman for the entire period that he was CEO. If Allbright ever felt he should have had the title of president, he never indicated it to anyone.

Before his promotion to executive vice president, Allbright had served as chief legal officer, vice president and treasurer, and secretary. While he had no firsthand experience in marketing—as he said, himself, "I have never sold a single policy"—agents and managers he had advised from his first days at the company were among his strongest supporters as he moved toward the top. They knew him as Dan, an easy informality that Allbright continued to encourage throughout the decade of his leadership.

Solid progress brought about by a sound organization characterized Allbright's decade. He came to the CEO's office with detailed plans, including an announcement three years before the date he chose to retire that he would like to bring into the company a successor from the outside.

It was his feeling, he told an executive session of the board, that someone with experience in other companies, someone with other perspectives—a fresh point of view—should be the next leader of AAIC. He further proposed spending a year finding that person, and then spending his remaining two years mentoring, grooming, teaching, and preparing the newcomer in every way possible to become CEO.

The directors were not hard to convince. The proposal was simply further evidence of the thorough planning with which Dan Allbright met all of his responsibilities.

A nationwide search, quietly conducted with the guidance of the country's most highly respected headhunter, settled on Duane B. Grissom, an executive vice president of an old-line company, somewhat larger than AAIC, with home offices in Philadelphia. Able, ambitious, and well-respected by senior officers in his own company, he was simply blocked from further advancement by equally young and able officers ahead of him. As the headhunter reported, Grissom's CEO was just eight years older than Grissom, and the president, promoted to the office only eighteen months earlier, was a year younger than Grissom. It all seemed to add up. Here was a promising young executive who must leave his company in order to advance. There was also a perfectly plausible explanation for Grissom's not being made president instead of his younger colleague.

Duane Grissom was interviewed by the executive committee of AAIC, of which Comstock was a member; everyone on the committee supported Allbright's choice of a successor. In short order the new CEO-designate met other directors and all senior officers and field managers. A date was set for his arrival as the new president of AAIC. If anyone had doubts, they were not expressed.

During the next two years, Dan Allbright did everything possible to prepare the new man for the chief executive's role. For his part Grissom responded with intelligence, hard work, and understanding. He was commended, especially, for his help in ironing out some particularly nasty hitches in the production schedules of the computer center. Allbright reported to the executive committee that Grissom, when he saw the snafu of the center, rolled up his sleeves and worked alongside the staff for two weeks, straight through the weekends, to get the problems solved. Those actions gained him new respect as word spread throughout the company.

Allbright retired as he had planned, settling down to a relaxed, part-time role in a real estate company his son had established, but only after he and his wife had spent three months on a round-the-world tour. For his part Grissom added chairman and CEO to his title of president with grace and dignity. Directors went home from the transition festivities, happy to be a part of such a satisfying chapter in the history of AAIC. Bill Comstock, who had witnessed considerable trauma in other corporate changeovers, was especially relieved.

Changing the guard at AAIC took place on June 30, the end of the company's fiscal year. Since August was vacation month with no meetings scheduled, a single meeting in July of the board's executive committee provided the group's only opportunity to hear from their new leader. All members would remember that meeting as routine, business as usual, but with Grissom in charge.

By September new plans were in the air. Comstock and other members of the executive committee heard them first. Nothing radical was in the wind, Grissom said reassuredly, just natural steps in preparation for further growth of the company. Then, as if to remove any doubt he added, "Things that Dan and I planned well before he retired are moving forward." By January, just six months into the new era, Grissom's reference to Allbright had changed.

"Those were Allbright's plans; these are mine." Duane didn't say it quite so bluntly, but the meaning was clear: Dan was right for the company in the calm, plodding, unchallenged period of the previous decade, but things are different today. The industry is undergoing a revolution, he explained, speaking as though he were teaching a class of ten-year-olds.

"Don't expect to see many insurance companies around a few years from now," Grissom declared. "There will be a few, and if we play our cards right, we'll be one of the survivors—and a giant in the business. Let those companies that want to do it go ahead and become financial conglomerates, selling everything from bonds to Oriental rugs. As for us, let's go after other companies. Growth by acquisition should be our course for the future."

Comstock and other directors listened in disbelief. Most were well aware that working out a merger with another company—acquiring control—was at best a chancy venture. What company officers are going to announce that they wish to sell their firm to another, except perhaps at a greatly inflated price? On the other hand, those prowlers looking for easy prey quickly smear an otherwise honorable reputation.

Who determined this was to be the path for AAIC? Directors were incensed. It was doubtful that anyone in the room jumped immediately to the conclusion that Duane Grissom had just driven the final nail in his tour as CEO, but that was the case. He never recovered from sawing himself off that limb.

A chance meeting at a local club with John Lorenzo, a fellow director and well-known lawyer whom Comstock greatly respected, offered an opportunity for a confidential exchange.

"John, I'm worried by some of the things I'm hearing at AAIC. Am I just ignorant, or do we have a problem?" Comstock asked.

"Did you know that Grissom has just fired Tom Rhodes?" Lorenzo's own question acknowledged that there was a problem. "As you know, Bill, I have done some work from time to time with Tom. It just happened at five o'clock yesterday afternoon, and Tom called me at home last night," John added.

"Tom Rhodes was one of the most highly respected men in the company I always thought," Comstock responded.

It seemed, as Lorenzo explained, that Rhodes had advised against the company's recalling a number of old policies and replacing them with new ones that lowered previously stated interest rates. He felt that such action, which technically might be legal, was nonetheless breaking faith with the policy holders. Grissom called Rhodes' action insubordination and promptly fired him.

As winter moved into spring, other cracks appeared in the smooth functioning of AAIC. Rhodes was replaced as chief counsel by a young lawyer from Grissom's old company—two experienced colleagues in the department were passed over without even the courtesy of an interview. The secretary of the corporation was moved aside and replaced, as the board learned later, by one of Grissom's college classmates. But the real bombshell came at the June meeting of the full board, just a few days short of Grissom's first anniversary, July 1.

"Yes, I directed every field manager and every agent that they could sell only our products. They were given 60 days to cut all ties with other companies they represent and to agree to handle only All American merchandise, or leave the company." Grissom was replying to a question from John Lorenzo. Another director quickly followed up.

"And how many of our total field force resigned?" Grissom's answer was less than clear. Some had done this and others had done that. The vice president for marketing, who volunteered nothing and spoke only reluctantly when pressed by Grissom, allowed as how as many as one-third of the group had chosen to leave. "And a lot of them were the deadwood of the company," Grissom quickly added.

It was not a confident group of directors who left the meeting that day. More than one believed that the separation of a third of the field force represented a significant loss for AAIC, but none was certain of what he should do about it. More discussion took place at the July meeting, and Comstock summed up the situation correctly with one of his favorite expressions as he and Lorenzo rode down the elevator together: "We have just listened to further obfuscation. And deliberate at that!"

September brought the expected and unavoidable confrontation. The five outside members of the executive committee had held two rump sessions during the August doldrums. Chairman Grissom, of course, was not invited. A few telephone conversations with Tom Rhodes, among others, gave a more complete picture of manpower losses among field personnel. Eight hundred of the two thousand had chosen to leave. Some were among the highest producers and were veterans with many years of service with AAIC.

As more and more questions kept coming from directors, Duane Grissom retreated to an ever weakening line of defense. Productivity had plunged, the 1,200 who remained in the field force were living in fear and with increased uncertainty. Two more senior officers were fired, and yet the CEO proceeded to discuss various aspects of the business plan. It was only in its first quarter, but the plan bore no resemblance to the one that had been put in place when the full complement of sales representatives was still on board.

"Mr. Chairman, how long will it take for the company to get back to last year's level of sales?" Comstock's question was wrapped in kid gloves, but it was vital. Before Grissom could respond, another director added the clincher: "How can expenses be reduced by 40 percent?"

Within the space of the three-hour meeting, a calm, seemingly well-organized CEO lost his composure. Unprepared for challenges, Grissom was red in the face and incensed that people who didn't know as much about insurance as he did would not accept his decisions. When he turned to his own staff for help, they were quiet.

Another rump session of the five directors followed just 48 hours later. It was decided that Dan Allbright must be invited back—by these same five directors—but clandestinely. They remembered Allbright's forthrightness, his devotion to the company, and also that he had picked Grissom to be his successor.

Since the group (the Fumbling Five, they branded themselves) had no chairman, that role fell to the senior member, Robert W. Flowers, who had recently marked his 30th year on the board. Rob was managing partner of a sizable accounting firm whose clients included both wealthy individuals and small corporations in the Washington-Baltimore area. He had joined two classmates from business school days to found the firm some 40 years earlier. Flowers, like many other good accountants, was observant and cautious. Although quiet, he could be bull-doggish when he needed to be. Bowing to the logic of seniority, he accepted the assignment.

Through his son's office, Allbright was quickly located some three thousand miles away on the West Coast. But the distance didn't matter; Flowers was soon in touch. Allbright had heard of some of the events back at AAIC; five field managers had called him over recent weeks to give him their versions of events. He was so concerned that he readily agreed to come to a meeting of the Fumbling Five. He brought his own strategy for dealing with the situation. It proved to be the right one.

Before seeing the five directors, Allbright called Grissom; he explained that he would be coming to the East Coast in a few days and would like to drop by for lunch. He wanted, as he later explained to the five directors, to discuss some of the matters with his successor personally.

He found Duane Grissom ready to expound. Few questions from Allbright were necessary. The new strategy for the company, according to Grissom, was something of which he was quite proud. A few years and AAIC, instead of plodding along in the middle of the pack, would be the leader. While other insurance companies would be all things to all people, his company (it had quickly become "his," not "ours") would be at the very top in insurance. And, to confirm the absurdity of the path taken by some other companies, he noted that one of AAIC's chief competitors had become "Great Northern Financial Services, Inc." No longer would the century-old entity be branded as an insurance company.

Grissom saved his strongest salesmanship to his old boss for his new strategy to grow the company. Picking up smaller insurance companies across the country would be as easy as picking ripe cherries off the lowest branches in a good harvest, he said. And they would be sweet and full of flavor–money.

"Name one such company," Dan Allbright challenged calmly.

"I'm not ready for that step yet," Grissom explained. "But investment bankers tell me there are plenty of candidates in all parts of the country."

Allbright needed no replies to his yet unspoken questions. Grissom was confident of the new direction for the company; Allbright's doubts came simply from one who was still living in another era, thought the new CEO. Having seen the complexities of proposed mergers, aborted acquisitions, and the animosities often aroused by corporate predators Dan knew that relying on growth as Grissom planned, was about as chancy as playing the lottery, and much more costly. How naïve.

Meeting the next morning at breakfast with Rob Flowers and the other four members of the rump committee, Dan Allbright was ready to face the AAIC crisis.

"Let me suggest a course of action," said Allbright after his brief but frank apology for making such a blunder in picking his successor.

"I suspect you invited me because you are convinced that drastic action was required. With that, I agree. I suggest," he continued, "that you ask Duane for his resignation. Faced with being fired or being allowed to resign, I suspect he is smart enough to choose the latter. Then you should name Gene Craver as interim CEO while you look for a new chief."

Dan had, indeed, read the minds of the five, fumbling or not, and had carefully mapped out a complete script for their next–and in his opinion–immediate steps. Craver was a senior vice president and chief actuary with many years at AAIC. He had chaired a number of task forces charged with working out various complex company problems over the years and had come away each time with praise from his colleagues. Endowed with a level head and a good supply of common sense, and within a couple of years of retirement, Gene Craver was unquestionably the best choice for the short-time assignment.

But the five directors were of a different mind—and they were unanimous. Rob Flowers spoke for the group.

"Dan, your suggestion is sound. But the five of us have another course to propose. We want you to return and head the company." Allbright was dumbfounded. It had not entered his mind that he might be asked to come back from retirement, from his new and very much changed lifestyle, to take up the responsibilities of the CEO again. Before he could respond, Flowers continued.

"Dan, there is more to the job now than just going out to find a new leader. From what we see, there is a lot of repair work to be done. The field force has to be revitalized; hopefully, at least some of those big producers who have left the company can be persuaded to return. Some senior officers have been brought in who may not be the right choices. Morale throughout must be restored." Allbright listened, still in shock.

"You were one of those most instrumental in building AAIC to what it is today, Dan." John Lorenzo spoke up,. "Now, the company needs you as never before."

Others made similar arguments, but it was the sincerity of all five that caught Allbright's attentions.

"Give me 24 hours to think it over, gentlemen, and I'll give you my answer," the former CEO responded, asking for a little time. No one faulted him for that.

What an upheaval for the already planned next chapter in his life, thought Allbright as he waited for his car to be brought up from of the parking garage. What would the family think? His son's business was thriving, but his own role, which by no means required his full-time effort, was still important. His own experience with real estate had been enough to prevent at least three serious mistakes from being made in his first year. Would his son feel that he was being abandoned if his father went back to AAIC? And for how long? There was repair work to be done—the corporate world called it "stopping the bleeding." There was also the none-too-easy task of finding another successor.

There would be no problem with Thelma, his wife, thank goodness. She would be the first to point out that AAIC was something he had spent his whole professional career in building. He could hardly stand by and let it be dismantled without doing what he could to save it.

He made up his mind before he reached home. He had to go back. The power he had happily given away would regrettably be his again.

As he expected, Thelma understood fully. She could help by taking a small furnished apartment near AAIC headquarters, making Dan's commute minimal. And that cruise to Scandinavia could be postponed.

Amazing, thought Dan Allbright! And wonderful! After so many years of married life, each not only knew the other's thoughts but also their very sentiments and inclinations as well as their likes and dislikes. Whether it was woman's intuition or intellect or both, Dan had come to respect Thelma's uncanny assessments of a person or a problem. She had been right so many times when he had been wrong.

Another day, another breakfast, another pleased five directors as they prepared their next steps for AAIC. Rob Flowers would arrange a special meeting of the executive committee that same afternoon if possible. Grissom would be asked to resign effective immediately. He would be told that Allbright was coming back. His contract would be honored. Granted, the executive committee didn't hold full authority to enforce the action, but if he challenged them, they would make a unanimous recommendations at a special session of the board the next day. With the signed letter of resignation in hand, the board could elect Allbright as CEO. It would not be either interim or acting, he would be chairman and president of AAIC, no strings attached.

But Duane Grissom refused to lie down and play dead.

"I refuse to talk to you," was Grissom's answer to the ultimatum carefully voiced by Flowers. "If that's what you have in mind, don't bother me. Talk to my lawyer."

"Mr. Grissom," John Lorenzo stepped in to meet Duane's challenge, "we want a letter of resignation from you today, tomorrow at the special meeting of the full board at the latest, or we shall put in your hands a letter relieving you of your relationship to AAIC." Grissom recognized the message was coming from a most highly respected lawyer.

Five directors waited for the CEO to speak. It didn't take long.

"I'll have an answer for you at eight o'clock tomorrow morning," he replied as he pushed his chair back and rose to leave.

Shortly after eight the next morning, Rob Flowers made a brief call to each of the other four directors. Grissom's letter of resignation, a simple one sentence statement, had been delivered by messenger to his front door a few minutes before eight. "And," he requested "can you please get to the board meeting today at least half an hour early so we may check signals before the others arrive?"

It took only a few minutes for Rob Flowers, who presided, to summarize events of the previous two days. Directors who were not members of the executive committee had been kept up to date by timely phone calls, so they needed little additional information. And, as arranged, Dan Allbright was summoned from a waiting room to join the group after he was elected.

He entered the boardroom to a standing, enthusiastic ovation; he knew then that he had made the right decision. When Flowers escorted him to the CEO's chair, happily relinquishing it himself, one director turned to Comstock and said, "You know, Bill, we are witnessing an historical moment."

It was a relieved bunch of directors who walked out of AAIC headquarters that day. The company, because of Duane Grissom, had major problems to resolve. But the board had done its most important job. It had just installed absolutely the best person available in the leader's chair.

How many corporate directors have walked away from meetings, leaving mountainous problems for the CEO, but feeling good because of their confidence in their leader? Comstock pondered the flow of power which had just taken place. First, it had gone from Allbright to Grissom. But the power had not traveled by way of the board; the transfer was direct from one CEO to his successor. Then the board pulled back the power from Grissom bit by bit. With Grissom's resignation, the directors had it all in their hands again–briefly. They quickly dished it out to Allbright. Like a hot potato, power–executive power, that is–didn't fit with directors, those people who had other full-time jobs. Their power was of a different nature; it was shared with all others on the board.

Bill Comstock explained it another way: "It is the one whose responsibility it is to exercise the power whose use of power is always on the firing line." A bit ironic, thought Midtown's president, that Dan Allbright, retired, relaxed, and away from AAIC could come back and overnight acquire more power over the company than he probably ever had before, or ever wanted. He could do just about anything he might wish to do with AAIC at that moment. The company was in his hands.

Allbright's return was in itself a major step in repairing the damage Grissom had done. The news was received throughout the company with genuine relief, a renewal of confidence, and as one field manager said, "a return to sanity." Directors could go back to their other responsibilities, relaxed in their restored confidence; every member of the work force could face each new day with renewed trust in AAIC. But the nitty-gritty of restoration remained to be done.

Dan Allbright moved decisively and rapidly. A quick message to all hands restored to every company representative a complete portfolio of products, both those of AAIC and of other companies. At the same time he set about wooing the 800 employees who had resigned, succeeding in bringing back many of the highest producers. Some, unfortunately, had carved out such satisfying new relationships with other companies that nothing offered to them could erase the damage done by Grissom's arbitrary action. It would take three years of aggressive recruiting to return the field force to its previous 2,000 level.

Duane Grissom was still fighting. Within a week of his resignation, he filed suit against AAIC, claiming "arbitrary and capricious action" by the board, resulting in "irreparable damage to his professional reputation." With the help of the friend he had brought in to head the legal department, he was able to create turmoil. In the end the company prevailed, but it was just one more problem which Allbright had to set straight as he worked to rescue AAIC.

Before much of anything else could be done, Allbright had to realign his management team, get rid of the Grissom cronies, appoint his own trusted lieutenants, and work out separation agreements with those who were leaving—as he said, "Clear out the debris."

The biggest task of all, finding the second successor to Dan Allbright, moved ahead—cautiously!

Determined not to repeat his previous mistake, Dan decided early that he would not rely on his own judgment alone. He would share the decision, the very selection itself, with the board's executive committee. So as the headhunters (another firm this time) went to work, he discussed their every step with Rob Flowers and his four colleagues. Bill Comstock saw it all from the inside this time around. He didn't anticipate the turn of events, but in the end personal judgment was pivotal.

It came about as the three finalists reached the finish line, and the committee, which included Allbright, was forced to choose from candidates the elimination process had brought to that point or back off and start all over again. Each of the three prospects had genuine strengths; each also had an exposed weakness; all were in the right age bracket, except one, and he was too young.

A senior vice president of the second largest insurance company in the country, one who had worked himself into his position after starting as a trainee upon graduation from college, Harry S. appeared to be the perfect new CEO. Like a ghost, however, he also looked too much like Duane Grissom, enough to frighten some members of the committee. James J., on the other hand, had 20 years with an insurance company. He was now in his fifth year as executive vice president of a large regional bank, which seemed to give him broader experience than the other two. But had he been away from insurance too long? Then there was Charles T. Why was he among the finalists? This company had never put one of its field managers in the CEO's chair, and most of the committee members believed this wasn't the time to take such a chance.

"Charles T. is here because he has survived all the cuts to this point," was the consultant's answer. "You may recall that he nominated himself in the early going by simply applying." Everyone remembered, and perhaps reluctantly, all wanted to forget. He was the highly successful manager of one of AAIC's smaller field offices, but could a field person become CEO? It had simply not been done.

Comstock, instead of discussing the candidates, was reading the CVs again. That of Charles T. was hard to ignore. His recommendations didn't all come from business and industry acquaintances. There was a glowing report from the president of his alma mater, a man Comstock had known and respected for several years. Charles was serving his first three-year term as a trustee of the university, an honor which didn't come to many people so early in their professional lives. Why not call his friend, thought Comstock, and get an even closer assessment of this young man? Why not, also, invite him back for another visit with the executive committee?

Allbright agreed with Comstock that Charles should come back, and as a courtesy, the other two were asked to return for another visit as well. After all, he didn't want to be saddled with all the blame should another poor choice be made. And the others went along because they were confident another, more extensive interview would reveal clearly that the young field manager's experience would be far too limited.

Comstock's call revealed that his friend held genuine respect and admiration for Charles. "His maturity, his judgment, his honesty will make you very proud should you choose him. There is no doubt in my mind that he is ready for such an important responsibility." After a few more questions, the fellow academic had persuaded Midtown's president that the young manager could be a winner.

As Charles' second visit moved along, each director became increasingly serious about trusting the future of AAIC to the young man. Arriving in the city the night before his interview with the committee, he was up bright and early for a private breakfast with Allbright, an invitation that was much more than a courtesy. Dan wanted another one-on-one meeting with the young manager, for Allbright had given him the general agent's job in the first place.

As the executive committee assembled for the midmorning re-visit with Charles, Bill Comstock had already decided on his own strategy for the interview, one he had used many times. He had seen others use it too, but he cautiously tried to hide it as a personal trademark. He would be the last to join in the serious questioning; he would let the others carry the heavy water, pursuing their own routes to gain further insights into the candidate's potential. Not until the last five minutes of the hour-and-a-half session did Midtown's president add his three or four seemingly casual questions to the discussion. Neither harsh nor patronizing, Comstock brought the interview to a close on a light note with a comment on Charles' role as a college trustee.

"Charles, we want to make a decision by the middle of next week, so you won't have much longer to wait, hopefully," Allbright explained. "We are committed to seeing the other two finalists, however." With that, everyone said good-bye to Charles and thanked him for returning for a second interview. When Allbright rejoined the group after escorting Charles to the door, John Lorenzo commented, "Young, but mature."

It didn't take long for a consensus to emerge, but it came only after Rob Flowers voiced the single strongest objection to Charles—the company had never before promoted a field person to CEO.

"I think it is time for our decision," Comstock broke in, "and to bring the matter before us to a close. I move that this committee recommend to the full board the election of Charles T. Adkinson as CEO of All American Insurance Company to take effect at a time to be mutually agreed upon by him and Dan Allbright."

Another hour passed before the motion prevailed, with pros and cons, doubts and assurances, and old ground spaded again. But the air was cleared, and the vote was unanimous. Six directors left the meeting firmly believing they had made the right choice. Each felt a tinge of adventure for having selected the first field person in AAIC's history as CEO.

They gave the headhunter the task of informing the other applicants that a decision had been made; their scheduled visits were unnecessary.

The selection proved to be a perfect fit. It didn't take long for forward movement to show. Pride and enthusiasm returned. Charles Adkinson's energy and well-worked-out plans, his willingness to seek expert help when he didn't know the answer to a problem, and his sound judgment were soon apparent. He had taken a small agency and built it into a winner. As the CEO, he took the whole company and did the same.

Although he enjoyed the full support of the many previously troubled directors, Bill Comstock went the extra mile to see that "Chuck Adkinson, our new CEO of AAIC," as he proudly presented him to business, professional, and academic groups in the Mid-Atlantic area, got off to a fast start. Comstock found it wasn't hard to do, for Adkinson's first impression, always favorable, remained constant with each subsequent contact.

Within a year, not a single doubt remained. Allbright went back to his well-earned retirement for the second time; directors reviewed reports, listened to senior officers discuss their activities without fear of criticism from the CEO, and saw company production once again move up the growth curve.

What a change! Directors again took their wives to company social affairs; happy days were back at AAIC. Power had been tossed back and forth, finally ending up in the right hands—resting with the board but fully delegated to the CEO.

PARTING WITH POWER: FIRED OR RETIRED?

Power, the ever present struggle for it! Wherever Comstock turned, he was reminded of its use and abuse. Each entity, large or small, the single policeman on the beat or the governor of the state, possessed some form of power. It seemed that each person, including the university president and the business leader, was always in the position of having to decide how much of the power of the office he would use. Then too there was the question of enhancing the power of the office by exercising more of it than his predecessor, more than normally delegated by governing boards, more than generally recognized by constituents. Common sense, reasonableness, fairness, and justification all came into play like power itself, they were difficult of precise definition.

Within academe, power was certainly shared. With the general public holding some, especially over public institutions, and with governing boards delegating certain authority to faculties, students, alumni, and the president, it was sometimes difficult to know just where one group's share began and another's ended. Tugging and hauling, the continuous struggle for power was a mark of the college and university. But within each group, Bill Comstock often saw power unduly concentrated in one person—a football coach, for example, who had so much influence in a state that neither a governor nor a university president dared criticize him. Many times, a small group—two or three trustees, a few members of the boosters' club, a handful of donors, or a group of powerful legislators—remained in control for years.

Over in private business, Comstock concluded that it was much easier for one—or a few—to grab power and use it to advantage. Stockholders seemed further removed from corporate headquarters, difficult to mobilize when management needed to be challenged, and, unfortunately, they were served by directors who often were only rubber stamps.

Back on campus, it took forever for a faculty to respond to a crisis. Students would march, demonstrate, sit-in, and protest—they acted more decisively than faculty members. And, of course, alumni, unless agitated over something such as athletics, were seldom aroused.

To prevent abuse and to head off damage to a business or university, Bill Comstock concluded that governing boards, since they hold the basic authority over the enterprise, must be held more accountable than has been true historically. Too many times, he thought, CEOs had been able to put the enterprise in jeopardy through fraud, personal aggrandizement, and downright theft before the governing board finally became aware of developments. In the university he had seen faculty all too slow to respond; in the corporate world it was the stockholder who learned too little too late.

"Don't accept appointment to the board unless you are prepared to accept the responsibility," became one of Comstock's guiding principles. Looking back over 40 years as CEO, trustee, and director, he used the advice for himself and gave it to others.

"No surprises," was the other half of his working formula. As Midtown's president, he tried never to surprise the trustees; as a corporate director, he made it clear that he didn't want to be hit in the face with the unexpected. Board members, said Comstock, have a right to know what CEOs are doing and what they propose to do. To follow such a procedure regularly is the only way a board can fulfill its duty and the only way a leader can be held accountable.

Good advice, but how easy to forget, to ignore, to circumvent!

Perhaps because the campus had been his life for so long, the most troublesome failure of a constituency to live up to its responsibility, in Comstock's opinion, was the all-too-frequent paralysis of a university faculty. A strange mixture of timidity and a don't-care, don't-bother attitude by professors, coupled with uncertainty of trustees, contributed all too often to a malaise that permitted a bumbling, ineffective, sometimes arrogant or occasionally dishonest president to remain in office for far too many years.

The attitude existed, Comstock sometimes heard, because professors were first philosophers or chemists or historians and then members of a university faculty. But there was also fear—fear of retaliation and fear of unseen power being used against them. Then too, he thought, perhaps academicians who were accustomed to talking their way through all sorts of mazes just stopped short of taking any action when discussion failed. No guts was the way Comstock looked at it.

Midtown's president believed Bertrand Russell was right when he wrote, "Teachers are more than any other class the guardians of civilization." He was deeply troubled when he saw a university faculty stand by and do nothing when a president or a trustee or a politician or any other culprit damaged the institution. To Comstock, professors ought to be in the front lines.

Trustees were portrayed as business and professional people, unacquainted with the nuances of the campus and, therefore, reluctant to take decisive action even when confronted with condemning evidence about their president. Such indecisiveness saddened Comstock. Invariably, the costs were counted in pain and frustration to many people and in longtime damage to the institution.

Could it happen in private business? Yes. Midtown's president had seen it.

Even when power was abused, it was hard for those who could recall it to take it back.

X

Campus and Workplace: Greater Understanding

There were flaws, and they could be corrected, Comstock concluded, both on campus and in the workplace. In America those flaws were not life threatening, at least not yet. The educational system was still providing its citizens with leadership in technology, production, and distribution. He was more concerned with the long-range prospects, and envisioned a national effort that would more nearly constitute the country's true potential. Since so many of our institutions and enterprises are governed by boards, he looked first at them.

Both a weakness and a strength of all such groups would always be the kinds of people who serve. Comstock saw flaws in academe as well as in corporate America. Looking at the campus first, he did not agree with the development over recent decades that placed students and professors on such governing bodies. At best such members were greatly restricted in their consideration of many issues, bound to represent only the point of view of their respective constituencies; at the worst, they were unable to shed the conflict of interest inherent in many agenda items. And the "sunshine laws," which opened meetings of all public bodies, guaranteed that differing interests would be exaggerated.

Of course, the sunshine laws brought other problems. They paved the way for membership on university boards to be used as a stepping stone for political office. What was best for the institution sometimes gave way to the member's public platform, a launching site for an upcoming campaign. It was another of those straws in the wind that led Comstock to move from a public institution to a private one.

Turning to the corporate boardroom, this academic leader had to shake his head time after time as he watched inside directors remain silent when their own leader often stated a position with which they could not possibly agree. Yet they were forced, at the risk of losing their jobs, to vote with their chief. Sitting in such meetings and seeing the scenario played over and over, Comstock concluded that most boards of America's industries would be better served if voting directors, with the exception of the CEO, all came from outside the enterprise. A good way to correct this weakness, he felt, would be to reduce the size of many boards by removing the insiders. Each member of the smaller body would then, in most cases, feel a measure of greater responsibility.

It was Comstock's further conclusion that most companies could and should arrange appropriate activities for frequent and substantive interchange between directors and other senior officers. They should attend meetings of the board and its committees and participate fully. Using social affairs and special events to bring the two groups together would be another way to strengthen rapport and enhance understanding. Such activities should occur frequently. It seemed only logical that directors, those who held the ultimate authority for the enterprise, should know as much as possible about the men and women who were serving in the highest offices. Unexpected twists and turns, an emergency of one kind or another, were ever present in the cycle of business dynamics. Too many CEOs seemed unable or unwilling to plan for such surprises.

How to improve decision making was another question that Comstock carried from the academy to the boards of other charities and on to the profit-making world. Improvement was possible in all three sectors, he was convinced. A tighter agenda rather than the always open-ended kind would help many university groups keep on schedule. For other charities most could benefit from more meetings, more reports, and more participation; and for many corporate CEOs the need is to slow down, conduct meetings at a more leisurely pace, and invite, even encourage, differing points of view. Resist the temptation, something he saw too often, to use the heavy heel of authority to stop discussion.

To correct those and many other flaws, the man from the campus envisioned a full partnership between academe and business; it offered the single best chance for America's continued world leadership.

Furthermore, the times seemed right!

As government pulled back and less government was an established trend by the nineties, our society could again rely more fully on the entrepreneurial energy of its citizens. Not even the industrial revolution could compare with the breathtaking changes of the computer age; technology continues to travel at awesome speed.

Comstock concluded that people had learned at least two things from big government: Too much from big brother destroys initiative; too little encourages greed and abuse. The pendulum had moved toward bigger and bigger government in the latter half of the twentieth century. Perhaps now, we are learning how to reach a better balance, Comstock thought.

Private enterprise and academe are closer together, less harnessed, freer to make the most of a new partnership. How then to proceed?

Comstock would argue mutual participation, complete immersion, each in the other's world. The nation has witnessed a long history of cooperation between the public and its educational institutions. Citizens got together in colonial days to provide for the local school; colleges were built in order to educate clergymen and teachers. In recent years voters, through their government, contracted with universities to provide all kinds of scholarly and intellectual opportunities. But as the entities of education and private citizenship grew together, they also grew apart. Each built a culture of its own, allowing an ever diminishing number from the other side to cross the divide. They must learn again how to talk with each other, Comstock reasoned.

Midtown's president searched for clues in his own experiences in both worlds during the half century from the forties to the nineties. He found persuasive developments.

He was a man who had been touched personally, as were millions of others. He learned to be a naval officer on a university campus; it was aboard ship that he and his shipmates used the results of academic research to fight a war; and it was to a campus that he returned for transition back to civilian life.

The post-World War II economic locomotive moved full speed into peacetime production. By 1960, Eisenhower had initiated the country's response to Sputnik, thanks to the scientific manpower called from America's campuses. JFK was ready to assume the presidency, bringing with him the best and the brightest, most of them from the campus. Comstock, then a part of New England U's educational effort, could not have been more optimistic.

In that heady, intoxicating era this academic leader was only one among many who saw the university as the pivotal institution for guiding the march to endless discoveries of new knowledge. Surrounded by an energetic and dedicated faculty, a hardworking and intelligent student body, a proud alumni group, and a not yet politicized governing board, Comstock saw few detours or rough spots in the road ahead. He could go before the governor, legislators, and the general public proudly reporting the day-to-day contributions of the institution to the state and to the nation.

Nothing deterred him. Comstock's respect for and his faith in the university was complete. He firmly believed that the university was society's best hope.

"Given a bit more money and a little more time," he said repeatedly, "the university can either solve or make significant contributions toward solving society's most aggravating problems." Disappointment came soon.

Comstock carried the same optimism to Midtown in 1965. Within 12 months, serious roadblocks appeared. Momentum halted in universities across the land. Comstock would never see full recovery. A new partnership with private enterprise was threatened.

Whether it was disease, poverty, or the shortcomings of democracy itself, efforts mounted on university campuses to resolve the conditions were met with increasing opposition. It mattered not that university research in earlier years had won major victories over polio, smallpox, and typhoid; that academic researchers had dramatically increased yields of corn, rice, and many other crops in the race to feed a growing world population; or that western democracies had guided scores of newly emerged countries in establishing governments where personal freedom and individual liberties would prevail.

By the late sixties disenchantment and disappointment had given way to confrontation, violence, and deep distrust. A national malaise had spread, enveloping all major institutions. The university somehow emerged as both culprit and savior and became the battleground. Corporate America, along with big government, became the targets of those who blamed both for Vietnam, the draft, and an otherwise uninterrupted march to Utopia. Academe and business found it advantageous to distance each from the other, and government became the vehicle for redress for the most critical voices.

Comstock saw the upheaval as an attempt of radicals to gain control of the university. At Midtown he witnessed students used as pawns by groups with both national and international roots. By disruption and confrontation they challenged the governing board, administrative officers, faculty, and all who represented the status quo. Teaching and learning took a back seat on many campuses.

As universities, some in desperation, sought responses to the new challenges, many reached for unproved and radically different programs, yielding to pressure and often compromising well-founded traditions. Pass-fail grading instead of the historic rating of students on the basis of their academic performance was installed on several campuses. Graduation requirements, curricular changes, and student behavior all came in for review and, in some cases, severe modification. For the first time Comstock saw campus authorities accept questionable points of view, a tilting of emphasis, and the modification of the content of courses, the forerunners of today's political correctness. Neither business corporations nor government agencies were eager for closer identification with institutions of higher learning. It was a period of further alienation of each of the three to the other two.

As the pressure from radicals persisted, often joined by political opportunists, universities canceled government contracts, particularly those with the defense department; corporate officers resigned from academic boards; and many public officials found excuses for staying away from campus ceremonies.

Grasping for ways out of the dilemma, universities ventured into activities far beyond the campus and for which they had neither experience nor knowledge. Some financed and operated low-income housing developments, others set up living accommodations for the elderly, and still others opened storefront activities, taking to the neighborhood everything from health care to collections of art.

Searching for appropriate responses to the tensions of the times, universities often found themselves simply tilting in the wind, swaying between longtime commitments and day-to-day expedience. "Dancing over hot coals," was Comstock's description of his own behavior when he refused to take five million dollars that had been raised for Midtown's new library and spend it on food for poor people then encamped on the Mall in Washington, a demand voiced by radical student groups and tacitly supported by a few professors and local clergy. Each confrontation, and there were many of them, pushed universities into further isolation from both business and government.

Comstock and Midtown weathered the five-year crisis in the nation's capital, but some of America's strongest institutions were rendered inert by strikes, protests, and takeovers. California's great university at Berkeley was among the hardest hit; Columbia and Yale joined Cornell and Wisconsin as other hotbeds of unrest. European, Asian, and South American campuses also felt the sting of disruption all too often reaching violent outbursts.

More saddened than angry with the turn of events, Comstock straightened his back and dug in, determined that the university was too valuable to be sacrificed on the alter of a confused society. But he also learned other, and for him, new insights into the institution he held so dear. He saw firsthand that universities are poor managers; decisions are difficult to make because campus machinery is so cumbersome. Endless discussions that seem designed to avoid reaching a conclusion, and yet are so vital to academic matters, become fatal flaws when relied upon in the management of crises. Again, a vivid contrast to decision making in the world of business and industry.

"Universities can't really manage themselves, very well that is," he observed, "so they should not be called on to run other things."

Sobered by the limitations he saw so clearly drawn over the university, Comstock was among the first campus presidents to reign in the institution. "Let's do what we do best," he said to colleagues who gathered from time to time from around the country to discuss mutual worries and to try to map a strategy for heading off new pressures.

"No," Midtown's spokesman said, "we can't house the homeless, we can't bring peace to the Middle East—or any other part of the world for that matter—and we can't eliminate racism. What we can do, however, is what we have always done. We can prepare people and teach people to work on these and all other of the world's problems. Make each generation of students aware of all that is in front of us and give them the chance to learn from teachers, scholars, and researchers, people who are spending their lives wrestling with such things. That must be our answer to the responsibility which our institutions carry. Do this well, and we shall again enjoy the trust and respect of a grateful public."

That became Comstock's soap box. He made no apologies for climbing to the top each day and proclaiming the obvious. It was his way of pulling the university back from an ever engulfing quagmire.

But the period of campus chaos—it was far more serious than just unrest—had shaken his confidence. Professors and presidents, students and politicians had debated and defined, dialogued and discoursed in a cacophony of utterances, many of which debased the university. Into this cauldron of misconception and misrepresentation any number of special interests entered, trying to bend the institution to their selfish purposes. It was not a happy time for someone whose whole being rested with the magnificence of an essentially sacred establishment.

How long might it take to retake, restore, and rebuild lost ground? When Comstock began to add up the damage and to look at still greater threats on the horizon, he could not be optimistic. He confided to friends that he didn't expect to live long enough to see universities return to the level of trust they enjoyed in the fifties and early sixties. Absurdities of misuse were not hard to find.

When gamblers moved in on college basketball in the fifties, public opinion was so strong and effective that no lasting damage resulted. But the tidal wave of problems that came in the late sixties brought a multitude of moral, ethical, and even legal infringements. How much could higher education withstand?

When a faculty member was fired from one of the country's most renowned institutions for giving students mind-altering drugs, alarms sounded from many corners. On another campus, a professor of theology wrote a sensational volume entitled, "God Is Dead." It came from a private, church-related, and very prestigious university. More than one campus museum exhibited the works of artists who found their subject matter in the human genitals. The media, always ready to pour gasoline on the first spark, missed no opportunity to magnify the damage. Midtown's president, a man so confident in earlier years of the unbounded benefits of the university, saw his doubts continue to grow. More than one friend from the corporate world would simply shake his head when the latest campus absurdity was mentioned.

Defining the role of the university in society was a never ending debate; Comstock was well aware of that. But recent troubles threatened to tear away the fundamental respect for learning, a matter that academic leaders all across the country began to fear. Could the amazing achievements of the three previous decades be continued? What would happen to the vital work underway in so many campus laboratories and libraries if the public simply turned away? Would government do that same research in its own laboratories? And would the great corporations do the same?

A debate which began in the first universities of the Middle Ages seemed destined to be aired all over again. Down through the centuries it had been a scholar's lot to wrestle with the abstract, unanswerable questions of the mind; to lay out moral, ethical, and religious theories; and to project philosophical alternatives and suppositions as guideposts for human behavior. President Robert Hutchins of Chicago was still defining the role of the university in such terms in the late 1940s. Things useful or practical, including the professions, should be left to training schools, places not to be confused with universities.

But science had already collided with philosophy, and science could no longer be ignored. Ironic that the University of Chicago should become the spot where one of the world's most fateful experiments in applied science should occur—the Manhattan Project. The industrial revolution of the 19th century had changed the campus; Hutchins and a few others simply refused to admit it.

Fortunately for higher education, business and industry stood on the sidelines during the worst of the campus troubles; they did not retreat to the locker room. As order was restored, leaders from all levels of private enterprise moved to work more closely with (and to benefit from) the advances of learning. Public policy makers responded by creating a new institution, the two-year college, which was destined to answer more directly than any already on the scene the rapidly changing needs of business. Within a few years they provided training for specific jobs, programs that were jointly designed and taught by campus personnel and industry managers. When governors used such leverage to attract new industries to their states, the whole country took notice. For Comstock a new level of campus/industry cooperation had arrived.

The community college was first established to offer a kind of trade school program to students who didn't have the academic strength to benefit from a four-year curriculum. It also provided the first two years of the normal four years of study to students who, for financial or other reasons, had to remain closer to home. But community college quickly became much more. In Illinois, the Carolinas, California, and many other places, community colleges provided key training for learners of all ages. As the computer era arrived and the new technology was carried into both home and workplace, these campuses provided technical training from basic literacy to sophisticated programming.

Gaining respect almost overnight, these institutions, with their multiplying satellite branches, became a source of local pride. Offering low cost and personal convenience, characteristics that marked these colleges from the beginning, they responded to the needs of new workers as they retrained the old, and established themselves as powerful players in the never ending struggle to create new jobs. Shoulder to shoulder cooperation between industry and education reached a new level.

Those guiding universities and four-year colleges soon took note; they carried programs of continuing education, both technical and liberal, to the two-year campuses, delivered by both full-time and part-time staff. In many cases the faculty personnel from the more traditional institutions experienced the new business/campus closeness for the first time. Public officials were not unmindful of the development. In many cases they were ahead of academic leaders in their vision.

Back on the main campuses of some leading universities, professors still debated applied vs. basic research. However, many others got the message of the need for intellectual response to daily problems, to the facts of international competition in business, and to the pragmatism with which public officials were forced by public opinion to react. The foundations of the ivory tower that for decades had been seriously challenged by the whole of the world's industrialization were continuing to give way.

In Britain where university education was available to far fewer than in the United States, C. P. Snow, a highly regarded intellectual, wrote "The Two Cultures," a treatise on the division he saw between science and the humanities in the world's greatest centers of learning. While he pleaded for more understanding between the two groups, he was not certain that common ground would soon be reached. It is, in truth, a flaw that higher education does not need. Added to the mix is a long-standing stereotype that humanists are all liberals and scientists are all conservatives. With such images persisting, somewhat reinforced by the campus crises of the sixties, it is all too easy for business leaders to view much of higher education as unfriendly.

While the seventies and eighties brought other identifiable cultural groups to some campuses—ethnic, racial, and political—some more confrontational developments took place. New Christian colleges sprang up, answering, it seemed, the challenge of public institutions judged to be secular and the already established centers of higher education built by the Roman Catholic Church. Special interests went so far as to subsidize "alternative" student newspapers in a few places.

As business and academic leaders looked ahead to the 21st century, another flaw still dampened prospects: Non-profit organizations were guilty of continued abuse. Politicians set up foundations to shield funds from taxes; individual cases of theft and fraud by senior officers of leading charities made the news; greed marked the behavior of some university presidents; and "administrative costs," a term used to cover high salaries of staff members, literally ate up the assets of more and more eleemosynary institutions.

Unfortunately, senior officers of America's leading corporations all too often added to the confusion by supporting the trend to higher and higher compensation for those who carried major responsibilities in the non-profit world. Consultants, with biases already known, stood ready to help. By defining the campus as paralleling industry in its complexity, the argument for higher pay for those in charge seemed only reasonable. Again, the component of service was forgotten. Whether in the United Way, Red Cross, Salvation Army, or a university, unreasonable salaries or other benefits were strong deterrents to public support. Stress on the individual, difficulty of the job, and experience necessary to perform satisfactorily were all carefully extolled as the case was made by the consultants for still higher remuneration.

Comstock was uncompromising in placing responsibility for such abuses—it was the presidents of colleges and universities and those who headed up other tax-exempt entities. Most of the time they sat around the same table, voicing no objection, to be sure, as governing boards, often working through closeted committees, pushed compensation higher and higher. Few had the guts to ask the tough question: Will this action weaken public support? Does the stress in this job exceed that of the policeman on the beat, the teacher in today's classroom, the nurse in the trauma center, or the cab driver in the inner city?

While Midtown's president wouldn't try to fix all the flaws that he saw in charitable organizations—and more and more crooks and deadbeats were appearing on the scene—he did see a way to remedy the problem in academe: Recruit academic leaders from the faculty.

Yes, he had learned very well that academic leaders to be successful must be good managers. But they managed academic affairs—learning and teaching—the all-important activities of student and professor. To put the world of scholarship in the same administrative mold as that of all other managerial tasks is to push out of sight the most vital part of the campus leader's responsibility.

Where should our next president come from? A professional manager from one of our great business schools? What skills are most important to his or her success—public relations, fund-raising, financial management, political influence, scholarly research, or what?

For the new president, or the president of any institution of higher learning for that matter, Comstock believed the most important and absolutely essential experience is that of faculty member.

The academic president should come from the classrooms and laboratories that are a part of the fundamental work of the campus—teaching and learning. Not to have such experience in one's background, Comstock reasoned, is to fail to understand the results that a college president's actions may have on the very fabric of the institution.

But doesn't the academic president need knowledge of finances? Shouldn't he or she be skillful as a fund-raiser? An expert in public relations? And a dozen other subjects? Of course. The president should have strong interpersonal skills, work easily and effectively with all kinds of people, have unlimited stamina, and on and on.

Yes, the Renaissance man or woman seemed to be on everyone's list. Unfortunately, there aren't enough to fill the many jobs for which they are needed. Then, thought Comstock, the one absolutely essential element in an academic president's experience, without which the institution is most likely to suffer, is the view from the professor's desk: All other qualifications must take a back seat.

From his own years as a faculty member Comstock remembered more about those who teach. Professors don't see themselves as cantankerous; they don't see students as unleashed teenagers; they don't see alumni as irresponsible critics; and, above all, they don't see the campus as a kind of anarchistic war zone. They see the college or university as a warm and friendly haven, protective of their right to search and teach, giving a continuing welcome to each arriving student or new colleague, and offering a guiding beacon to all who come within its reach. They see alumni and parents of present students as the best and most interested friends of the institution, standing ready to help wherever needed.

Would faculty leaders, deans, department heads, academic vice presidents, and popular professors be willing to step forward to be considered for the presidency under such ground rules? Yes, Comstock knew. To him governing boards were continuing to mold the academic presidency into a non-academic office.

Ah, yes, the university had its flaws—some serious, many frivolous—none, he thought, life threatening. But underneath the more obvious shortcomings were a number of basic misunderstandings, some with a long history.

Academic freedom was a concept born many years ago in the first days of the university. Individuals could be found even among the earliest professorate who challenged the popular wisdom and often refused to be silenced. Seldom in the history of universities is there recorded a period of any length that could be described as free from intellectual or scientific challenges springing from the writings and pronouncements of scholars and researchers.

Perhaps due in some measure to our world of instant communication in more recent years, we are now assured of immediate challenge or criticism of unpopular claims from a campus scholar. Comstock had seen public officials demand the expulsion of some such individuals from the teaching ranks in public institutions, and donors withheld their contributions when opposing similar situations in private universities. Presidents, often courting both public officials and private donors for increased financial support, were often caught in the middle. Comstock was just one of many presidents who, in coming to the defense of the scholar, found academic freedom a condition seldom understood.

Governors, legislative leaders, and business executives were among the first to call for the controversial professor's resignation only to be told that the scholar in question was protected by tenure. Of course, academic freedom and tenure go hand-in-hand; neither can be found in the same measure any other place in society.

But Comstock and the others who understood the conditions necessary for unbiased scholarship recognized that the only path to truth is freedom. "The freedom to pursue truth wherever it may lead" has become the banner under which university researchers now march.

While far greater understanding exists today than ever before, academic freedom requires constant explanation and defense. Comstock was not alone—and it was a good thing—since each day brought new challenges to one campus after another. Public institutions were most often the scene of attacks, made sometimes by legislators, governors, or those seeking such offices. To court favor with voters could be seen as the motivating factor all too frequently.

The strongest private colleges and universities were better able to withstand public criticism, but even they were threatened at times by supporters who withheld or threatened to whithhold funds unless or until some scholar was silenced. Perhaps the best insulated of all were the researchers who were staff members of special institutes or foundations. As Comstock came to appreciate, all such voices helped to protect the basic freedom to find new knowledge and to make it known to the world.

Universities also shared, unfortunately, the weakness of injustice for women. Perhaps, Comstock's sharp sensitivity to this matter came as a result of his feeling of personal guilt. Free to admit that he came late to the realization that fairness to women lagged in academe, he began to examine the many other corners of society where the same shortcomings could be found. It was to his credit that he worked hard and effectively to improve the lot of women in all the circles that he reached, but he retired dissatisfied with the gap that remained.

Equality for women was a self-evident truth to Comstock, one that history had ignored. Slowly, progress was being made, but all too many women close to home and millions around the world would have lived a full life before justice could reach them. Government through laws, corporations through enlightened actions, religions through new teachings, and the professions through collective resolution must all lend their power to set aright the centuries of injustice. This was a weakness in which the university must be one of the team members, enlightening others through research efforts but teaching by example.

The difficulties could not be minimized. Basic teachings of many of the world's major religions would require change; modifications to the traditional roles of men and women would be necessary; and the foundations of the male-dominated culture must surely be torn away. Comstock was among those willing to take each step as the opportunity arose, impatient with the rate of progress but happy with the direction.

Deeply ingrained on both sides of the academy-business divide was the historical stereotype of the liberal campus aligned across the philosophical stream from the conservative corporate world. Comstock had seen so many exceptions that he refused to accept the generalization. True, he would admit, those in the social sciences and humanities were more often on the liberal side of most arguments. It was easy for them, with their studies of human behavior within the context of human suffering, to look around for ways to correct societal inadequacies. The only institution with enough power and outreach was easily identified—the government! Why, they often asked, should not our public officials dedicate themselves to correcting such ills? Only when specific remedies were chosen, the costs were faced, and the results measured did the objections arise.

Many in the general citizenry as well as the business community failed to recognize that working alongside the liberals on campus were those in the hard sciences who were predominately conservative. Schools of business and engineering were more often bent toward the conservative side. Then too, exceptions were to be found on every campus, making generalizations both inaccurate and unfair.

Turning to the for-profit world, Comstock saw similar individuals who could be expected to take the conservative side on many of society's knottiest problems but who looked instead to even more liberal solutions than some of the most vocal among campus liberals. Here again, the strongest colleges and universities were able to delineate the areas of disagreement and build the bridges necessary to the business community, retaining both understanding and support. Left to their respective worlds and recognizing their mutual interests, the academy and corporate America would be able to live together in mutual support; it was the politician who exaggerated the differences, usually driven by personal motives.

More than one philosopher has observed that to be liberal is to be youthful—to become aware of a few troubling problems in society and to insist upon correcting them without delay; whereas the more mature see the complexities of those same problems and realize that some remedies may do more harm than good. Since campuses are populated by the young, Comstock could see their views change as graduates became parents and parents became grandparents.

Returning to campus, his ever welcome home, Comstock came to realize that the university is both a reality and a vision. Reality is the here and now; it is what we must work with and what we see each day. The vision is the dream, combining *what is* with *what it will someday become.*

From a lifetime on campus, this executive saw in the university a unique spirit, a force to lift people—the young and the old, citizens of today and tomorrow—to a higher level of both achievement and behavior. He felt the pain personally when one-time aberrations cast shadows on the institution; he worried endlessly when he missed an opportunity for correcting an injustice, a young athlete had lost his way, or a woman had been passed over for advancement.

Comstock believed that a university must be a model providing a beacon for other human endeavor. Yet he knew that everything in which people are involved is subject to human frailty. It was a haunting feeling that never left him. Somehow the institution that he saw as man's noblest should be impervious to stain or blemish. This did not, however, blind him to changes he wanted to see.

Beginning with what he knew best, Comstock suggested that professors travel more frequently to the world of business. To do so, he argued that universities should give faculty members the opportunity to spend periods, such as a sabbatical semester or a full year, actually working in the business establishment. It would need be in a position that would allow the academic to make a reasonable contribution (not just busy work) and also to see the broader effects of corporate policies on employees, customers, and community. Most universities now define rather rigidly what is acceptable as appropriate activity for a sabbatical, and bona fide work in private enterprise is rarely included.

To get more people coming in the other direction, membership on visitor or advisory committees should be greatly expanded. One experience stood out at Midtown.

Comstock remembered the enthusiasm that former trustee John White brought to each meeting of the advisory committee of Midtown's business school after the dean organized the group. It was the first attempt to invlove citizens from outside the university in actual decisions affecting the school. Department heads and professors met around the table with persons then fully immersed in work beyond the campus. White, a graduate in engineering from Midtown many years before, had spent his career in transportation, first with the railroads, then with trucking. Experienced as an executive in both industries, he had much to offer students preparing for their first jobs. He had sound advice, too, for faculty members, some of whom were complete strangers to private business.

Another member of the group was the owner of a large automobile dealership. Joining him was the vice president for personnel of a sizable department store, the owner of an upscale dress shop, and the office manager from the local chamber of commerce. They looked at the business school curriculum, talked with students, exchanged ideas with faculty members, and some, for the first time in their careers, gave serious thought to the formal training of those of the next generation who were headed for private industry.

Before the dean retired some three years later, "The Advisory Council," as it was named, forged several important initiatives for the business school.

The idea for such an advisory council was not new then, and it isn't new today. Any number of business schools, including Harvard, Wharton, Dartmouth, Stanford, and others, now have such groups permanently anchored. At Midtown the effort was allowed to die when a new dean arrived, unfortunately unsympathetic to that kind of involvement.

The business school experience was not Comstock's only exposure to such cooperation. He had seen it used at the department level for special institutes, programs, and, in one instance in which five major universities were involved, for a foundation-financed research effort. If the idea is so sound, why hasn't it caught fire? Not until after retirement did Midtown's president look more broadly at the matter.

Many reasons could be found. Department heads often carry a full load of teaching and research; deans prefer to spend time in the classroom, something it is difficult to argue against; and, not surprisingly, few administrators have had experience in dealing with an advisory body. They may be suspicious and even somewhat fearful if encouraged by their senior leaders to create programs involving the business community. Might visitors see embarrassing weaknesses? Still another rationale or excuse could be: What do they know about today's subject matter? We academics are on the cutting edge of new knowledge.

On the other hand, as campus meets the public, understanding leads to trust; the process goes both ways. After all, education of students must be the concern of the public, of the professor, of the family, of the employer, and of the community. That common interest is the prime responsibility of all. Why not come together in that young person's behalf?

Upon coming together a whole world of mutual interest will be discovered. What knowledge? What skills? Relevant questions whose answers should be sought by all—student, parent, professor, and employer. Any barriers to the problems of keeping pace? Outdated laboratories, inadequate library, or ineffective on-the-job effort? What must we do *together* to correct the weaknesses? To remain a leader? All can be exciting for those who become intimately involved in the campus learning process.

Dividends abound, however, for those on a campus who will take the time to build bridges to its chief constituencies, even though some may reach around the globe. Since most colleges and universities now have alumni and friends in all corners of the world, it's all the more important to keep in touch. Such efforts constitute a long-range investment to be sure; but these institutions are here, most of them at least, for the long pull. Their leaders, as they prepare for the future, must be farsighted. Through advisory groups or other means, keeping communication alive is in the best interests of all concerned.

What we are after here, this academic reasoned, is greater understanding, but we will never get it until both academe and business open their doors to each other. They must realize that each is increasingly dependent on the other.

Too often, membership on an academic board is reserved for the CEO. That simply isn't enough, Comstock believed; neither is it sufficient to engage just the senior officers of educational institutions and major corporations. Why not involve far more people, particularly those from small business. Isn't this the place where more and more young men and women will make their start?

It is true that some schools and colleges across America bring skilled tradesmen, members of the professions, and others with various talents to the classroom to share their insights with students, but in all too many communities those activities are at best irregular. If institutionalized, argued Comstock, millions more would benefit.

In this regard the two-year colleges were breaking new ground. It could be, observed Comstock, that these institutions, which were set in place in the fifties and sixties, could show the way for more fundamental business/campus cooperation.

Could the close association that the two-year colleges are developing with industry be carried through to include four-year institutions and universities? Comstock was firmly supportive. Campuses have been too aloof, too self-satisfied, too snooty—an attitude of "holier than thou." Thus people in business can easily conclude that academics are daydreamers, impractical nerds who don't live in the real world. Since they don't see enough of each other to learn better, the limited views keep both groups myopically imprisoned.

But there may be another basic change at work in our society, thought Comstock, which will encourage more direct cooperation between the two parties. As the citizenry accepts—or even forces—less government, changes in public policy that were previously determined politically may now be achieved only through direct action. In the case of education it may be increasingly difficult to find timely direction from legislation or executive orders. The guidance that is necessary, as well as the financial resources, may be more readily available from business and industry. Looming large is the ever present knowledge that each enterprise, large or small, is now in an international market with success or even survival dependent upon quick response.

The whole scene simply made more urgent than ever to Midtown's retired president the absolute necessity for a strengthened partnership of academe and business—and for free enterprise to have the freedom to move quickly in an environment of responsible corporate citizenship.

Of course, Comstock acknowledged, there is traffic between campus and industry, school and business, and it has been around for decades. The problem is that such interface reaches only a small minority of students and professors, workers and managers. All too many youngsters grow to adulthood without a single glimpse of the productive machinery that creates the nation's wealth. Parents, with few exceptions, either don't know how to interpret the massive world of free enterprise to their children or don't see such activity as important. The same can be said for educators when only a few teachers and professors know the trails of understanding well enough to navigate the twists and turns with confidence. A great majority in each school and community or campus is left in ignorance or, at best, left to find answers through trial and error.

Just as there are reasons why too many adults can't read, there are also reasons why more citizens don't understand the role of private enterprise in our society. In both cases it is a matter of neglect, neglect of the young at the time when the appropriate skill and knowledge should be a regular part of the person's maturation. Comstock reflected on the conditions.

Most basic to all, he thought, may be the feeling that each—learning to read or reaching some familiarity with our economic system—will somehow take care of itself. If I don't take time to read to my child, a parent may conclude, it won't have a vital effect in the long run. Someone else, perhaps a baby-sitter or teacher, will do what I can't take the time to do. A similar rationalization can easily take place when the time comes to visit the workplace, discuss a summer job, or hear an accountant discuss his career. Such opportunities to learn a critical skill or to meet a timely problem are lost, leaving the young child or advanced student still in ignorance. Since the problem when first faced was judged to be too simple or too unimportant for timely attention, that most opportune moment was possibly lost forever.

Still another barrier to increased traffic between academe and business is a mutual feeling of superiority. Each side tends to hide behind a kind of smugness. Academics suggest that since they read and study more, they are wiser, have deeper insights, and, therefore, should be listened to more seriously. Those from business achieve their complacency through work and action, never yielding to wrangling and procrastination they think. Such may be a smoke screen in both camps, a kind of uncertainty that leads to reluctance to engage in serious exchange. Whatever the cause, the effect is the same—serious losses for both the individual learner and for society.

Is human nature so negative, is knowledge so ineffectual, are we as a people so transfixed that we cannot bridge the chasm? Of course we can, Comstock concluded. We know the way. We are doing it now for a few. Extend the net, he thought, and reach more and more every year.

Business and industry of the private enterprise variety coupled with the full range of educational institutions would give to America and its people a partnership strong enough to meet every challenge of the 21st century. The direction is clear, even the route has been pioneered; all that is left is the will. It is the role of education and the special responsibility of the university, Comstock believed, to demonstrate the urgency and to make clear the stakes. With that accomplished, citizens will respond. Of that Comstock was convinced.

Turning to the campus for one last look, Comstock continued. "You plow on," he thought. The goal is the continued strengthening of the university. Every decision is to be made on the basis of one simple question: "Will it help or hinder the institution?" Other questions must be asked. "Is the proposed action both morally and ethically right? Will it be viewed as uplifting or with suspicion?"

A stronger university, the president believed, can better serve humanity if it is to that end that all energies and resources are devoted.

For such a glorious purpose, Comstock reflected, I offer no apologies. Neither do I hesitate in asking leaders from all walks of life—government, business, industry, and the professions—to give of their time, their talent, and their wealth. Those of us who are privileged to be a part of the university must forever treat our role as a sacred trust. He added a further thought: Professors and campus administrators must meet the men and women from business where each may discover the high level of idealism and hope that abides in the other. They must take time to understand.

From worried freshman to graduate student to inexperienced instructor to professor to administrator to president, William Comstock's fifty-five years on eight different campuses, with an absence of four years for

World War II, had given him every possible view of his cathedral of learning—the university.

Correct the compromises that marked campus life in the late sixties; meet the occasional aberrations of misconduct that flare unexpectedly from time to time; and develop long-range policies that protect the integrity of the university from chronic infections such as athletics. In this way, he firmly believed, the institution will retain its rightful place of honor and respect.

If these things are done, the great engine of private enterprise—that ingredient of American life that has proved so necessary to the preservation of economic strength and political freedom—can be counted on to expand its partnership with the university, the veteran president thought confidently. That relationship has truly provided the muscle for the country's well-being and continued world leadership. It can be counted on to continue to do so if nurtured properly.

For Comstock, one educator whose good fortune had allowed him to glimpse both sides of this dynamic phenomenon, the struggle in its pursuit had led to a busy, challenging, and altogether satisfying life.